★

Advance Praise for *The Ignorance of Bliss*

"You've captured the essence of the people and the country of Vietnam at a time before all hell broke loose. You tell the story from the perspective of a child who is old enough to be aware, but whose memories come from a place of innocence. You have such a gift for nailing the descriptions of your siblings' characters and motivations. It is unique on so many levels."

 —Lucie Haskins, Writer and Wife of a Vietnam Veteran

"Powerful. Crazy. Growing up at a perfectly awkward time in life and history."

   —Jerry Waxler, Author, *Memoir Revolution*

"Immersed in your wonderful book and can't put it down. Fresh, funny, tragic, and rich with unforgettable characters, this ten-year-old's vision of wartime Saigon will captivate every reader."

 —Arthur P. Johnson, Author and Baby Boomer

★

The Ignorance of Bliss
AN AMERICAN KID IN SAIGON

SANDY HANNA

Post Hill
PRESS

A POST HILL PRESS BOOK
ISBN: 978-1-68261-794-6
ISBN (eBook): 978-1-68261-795-3

The Ignorance of Bliss:
An American Kid in Saigon
© 2019 by Sandy Hanna
All Rights Reserved

Photography Courtesy of Colonel George T. Hanna
Cover Composition by Cody Corcoran
Cover Art: The Spy by Sandy Hanna
Cover Design by Alicia Milosz
Author Photo by Jeffrey Apoian

Post Hill Press
New York • Nashville
posthillpress.com

Published in the United States of America

This book is dedicated to my parents,
Ruby Nell and Colonel George T. Hanna;
my siblings, Patijean, Robert, and George T., Jr.;
as well as to my husband, Jeffrey,
who have all played a part in my life's journey.
A special thank-you goes to my older brother for
memories and details that eluded me in telling this
story. For all the friends and relatives who listened
to this story so many times, I thank you for your
patience, suggestions, and encouragement.

TABLE OF CONTENTS

PART II

PART III

PREFACE

*T*he *Ignorance of Bliss* is the story of a time when ignorance set the course of events for a small country halfway around the world, when propaganda and paranoia created the facts upon which decisions were based and actions taken in Vietnam. This memoir is about a military family that blissfully found itself in an exotic land living a life of French decadence during a time of transition to war. The years were 1960 to 1962. This Paris of the Orient, Saigon, so aptly named by the French, was a magical place in those early years, especially for a ten-year-old child, the first-born daughter of an American military officer, the Colonel.

The life of military-dependent children is different than that of most. It is an ever-changing life that requires the ability to adapt as their worlds change around them. These children travel to foreign lands and experience things that most can't even imagine. This story will bring you into such a life and allow you to be part of an experience that is unique. The fact that American children grew up in Vietnam is little-known. There weren't that many children who went to Vietnam in those pre-war days, but those of us who were there form a tribe of our own. We call ourselves "Saigon Kids" and have begun to connect after so many passing years.

In Saigon, the Colonel was part of the Military Assistance Advisory Group (MAAG), serving in an advisory role as Chief of Ordnance Corps to the South Vietnamese military in the Ngô Đình Diệm regime. This political regime had come into power with the support of the United States after violating the Geneva Accord. This was a treaty agreed upon by the Allies of World War II when the French could no longer hold on to the country. The Geneva Accord had promised a truce between 1954 and 1956, culminating in a countrywide election. It was intended to remove all foreigners from interference in Vietnam and give it the independence it so desperately sought.

A brief history of Vietnam might be helpful to understand the progression of events that occurred before and after my life in Saigon. For two thousand years, the Vietnamese had struggled to be independent of foreign rule. The French were in control of Vietnam before WWII. During WWII, the Japanese had taken over Vietnam, primarily for its ports, granting the Vietnamese independence at the end of WWII. Hồ Chí Minh had fought alongside Americans with his Việt Minh nationalists against the Japanese. The Allies, the countries that fought together against the WWII Axis powers, agreed to return territories to the countries that had ruled them before the war. The French requested the return of Algeria and Vietnam.

The French returned to Vietnam after WWII to reclaim its former territory, only to find itself in a war with a country not wanting foreign rule. Indochina War I was fought against the French and the Japanese between 1946 and 1954. The Geneva Accord, created by Allies, after WWII established a truce with France for this war after France's defeat at the battle of Điện Biên Phủ. This Geneva Accord called for a cessation of hostilities and the opening of the border between South and North Vietnam at the 17th parallel from 1954 to 1956. In the interim, Hồ Chí Minh would govern North Vietnam, and Ngô Đình Diệm would represent Emperor Bảo Đại in South Vietnam as premier. At the end of that two-year truce in 1956, country-wide elections were to be held to decide who would rule the entire country of Vietnam.

South Vietnam Premier Ngô Đình Diệm held his own independent election prior to 1956. Diệm knew that he would not win as a Catholic in a country that was eighty percent Buddhist, where his only political support was through the efforts of his brother Ngô Đình Nhu. Diệm credited more people than existed in the whole of Vietnam with his win. He created the Republic of South Vietnam and declared himself president. The United States of America supported this violation of the Geneva Accord, going against the other Allies and Hồ Chí Minh, backing Diệm and a regime that would later be revealed to not be pro-American. The rest is history. Americans had no understanding of the history or the culture of this small but fiercely independent country at the time they joined the conflict. I hope to bring an awareness to a time and a place that seem to be remembered only for the wartorn bloody days of the conflict between the Americans and the Vietnamese. This is the story of an American child growing up in a country determined to gain its independence. Hopefully, this story will foster some understanding about the events that led up to that moment when all became chaos.

The Colonel, my father, asked me to tell the story you are about to read. He gave me an exposé written by his military counterpart, Colonel *Lê Văn Sâm*, Chief of Ordnance ARNV. It came as a direct order, something never to be disregarded. He wanted me to write something compelling, because he believed that if you don't understand history, you repeat it. He knew Americans shied away from anything having to do with Vietnam after the cessation of American involvement in the conflict, as if by ignoring it there would be no need to understand the *what* and *why* of it. He felt that Americans' lack of understanding about what had led to our involvement in Vietnam has left everyone in a state of ignorance about the past, the present, and what would happen in the future. He said the mistakes that were made in Vietnam were being repeated in the Middle East and bringing disaster on all fronts. I've attempted to make this story palatable by telling it through my eyes, those of a ten-year-old child of a military family.

Realizing that much of the history of that time has been forgotten, I have added "A Moment in History" to various chapters. These sections detail events that had occurred earlier or had consequences later, years after my family and I left Vietnam. It is intended to provide information that might be helpful in the overall understanding of the time and the place. The story of Vietnam is little understood and I encourage the reader to access other publications to fill in what I might have only scraped the surface of in my story.

As time passes, the younger generation seems to have little knowledge or understanding of this critical time in world history. For those who remember and lived through that period, it is often with great sadness and unanswered questions. For those of us who, as children, experienced the years before the United States became submerged in a state of war, it was an extraordinary experience. Perhaps a different conversation will emerge from hearing about the days that preceded those unfortunate fully-engaged war years. I hope that you, the reader, will access a broader understanding of that period of time and its people. I welcome you to my Vietnam: *mon* Saigon.

A Moment in History

"AGREEMENT ON THE CESSATION OF HOSTILITIES IN VIET-NAM, JULY 20, 1954

The Geneva Agreements theoretically ended the war between French Union forces and the Viet Minh in Laos, Cambodia, and Vietnam. These states were to become fully independent countries with the last-named partitioned near the 17th parallel into two states pending reunification through 'free elections' to be held by July 20, 1956. The United States and Vietnam are not signatories to these agreements."

—U.S. Congress, Senate, Committee on Foreign Relations, 90th Congress, 1st Session, Background Information Relating to Southeast Asia and Vietnam (3d Revised Edition) (Washington, DC: U.S. Government Printing Office, July 1967), pp. 50–62

The United States provided military advisors to Vietnam until the Gulf of Tonkin was used as a ploy to involve the United States in a full-scale military assault. The Gulf of Tonkin Resolution, or the Southeast Asia Resolution, Public Law 88-408, 78 Statute 384, enacted August 10, 1964, was a joint resolution that the United States Congress passed on August 7, 1964, in response to the reported Gulf of Tonkin incident. Documents were released later by the Library of Congress saying that the incident in the Gulf of Tonkin never occurred. This resolution gave U.S. President Lyndon B. Johnson authorization, without a formal declaration of war by Congress, the use of conventional military force in Southeast Asia. Specifically, the resolution authorized the president to do whatever was necessary to assist "any member or protocol state of the Southeast Asia Collective Defense Treaty." This included involving armed forces.

—Library of Congress

Vietnam would prove a whirlwind of political and military intrigue for the Colonel, my father, during our two-year posting in Saigon, 1960–1962. It would also be an exposure to a culture and history of a country that would create a different world view for him. Colonel George T. Hanna at a Buddhist temple in Huế.

"The Vietnamese are indeed not a reliable people. An occupation does not last long before they raise their arms against us and expel us. The history of past dynasties has proved this fact."

—*Eighteenth-century Chinese emperor*

PART I

"What is history but a fable agreed upon?"

—Napoleon

CHAPTER 1:

ASHES, ASHES,
WE ALL FALL DOWN

November 11, 1960
Saigon, Vietnam

S aigon was a world of crushing poverty and extraordinary
beauty. It was also a world of streets, villas, and brothels
where politics and intrigue resided amid plots and counter-
plots. It was a world where I grew up as a ten-year-old with
my brothers and sister between 1960 and 1962. As children, we lived in the continuous present—perhaps the only
way children can live. It was a present that was ancient,
pastoral, and so often veiled from those of us not from this
exotic and complex country. However, my siblings and I
simply adapted to the change, as all good military kids do.
We made it our own without a second thought.

A government sedan sat motionless in the compound
driveway outside the ancient villa. It had arrived with a
uniformed driver in full military attire early that day and

had been waiting for nearly half an hour with the motor running. Having already gone through at least three cigarettes, the slim Vietnamese man was now lounging outside the driver's seat in the shade of a nearby flame tree. Leaning against the fender of his shiny black car, he seemed lost in his own thoughts. He was not particularly interested in the four children playing dodgeball near him. Suddenly standing to attention, the driver hastily tossed his half-smoked cigarette into the nearby hibiscus bush. He rushed to open the passenger-side door.

Four sets of children's eyes fanned from him to the villa's front portico. Our parents had appeared in the doorway. Our mother, Ruby Nell, was beautifully attired in a dress she had recently copied from a fashion magazine and had made in Hong Kong. Short-sleeved and tight at the waist, it showed off the trim, fit figure of an attractive woman who knew how to carry herself. The Colonel, our father, was in casual military attire. His dark features and playful sparkling eyes were distinct. Although he was ranked as a Lieutenant Colonel, we called him Colonel.

Mom slid across the shiny leather back seat, carefully smoothing out her dress to avoid any creases. The Colonel followed. Closing the car door softly, the driver quickly took up his position in the front seat. The tinted sedan windows were rolled down. "You kids be good" were their parting words. We had no idea where they were going this morning. We could see them sitting in the back talking. As they drove out of the driveway, the tall, ornate oxidized metal gates were closed behind them. The sound of rusted metal rubbing followed the creaking of the bolt lock as the servant slid it into place. The car turned right onto Đoàn

Thị Điểm, our street, and disappeared. It was Saturday morning, November 11, 1960.

The servant made her way back toward the house, shooting an irritated glance in our direction as she passed. She had wearied of waiting for us kids to follow her inside the villa earlier. With a slight shrug of her shoulders and faint muttering, Anna went back to her work. She was to be in charge of us today, but that simply meant we would do what we wanted. She in turn would ignore us. We'd established this pattern in the four months we had been in Saigon.

We four kids continued playing dodgeball in the garden with our thirteen-year-old brother's cherished American basketball. This basketball was his identity. Tom had clung to this symbol of America from the moment we started our global trek to Vietnam in July. Tossing the ball, we occupied ourselves with this inane game. Tom, now out of adult view, was hurling the thing as hard as he could, hopeful of maiming one of us.

"Hey! That hurt!" I screamed, having taken a direct hit when I'd turned my eye off the culprit. "You cheated! Oh, what the heck. This is a stupid game anyway."

I collapsed to the ground and sat nursing my arm. Tom seemed pleased with himself. His sideways smirk always gave away the pleasure he was feeling at injuring one of us. I knew better than to take my eye off him, but I had been distracted. Outside the compound walls, muted sounds could be heard. "Get over it," Tom said, now lounging on the ground. He leaned back on his elbow. The two younger kids were staying out of range just in case. Tom always seemed to have a chip on his shoulder when he was left with his siblings and told to watch them. He was the next in charge after Anna, the servant. We usually tried to avoid any of his mood changes. It was purely a survival move —something we were all very good at after years of trial and error.

The ball had rolled off to the side of the driveway, but none of us bothered to get up to retrieve it. Melting down to the level of the earth, I surveyed the exotic world that surrounded us. The garden's grassy area was filled with every imaginable fruit tree and flowering bush: hibiscus and forsythia, Chinese pear trees, lemon and lime trees, fuchsia and jasmine flowers covered the grounds. A footlong blue-headed lizard occasionally made its presence known whenever we kids were close enough to disturb it from its flowery haven. Today, it stayed hidden from us, although Bob attempted to rouse it now by kneeling and thrusting a stick into the thick vegetation. I sat cross-legged, holding my arm, watching. It was another hot day.

"Leave him alone, Bob! One of these days he is going to rush at you and grab your little ass!" I yelled.

"You know Mom said not to sit in the grass or walk on it without shoes. She says worms will get into your skin," Pati said, remaining seated. She was eight years old and liked having unique information to impart to her five-year-old brother.

"Ugh!" Bob yelled as he jumped to his feet, immediately brushing himself off and checking the bottom of his shoes, the back of his pants, and anything else that he could inspect.

The sounds of cicadas and the rustle of the leaves in the flame trees towering over us were interspersed with clearer sounds of rumbling machinery. It was coming from somewhere far away. If we had been back in the States, I'd have sworn it was a military parade. There were always parades on military bases, complete with tanks, marching troops, and sometimes a band. Being in civilian territory now, I was surprised and not sure I was hearing right.

"Hey, everyone be quiet. Hear that? I think I hear a parade," I said now, clearly catching what seemed like the illusive rumble of rolling tank treads somewhere beyond the gate and walls of the compound. It was a dull sound, not much more than that. Not waiting for an answer, I jumped up, forgetting about the arm I'd been clutching. At ten years old, I was ready for anything.

The younger kids cocked their heads, smiling. I started toward the gate. There wasn't anyone around to stop us.

"Oh, no, you don't, Sandy! You aren't going anywhere. None of you are. I'm in charge and you'll stay here. I'm going out and I don't want to have to be bothered with any of you little snots, thank you," Tom said as he headed toward the gate, scooping up his basketball in one clean swoop.

Guess he figured if he didn't find any action, he'd head on to the Cercle Sportif Club and maybe get a game going. His mood seemed to brighten as he walked by his brother and sisters. Opening the big metal gate for the second time that day, he allowed just enough room to slide through. Crushed, we younger kids silently watched him as he easily slipped out onto the dirt pathway that ran between the road and the outside wall of our villa. No one in the household paid the slightest notice to any of it.

"That's not fair. He always gets to do the fun things," Pati said, sitting back down in disappointment. Bob collapsed on the ground next to her, forgetting her earlier warnings.

"Well, I'm not staying here! You two coming?" Pausing at the gate, I waited for them.

Pati and Bob scrambled back to their feet. "When we get closer, Tom won't want to have to come back here with us. He'll let us stay then," I said, sure that we'd be okay. We just had to stay out of sight.

We didn't latch the gate completely as we slipped through the opening, just in case it would make the creaking sound we'd heard earlier. In single file, the three of us, oldest first, youngest last, walked down the narrow and dusty path. We could see Tom ahead of us.

Shaded by a magnificent canopy of towering eucalyptus trees, we dodged in and out of their wide trunks, staying hidden. It was a glorious day. There wasn't a cloud in the sky. A gentle breeze rustled the overhanging leaves. The air was permeated with the scent of jasmine. With a sense of pure freedom, I felt unburdened and happy. The city was beautiful and vibrant today. Glancing at Pati and Bob, I could see that they both had grins running from one side of their faces to the other. They were trying hard not to giggle. Tom was ahead of us, busy bouncing his basketball along the dirt path, distracted, caught up in his own thoughts and ignoring everything around him.

Ragged huts built from tin and wood scraps leaned against the solid concrete stucco-covered walls that ran between the buildings and down the alleyways. These were many. They formed little hamlets attached to the tall, white-washed walls of their neighboring villas. With Tom still bouncing the basketball, its rhythmic sound determined our pace as we all moved along. We were a sight to see. Three pale, skinny American kids secretly following their thirteen-year-old leader in a duck-and-dodge manner. In our colorful Sears Roebuck outfits, we were a bright blur in contrast to the white walls and the stark setting of the surrounding shacks.

Women and children stuck their heads out of their tiny huts. They looked up from their boiling pots over open fires to view the curiosity that was passing. Blond Caucasian children, except for Bob, who had brown hair, in starched clothing and spotless Keds tennis shoes filed passed them seemingly without a care in the world. The small Vietnamese children with only shirts on their backs, standing naked from the waist down, pointed and giggled at the sight of us. Old ladies squatting in front of their hut doorways sat grinning, showing off full sets of either red or black teeth, the result of years of chewing betel nut leaves.

We younger kids moved along with awkward, jaunty steps on the uneven earth, keeping time to the sound of Tom's basketball hitting the hard, tamped ground. It didn't help that the ball suddenly took a sharp right into a nearby hut and had to be retrieved, to the startled surprise of its inhabitants. They held it out to him with wide smiles as he dashed in to retrieve it. They seemed so selfless and innocent. Sitting on their haunches, they were simply humored by it all.

Taking in everything around us, we took our time. No talking, just the hush of excited anticipation with a purposeful gait. We moved toward sounds that were slowly becoming more and more audible. Usually, we caught a taxi or a *cyclo-pousse*, a bicycle-driven cart, directly in front of the villa on Đoàn Thị Điểm when we went anywhere. Walking the route now on foot was new to all of us. We had to go quite a distance before we reached a gathering of people, a crowd. Sound can play tricks on you, and I was surprised at how far we had walked. I didn't care though. We were out on our own and having an adventure.

"What the hell are you kids doing here? I told you to stay in the yard!" Tom said, having caught sight of us while we were looking at everything but him. He was mad, but you could tell he didn't want to have to go back home right now. Something was happening, and he wanted to see what it was.

"Okay. Stick together and don't let me hear a word out of you. No complaining and no asking for anything. Got that?"

"Umm-huh," I said, trying not to say a word. Pati and Bob simultaneously nodded in agreement.

Armed South Vietnamese soldiers blocked the way. They were holding guns and discouraging everyone from getting through. Guns are a familiar sight for military kids. We weren't frightened or discouraged by their presence. We were veterans of these on Army posts, with their tanks, soldiers, and guns. Our small squad quickly slipped by the soldiers. Our illustrious leader had spotted an opening that the guards had neglected to cover, and we quickly dove through it. No one seemed to notice. A mass of people crowded the long tree-shaded boulevard. Easily sliding by each row, being smaller than the Vietnamese, we finally broke through the throng of bodies. We found ourselves at the roadside edge in front of the mass. People lined the street as far as the eye could see. This parade didn't seem to have a band, though. Our military parades always had a band. We strained our necks looking up and down the roadway. It was a wide street, one that led to the President Diem's Independence Palace. I guess you could say, for us kids, it just didn't get any better than this! Squeals of delight erupted from us. I looked around beaming. The Vietnamese people on either side of us just stared in wonder at the small, colorful figures standing next to them.

Military equipment and soldiers were moving along the roadway. I tried to peer around the bodies packed in next to us, managing only to look directly at Tom. He stood holding the basketball under his arm, resting it on his hip. He wasn't saying anything. He had a hardened smile. I'm sure he would have preferred to be without his three younger siblings.

Suddenly, a jostle of people from behind knocked the basketball from under Tom's arm. It bounced and then rolled onto the roadway in front of us toward an oncoming tank. We were frozen. No one had the courage or will to run after it. Breaking ranks wasn't allowed on the Army posts. We watched for what seemed forever. Each rotation moved the ball closer to the oncoming tank. The word "Spalding" appeared again and again, turning, round and round. The ball moved slowly toward the shadow of that monstrous tank. Just as it reached the tank, my eyes shifted to fix on what looked like a boy marching next to the tank. Maybe he was young. Maybe he wasn't. It was so hard to tell anyone's age here. He had a rifle and was in the traditional military attire of the South Vietnamese Army. He was carrying a gun, a real one. I stared at him. As he raised his head and looked up, our eyes met. His dark eyes looked straight at me. My singularly blue ones stared right back at him. The strangeness of the situation began to register for me.

"Look at that guy," I said, surprised by his gaze. "He is looking right at us." He seemed nervous and jittery. His was a look of doubt and determination, mixed into one.

All of my attention suddenly shifted back to the ball. The American basketball, Tom's treasure, was now rolling under the tank. Moving between its noisy treads, it disappeared. The last thing visible as the ball slipped into the shadow of the huge metal beast was the word "Spalding."

A green military truck full of antagonistic-looking ARVN (Army of the Republic of Vietnam) soldiers was passing by on the other side of the tank. They looked so young, these men, all carrying M1 rifles. Giving menacing and hostile looks at everyone on both sides of the road, they nervously pointed their guns at the crowd. At that exact moment, something sounding like a firecracker went off somewhere behind the crowd. It rang out close by. The sound resembled that of a bullet being fired. Snapping to attention, the soldiers drew their weapons and began shooting. It was deafening. It was that loud bang that accompanies an explosion. The sound pierced our ears. Both Pati and Bob instinctively put their hands up to cover theirs. We all crouched down. It continued. *Rat-tat-tat. Rat-tat-tat.* The crowd convulsed around us. Like a wave that reaches the shore and is suddenly pulled back, everyone was moving away from the road and the soldiers. Beyond my older brother by only a few people, I saw figures falling to the ground. The crackling sound of gunfire was all around us now. The rapid firing was mixed with the high-pitched sounds of people crying out. Chaos had erupted. We could no longer see anything other than the figures that enveloped us in the raging crowd. With a sudden yell from Tom, we responded. We now moved as if we were one entity following his direct orders.

Grabbing hold of each other, we pulled back into the crowd, pushing our way out of the mass of people. Tom was in the lead, determined, yelling, holding on to my arm with a deathlike grip. "Grab the kids!" I had Pati's hand clutched in mine. Pati's arm was locked around Bob's neck. She would probably have had her arm cut off before she would let go of him. We saw an opening and literally dragged each other through it, our narrow legs flying. We ran. We were now beyond the swaying crowd of people. We didn't stop as we ran back in the direction from where we had come. The shacks, the walls, the eucalyptus trees, all flew by us in a blur.

Finally, we released our hold on each other. I moved to the back of the line to be sure the younger kids weren't left behind. Screaming at each other to keep up, we ran until we reached the gate to the villa. We shoved it open, our feet moving at full speed. We shot across the driveway. Scurrying up the stairs of the entry vestibule, Tom slammed the screened door to the house wide open. A single mass streaked past the servants in the living room. Running up the circular stairway, diving headlong across the cold marble floor, sliding one after the other, we deposited ourselves under the first bed we reached. Gasping for breath, we eyed each other. Our adrenaline was still pumping. The silence assumed a huge proportion. We waited.

"Well, I guess that wasn't a parade after all," I said, having finally caught my breath. "Did you see those people who got shot?"

I was addressing Tom, our all-knowing leader. I hoped he might have some words of wisdom or maybe had seen more than me. He gave me that cold look of his, the one that basically said I was bloody tiresome and required no response. I guess he was still sulking over the loss of his basketball.

"Well, no one is going to tell. Got that? I'm not going to get in trouble on account of having you all out there with me. So, no one tells or else! And I don't know anything about any people getting shot! Okay?" He sneered with a determined air.

Older brothers have an advantage. They can threaten you, and generally, you know better than to cross them. They are just bigger than you. You aren't going to win in a physical battle, so there is no point to it. He didn't say anything more. He just sulked and played with the pocket-knife he'd pulled from somewhere. He could turn that thing over all day and not say a word to anyone. I don't know if he was scared or just plain mad. How would I know? He didn't confide in me, and for good reason. I wasn't trust-worthy. He had lost that stupid basketball after carrying it with him for the entire trip from Illinois to Saigon. That was burning him up. And why didn't he want to talk about those dead people? Well, they might have been dead. How was I going to find out?

We didn't say anything more to each other, but then again, we didn't bother to get out from under the bed either. Our adrenaline had finally subsided to a reasonable level. We eventually dozed off on the cool marble floor waiting for our parents to return. The servants brought food and drink upstairs. It was slid under the bed to us since we were making no signs of leaving our encampment. They didn't want to get in trouble for not feeding us. They looked at us as you would a pack of strange animals. We ignored them. We were still getting used to having servants. Frankly, we weren't comfortable with all this being-waited-on stuff, though I liked the fact that I didn't have to make my bed anymore. It was a new thing for us. We ate everything and stacked the dishes near the wall. Eventually, we fell into that comfortable state of being between dreaming and waking.

I remember sleepily surfacing to the warm, incoherent sounds of my parents' voices. "They're here!" Mom and the Colonel were both bent over looking under the bed with a somewhat alarmed expression, not saying anything further. They didn't ask. We didn't tell. Our silence now bound us kids together. This would become standard operating procedure in our sibling lives with each other. We four kids would never disclose to our parents what we were up to unless asked directly. It was easier that way.

The Colonel returned from work a few days later with a flier in hand. He read it out to all of us that night as we sat around doing our school homework. Our father was the Chief of Ordnance Corps for the Military Assistance Advisory Group (MAAG) stationed in Vietnam. He told us that there had been a recent coup against the current Diệm regime. He stressed that we were now not to go anywhere unaccompanied. All of us kids played dumb regarding knowing anything about what this was about. We eyed each other as he read the flier.

Appeal of the Colonel
Commander-in-Chief of Military Region 5

This is the powerful military force of the 21st Division of Military Region 5 including armor, tank, and artillery, who went and liberated Saigon and put down the rebel force.

Fellow citizens—be calm, peaceful and keep order: the rebel forces have been dissolved and a number of rebels have surrendered and returned to the government and have determined to support the president.

Soldiers who have gone down the wrong road—repent and don't listen to that band of officers who are selling their country, Thi and Đông. They received money from the communists, intending to rebel against the people and injure the country.

Soldiers who have gone down the wrong road—return to the government, support the president in order to protect our country's independence, and in order to guard the republican regime.

The president is ready to forgive all you friends.

Commander-in Chief of Military Region 5
Colonel Tran-Thien-Khiem
Army of the Republic of Vietnam[1]

The Colonel proceeded to explain that there had been a coup. It was the result of discontent among officers in the South Vietnamese military about the current South Vietnam regime of President Ngô Đình Diệm and his brother Ngô Đình Nhu. The contents of this flier seemed strange to me. Diệm would forgive them? It wasn't a rebel force, that of the Việt Minh; it was his own military that had orchestrated the coup. The Colonel told us that four hundred people, mostly civilians, had been killed in the coup. We listened quietly with our eyes wide open.

Throwing an all-knowing glance toward my older brother when he looked my way, I stuck my tongue out at him. I was right after all. Those were bodies dropping down around us!

This childhood universe of ours had been altered in a single moment. We were to soon discover that we had entered a time of good and evil in Vietnam, when politics ran amok. Our Paris of the Orient would prove over the coming years to be an exotic place that hovered between illusion and reality. Our real indoctrination into the world of Saigon had begun.

The 1960 coup against President Ngô Đình Diệm's regime in November was orchestrated by his own military. The vehicles carrying young ARVN soldiers equipped with M1 rifles rolled down the main boulevard to Independent Palace, the residence of President Diệm and the Nhu family. The coup failed, and over four-hundred civilians were killed.

CHAPTER 2:

AS THE WORLD TURNS

In 1960, I had never heard of Vietnam. I don't think many other people in the United States had either. No one was paying attention to what was happening in this small country halfway around the world. The 1950s had left America under the shadow of a "Red Scare," believing Communism would take over the world. The domino theory was solidly in place. The party line was that if Vietnam fell, so would all of Southeast Asia, one country after the other. No one seemed to have any grasp of the history of this ancient country or know anything about its culture. Anyone in the United States government who had any previous knowledge of Asia was thought to be a Communist and removed. President Eisenhower was still submerged in the legacy of the Cold War and couldn't see beyond that. The military advisors (MAAG) who were sent to Vietnam in 1960 would find themselves steeped in the same mire.

Before my family moved to Saigon, my world was insular and defined, as it should be for a child—safe and structured. My family and I were edging toward the completion of our two-year posting in a suburb outside Chicago. The Army had sent the Colonel to the University of Chicago for an MBA, a master's degree in business. He already had a bunch of degrees, but the Army must have thought he needed another one. We had moved there in 1958. It was now 1960. We were an Army family, and that meant that we moved every two or three years, when the Colonel's transfer orders came through. We never knew when we would receive these orders, however. I say "we" because we moved more like a small military squad than a family. It just seemed that the day would come when we were to be transferred again, and the only warning we had that change was brewing was the spinning of the Colonel's world globe. It was a ritual in our family. This event happened a few weeks before school was to end in Hinsdale, Illinois. This had been our last assignment and one that involved living with civilians. In Hinsdale, the entire family was posing as civilians.

I refer to my father as the Colonel, though his name is George. My older brother, Tom, simply calls him "the old man." I grew up as a military kid, along with my older brother and two younger siblings, Pati and Bob. Our mother, Ruby Nell, was the perfect officer's wife, completely supportive of her husband's transient life. We traveled the world together following the Colonel on each of his Army assignments. We were told we represented America—so shape up and fly right! We conducted ourselves accordingly, with the tendency to bow and curtsey without the least provocation. We had accents, but none of our accents was the same, due to a constant schedule of moving.

We, the squad of six, lived in a brick house on a maple tree-lined street. It was an Ozzie and Harriet–type of neighborhood with well-groomed lawns and cookie-cutter families. We blended in quite well, I thought, but we weren't like them at all.

We children of military personnel are referred to as BRATs, a title we all wear with pride. The acronym BRAT was created a long time ago and stands for British Regiment Attached Transfer. It is the perfect way to describe our extended gypsy family. We are the "attached" dependents who go wherever the military transfers take the Colonel.

"Adaptive" would be the best word to describe us BRATs. In a way, we are a tribe unto ourselves. Making friends quickly, we depart our assigned posts without a goodbye or any chance of future encounters. We pick up languages and accents quickly. Material things just aren't important to us. We leave them behind us as we do our lives, our friends, our pets, and our teachers. Nomadic and in some cases feral, we bond immediately with kids who are like us, displaced and transient. We recognize fellow BRATs in an instant, seeing a reflection of ourselves. At the same time, we view civilians as strange creatures that we do not understand, and they in turn don't understand us. We just don't fit in with people who have been and will be together for the rest of their lives. Our lives are just so different than theirs.

My real awareness of the world around me began at the age of eight years old. This was when I became a self-proclaimed spy. At that time, I was just a kid with no secretive activities other than the normal things kids do that they don't tell their parents, like slugging your kid brother just because you can or sneaking money out of your mom's purse so you can buy that candy after school. Small stuff. Nothing that could result in a serious loss of freedom. But that all changed the day I decided to break into the Colonel's makeshift darkroom in the basement bathroom in Hinsdale, Illinois. My official spying activities began that day. I'd become more than curious about that room in the basement that the Colonel would disappear into during the evening hours. He'd spend long nights locked inside with only the red light seeping out from under the doorway. This behavior seemed odd to me, since as far as I knew, the room was a bathroom.

The house was unusually quiet one day. I was alone, a rare occurrence. After all, there were four of us kids. Going down the basement stairs to the bathroom door, I opened it, switching on the light. It wasn't red but white. The red bulb seemed to be in a clip-on light that had a separate plug. All types of photo equipment were in this small room. A board had been put across the toilet lid to make a place for things to sit. Black plastic tubs had liquids in them. On the floor nearby, a wooden box held curled-up rolls of developed film. A clothesline ran across the room with strips of paper attached by clothespins. Pulling the nearby stepstool over, I climbed up to have a closer look at the small black-and-white images in blocks on the strips. The first few pieces of paper had pictures of military equipment and soldiers. It was the ones at the end that shocked me. They were pictures of bodies in piles: skeletons clinging to wire fences, people who appeared to have no hope, all half naked or dressed in faded striped rags. These were the Colonel's World War II memories, captured and later hidden in a wooden box. These were things he had seen and couldn't talk about. I realized at that moment I knew nothing about my father.

At the time, I was enrolled in the Brownies and had what I considered to be an incredible uniform. The Brownies are the beginner level of the Girl Scouts, an organization for young girls that is supposed to teach life skills. I thought this official uniform lent great importance to what was now my self-proclaimed mission as spy. I would don the uniform whenever I was on a serious stakeout. I was determined to develop my skills of observation and stealth. My mother would often catch me, confused by the change of clothes on a non-Brownie day, telling me to get out of the uniform so I wouldn't soil it. She already had enough laundry to do, she said.

Trudging home from Lane Elementary School one late spring day, Pati and I were surprised to be greeted at the door by both of our parents. They stood before us wearing ridiculous smiles on their faces. Something was brewing, that was for sure. They loved to travel. The two-year stay in Illinois had been long enough, especially for our mother. She missed the officer's club and the groups of friends she'd make immediately on post. It didn't work the same here. Neighbors stayed to themselves, and no real effort was made to be social, though Mom gave it her best shot. I'd made only one friend in all the time I'd been there: Ellen Wright. I wouldn't be leaving a lot behind when we moved other than her and my beloved fourth-grade teacher, Mrs. Grace Hibdon.

My older brother, Tom, was a veteran of the Colonel's transfer-announcement process. He was the one who would dig the world globe out from who-knows-where once he picked up that change was in the wind. He was ready for any announcement that would get him out of this town. He hated it and for good reason. He was in seventh grade, relentlessly taunted and teased by the kids his age. He was shy and slightly heavy, a bad combination at his age. The two years had been a real trial for him. He put it a different way: "It was hell!"

Standing in the doorway of the kitchen for just a moment, Pati and I entered a room already full of excitement. Our brothers were seated at the table. Everyone was on pins and needles. The world globe sat in the middle of the kitchen table ready for its single spin. Our globe was an old one. It had been with the Colonel throughout his life. He'd had it when he was a student at Texas A&M. Some of the names of countries had changed in the world, but not on this globe. The Colonel stood in front of us ready to set the world in motion and us with it.

Whenever I took the time to look at the Colonel, I was always amazed at how striking he was. Tall and with dark hair, he had a slim figure. There was always a twinkle in his dark, mischievous eyes. I thought he looked a lot like Gregory Peck. He had a face that seemed to move constantly between being serious and being completely humored. He was a handsome man. Mom said he was a bit of a "fox" when she had first met him. Mom had that same type of changeable face. She too was strikingly beautiful, a former high school beauty queen. The Colonel attempted to look serious now, but I could tell he couldn't wait to get started. His eyes sparkled. We all sat in a hush of anticipation. We were a restless family.

"We are going to South Vietnam," he said. The Colonel was beaming. All four of us kids stared wide-eyed as he set the globe spinning on its axis. The sphere whirled around and around, blending the continents' and oceans' colors together. After several orbits, as it slowed down, the individual countries and oceans could finally be distinguished one from the other. He placed his finger on a long strip of land that had the China Sea running its entire length. Instead of the name "Vietnam," it read "Indochina." On this globe Indochina was made up of Vietnam, Laos, and Cambodia, the names all written in smaller lettering. My eyes wandered away from the globe to scan the table. Next to the sphere sat a newly purchased set of records, titled *Learn French*, and a book printed on newsprint with the title *Speak Vietnamese*. The book looked like military issue.

The Colonel enjoyed this way of telling us where we were going. His eyes shone with delight as he continued to turn our world inside out. He stood before us in civilian clothes, not regulation military fatigues, devoid of the starched uniform he'd soon have to wear. A lit pipe hung from the corner of his mouth. He backtracked with his finger to where we currently lived, Illinois. He proceeded to lay out the journey we'd be taking. We'd drive from Illinois to Kentucky, then on to the very bottom tip of Texas, Brownsville, eventually traveling across the desert to Los Angeles. He rotated the globe slowly to illustrate the journey.

"We'll be going to Disneyland when we reach Los Angeles," he announced to four children's absolute surprise. Thinking I'd misheard, I came to full attention. The mouths of all four of us kids had dropped open simultaneously. We gave loud whoops and shouts of sheer joy. This was better than expected. Who cared where we were going? We were now more than ready for the move.

"Your mother has saved all her fifty-cent pieces from these last two years running her daycare so we can all do this. Maybe now you won't feel so resentful of her efforts and having to share her time with other people's children," he said. He knew we were angry at the fact that Mom ran a daycare in our house. It had been irritating to have to share her with these strangers who filled the basement and used our toys every day. They were the enemy. This was something all four of us could agree on.

The Colonel continued adding more details to our itinerary. His voice was melodious and smooth. Our last stop in the United States would be San Francisco, Travis Air Force Base, where we'd catch a four-engine Constellation MATS (Military Air Transport Service) plane piloted by a Navy crew. We'd fly out from there to Hawaii, Wake Island, Guam, and the Philippines, finally reaching Southeast Asia. Our final stop would be the capital of South Vietnam, the city of Saigon. "The French have always called Saigon the Paris of the Orient," he said. My mind soared with images that probably had nothing to do with where we were going, just the collage of images a child collects from books and television. A world only half-imagined.

Taking the globe with me to school the next week, I stood before my fourth-grade class and repeated the Colonel's story of future travels. I was normally shy and quiet in class, but I told the story with elaborate gestures to the surprise of my mesmerized fellow students. I traced the journey along the moving globe just as the Colonel had done. It was truly a moment of creative storytelling on my part. All the other kids were glued to the edges of their seats. It made me a bit popular for the few weeks we had left in civilian territory. They held a going-away party on my last day there. I was given a green leather-bound diary complete with a small gold key. We left Hinsdale several days later. I took Mrs. Hibdon's mailing address with me and would write to her on and off over the next two years. Many years later, after we had returned to Illinois, I met a former student of hers who told me that Mrs. Hibdon read my letters to her new classes. She wrote to me as often as I did her.

During those last days in Illinois, the family had to go downtown to Chicago for immunization shots at the Great Lakes 5th Army Headquarters Dispensary. I'm talking every possible shot you could imagine: for cholera, typhus, polio, tetanus, and more. It just seemed like the staffers would put two in each of our skinny little arms whenever they could get a hold of us. Next came the passport photos. I was on one with Pati, Bob, and Mom. Pati and I stood like deer in headlights with the new perms she had given us specifically for the photo. I had a bird's nest of curls on top of my head. As usual, Pati and I were dressed in somewhat matching outfits. Bob had on a smart little suit jacket. Where that one came from, I'll never know. Tom had his own passport separate from us. He paraded it around with pride, flashing its glossy photo at us. He let us know that he was no longer a child to be grouped with us underlings. The Colonel had his own as well.

We were now ready. Documents were in hand and orders cut. The packing would come next, but not before Mom shipped us three younger kids down to Horse Cave, Kentucky. Sent to our Aunt Minnie, Uncle Tink, and Cousin Wanda's house, we would wait for our parents to complete the last details of the move. Tom had refused to be included on this trip. He wasn't partial to outhouses, taking care of his younger siblings, or having to take baths in a metal tub in the center of the kitchen floor. No, he'd stay right where he was, thank you. He'd see us later if we were lucky. "Maybe they'll forget about you," he'd tease, though I think he was hopeful. I smiled and shook my head. I wasn't worried. I always memorized how to get back to wherever we had come from. It was one of my survival tactics.

I decided to become a spy at age eight when I came across the Colonel's stash of photos from WWII. I considered my Brownie uniform to be the perfect attire for such covert activities as spying on my father. I would continue this behavior into our time in Saigon.

CHAPTER 3:

DESTINATION SAIGON

The South in the United States is a place of conflicted memory for me, permeating the very air. Stifling and unbearable. I only had to cross the Mason–Dixon line before I'd feel its weight on my chest and the blurring of my vision. Most of my childhood summers were spent in Horse Cave, Kentucky, with my mother's relatives.

We traveled down the paved roads we always took on these trips south. Passing familiar road signs, we sped toward our Kentucky destination. Big Otter, Jane Lew, Mink Shoals, Little Sandy River, Salt Lick, Cheat Lake; these were places where people lived but no one else had ever heard of. We'd stop along the way at little independently-owned gas stations that had signs posted separating whites from blacks, not so nicely phrased in those days. "No Drinking for Colored" signs hung next to the water fountain. "No Colored Served Here" written on placards set in the windows of greasy-spoon food stops. These were horrible ugly words displayed everywhere. Each year it was like seeing it again for the first time, this timeless, senseless hate. These Southerners knew it as a way of life that had always been and, as far as they were concerned, always would be. I found these prejudices confusing.

Southerners are polite and friendly, I always said, so the juxtaposition was always jarring. The Colonel would tell us kids to not make trouble when we'd make our bathroom or food pit stops. I wondered what trouble I could possibly make. Although, it did often occur to me that I should go over and use the "colored" drinking fountain just to see what would happen. The unblinking stares of the listless white men hanging around chewing on their wads of tobacco always made me think twice. I found myself surrounded by two seeming opposites during our summer stay before we headed to Southeast Asia: religion and prejudice. I soon discovered that the Ku Klux Klan and the Baptists ruled the region, and they weren't as separated as one would think. In fact, most were members of both groups.

Religious activity was a full-time thing in the South, and our aunt made sure we participated in all of it. We younger kids stayed in Kentucky for an entire month and found ourselves engulfed in every form of religious activity you can imagine: Sunday school, Sunday church services, revival meetings, and summer Bible school were all held just down the dirt road from the farmhouse at the Horse Cave Baptist Church. Having attended "all denomination" churches in the military, this southern version of religion was overwhelming.

Nightly revival meetings that, for the uninitiated and uninformed such as my siblings and myself, were frightening and daytime baptisms in smelly sulfur spring pools left us wondering if the preacher was trying to drown his "saved" souls. The finale to these religious encounters for me came on the last Sunday of our visit.

I triumphantly entered the church with my Bible, the one that had been given to me on my first day there, tucked under my arm. I decided to sit up in the front row for a change. I told myself that he didn't scare me, this blustering preacher with all his threats of sin and damnation. A short robust fellow, he entered from the back, making short stops and bending over on his way to the podium. I was engrossed in something and wasn't paying much attention.

"Brothers and Sisters, there is a non-believer in our midst," he said glaring in my direction. I turned around to see who he might be singling out. "I happened to find these four-leaf clovers along the aisle as I entered today," he said waving them over his head. "These are false idols and will lead you away from the one true God." He was off and running.

I sat completely still, but I could feel the heat rising in my face. I had been pressing these small treasures in my Bible. My face was probably as red as a country fire engine. Not only had I lost my four-leaf clovers and all that good luck, but that dang fool wanted to send me to purgatory.

At long last, the family station wagon arrived, its top-loader stacked high with luggage, pulling a trailer piled to the brink. I was ready to be on our way. Our official trek to the Orient was finally starting. We left Kentucky and followed the route the Colonel had shown us on the spinning globe. We traveled further south through Texas and across the wide-open King's Ranch. Two weeks would be spent with the grandparents, fishing in the Gulf of Mexico for ocean trout and eating the fresh tortillas the Mexican workers cooked over the outdoor fires by my grandfather's orange and grapefruit orchards. Before we continued our journey, the entire Hanna clan camped overnight on Boca Chica Beach, night fishing and telling stories around a huge bonfire.

For some reason, the next day, the Colonel decided to show Tom and me how to fire his WWII vintage .45 automatic. I guess he figured this was as good a place as any to do it. This was a weapon he had gotten from his older brother, Harold, when he had built levies along the Mississippi River, right after WWII. He was intent upon both of us kids knowing how to use it. I don't think Mom had a clue as to where he was taking the two of us that day. He owned a few cotton fields just outside of town, and we headed in that direction. I thought we were just going to take a look at them when the car came to a stop and we all climbed out. He set up a target of bottles on a stump and pulled both of us over to the side. He handed twelve-year-old Tom the gun and gave him some preliminary instruction. With the gun pointed, Tom struggled balancing the darn thing. I put my fingers to my ears. *Bang!* it cracked, and the kick from it sent Tom backward with the full force of the blast. It was a canon of a thing! Tom managed to stay on his feet somehow. I found out later that the Colonel had done this same thing with him when he was eight. Then, the Colonel had neglected to instruct him to keep his elbow locked, and the darn thing had come back and hit him square across the face. Mom had the Colonel's hide that time, as Tom was saddled with a bruise that ran across his face from his forehead down to his cheek by the time they arrived home. This time, he avoided injury.

The Colonel motioned for me to step up for my turn. I had already decided I wasn't going to have anything to do with that gun, and trudged back to the car, ignoring his commands. Exasperated, the Colonel now told us both to get back in the car. These rites of passage with the Colonel would continue throughout Tom's and my young lives. I could get out of most of them simply by the fact that I was a girl. There was no refuge for Tom.

We left Texas and headed toward the West Coast. The Colonel drove all night, stopping at motels with swimming pools during the day. This way, our parents could count on us kids being passed out in the back seats sleeping. We four kids swam and played while our parents slept. The station wagon's air conditioner gave out as we crossed the desert. A weird bag-of-water thing was hung on the window to create a kind of air-conditioned effect. It didn't work. It was still just plain old hot in that car. The trip was long, and we fought like cats and dogs, sang stupid songs, and played tic-tac-toe games. Mom told us that she'd give a dollar to whoever spotted a white horse first. Like we were ever going to see a white horse in the desert! Packed in between pillows, blankets, bags, and toys, we were miserable! The Colonel used the trip as an opportunity to make me learn my multiplication tables. When we reached California, I was up to twelve-times-anything. Nerves were frayed, and all-out war would break out often between the four of us kids in the back seat. Only the Colonel's threats of not going to Disneyland would stop the battles. We finally reached Orange County, California. Disneyland. This was something that did not fail to live up to all our wildest dreams.

Tom kept a notebook about our journey, where it began and where it ended. He'd crouch down wherever he was to scribble his notes like he was a secret agent. Forget getting him to tell you what he was writing. It was beneath him to confide anything to us lowly siblings. Even though our parents picked up my little brother, my sister, and me on the way through Kentucky, he failed to make that entry. He simply stated that they left Chicago and drove to Texas. Tom didn't consider Horse Cave a stop he wanted to be part of. He probably didn't want to acknowledge that his younger brother and sisters were going to be part of his life again. Tom's notebook entries read as follows:

June 1960/Left Hinsdale, Ill.—Went to Texas to visit my grandparents. 1957 Ford Fairlane Station wagon with top-carrier and pulling 'the trailer' my father had built during WWII.

June-July/1960 Left Texas—Drove to Anaheim, CA. Crossed desert without air conditioner working. Found a motel with swimming pool—stayed three or four nights. Went to Disneyland—two days I think, maybe three. Bob left his mark by throwing up in the pool, something that kept us out of it for a day. Luckily, we would spend the day at Disneyland.

July 1960—Drove to San Francisco. We'd be staying with friends of the family there.

July 14 thru 16, 1960/Flew from Travis AFB, CA to Saigon, Vietnam. The Colonel took a picture (slide) of the plane on the tarmac at Travis: a three tailed Constellation MATS plane with a US Navy crew. Flight took three days. Aircraft was full, all seats were taken. No stewardesses and no real food, just c-ration boxes with unidentifiable items in brown cans.

He was right. The Colonel took a photo of the transport, the MATS plane sitting quietly on that black tarmac. He also took a picture of us kids in the military bus as we were being driven out onto the tarmac. Pati and I sat together in one seat, with Bob and Tom together in another. In the photo, we are all peering out the bus window. That singular moment, preserved on film, would prove to be an image frozen in time, recording what I consider to be the time of our innocence. We were children who had been sheltered as best as a military family can be. The faces in the windows were the faces of seemingly normal American children. Then again, "normal" is a relative term at best. Loading onto the plane, we listened for the close of the doors and the engine's propellers to twirl.

All that seemed visible now from high above was water, water, and more water. We peered out the windows of the plane, a view available only after a squabble to gain rights to them. The cerulean cloudless sky soon became a monotonous view. Blankets and C-ration boxes would be handed out by a Navy ensign. The food was in brown cans and boxes with no identifying names. This didn't change for three days. The same boxes, with the same unidentifiable contents, were eaten by all. The makers of Spam must have had a contract with the military, along with the company making saltine crackers. They were in every box.

We four kids pinched, slugged, sneered, and insulted each other throughout the entire three-day flight. Tom was brilliant at looking completely innocent while most definitely being at the center of the unraveling of sanity on the part of us younger kids. Our mother was at her wit's end. The Colonel simply ignored it all, lost in his own thoughts and removed from the ruckus that constantly erupted. The battle for the floor space under the seats was constant. It was a contortion act trying to get comfortable in what were some of the most uncomfortable seats ever designed. The military way of trying to toughen you up, no doubt! There were no other kids on the flight. This caused Mom to be even more attentive to our shortcomings than usual. She was trying to pull off an image of a well-behaved family to the military personnel around us.

Mom finally drew the Colonel into the fray. His strategy eventually became one of trying to get our brains working instead of our mouths or fists. His hope was to reduce the amount of fighting and squirming that was going on, if possible. He pulled out a small paperback edition of *Vietnam's History at a Glance*. It was military issue, something the State Department had put together, with a simple listing of historical dates and activities. It was merely a glance without any earth-shaking understanding of the country we would soon find ourselves in. I must admit though, some of it was amazing. The list of dynasties, invasions, the splitting of the country, and changing rulers was extensive. One fact stood out. No matter how many times the country had been divided, it was always reunited. Its history dated back to 2879 B.C. Can't say that about American history, that's for sure! The fact that the Vietnamese beat Kublai Khan's armies in 1288 had my mind swirling with visions of great battles fought on water buffalo and of amazing emperors in exotic palaces.

Tom's diary detailed the plane's refueling stops. We looked forward to these refueling stops as much to get out of the plane as to get out of the history lessons.

Refueling stops (Tom's diary continued):

Stop 1—San Francisco, California to Honolulu, Hawaii—six-hour layover in the middle of the night. Ladies with leis standing outside the plane put them on Mom and Dad.

Stop 2—Honolulu to Wake Island—two to three hours during the day—very hot. Ushered us into a large Quonset hut with no air conditioning. Served us pot roast. Wreckage left from WWII on the beach.

Stop 3—Wake Island to Guam—US Airforce Base— six hours. During the day, I got a haircut. The barber asked me a lot of questions about who 'the old man' was and where we were going. I made up some stuff and then told Dad after about the questioning. Not sure what Dad did if anything.

Stop 4—Guam to Clark Field, Philippines—6 hours. We were like zombies by now and hated each other's guts.

Stop 5—Clark Field, Philippines to Saigon, Vietnam—Walking out the door of the plane was like walking into hell it was so hot.

On July 17, 1960, we arrived in Saigon, Vietnam. It was Tom's thirteenth birthday.

A Moment in History

"Only a few scholars know that Viet-Nam has been thwarting Chinese southward expansion for 2,000 years. Fewer still know that the Vietnamese have defeated at least half a dozen Chinese attempts to penetrate the rich rice bowls of the Indochinese peninsula. Much has been written about the 100 years of Western colonial exploitation which came to an end only after one of the longest, most cruel and politically most perplexing of all colonial wars. (The Indochina Wars). But the Vietnamese had fought against Chinese colonial exploitation and political domination for more than 1000 years before the coming of the French. Even partition of their country is not a new experience for them. During the last 500 years, the Vietnamese had lived through two long periods of a divided Viet-Nam and have come out of them stronger and more united than before."

—*Joseph Buttinger,* The Smaller Dragon: A Political History of Viet-Nam. *New York: F.A. Praeger, 1958*

A three tailed Constellation MATS plane waited on the
runway tarmac in San Francisco as the Hanna family waited
to be transported to it via military bus. The naïve and
innocent faces of me and my siblings peer out the window
in expectation of the adventure that would soon begin.

CHAPTER 4:

THE ESSENCE OF LEMONS

We always seemed to be arriving places on my brother's birthday. When we returned from England in 1955, another military posting, Tom had just turned seven years old on the day the ship docked in New York. I was four years old. We sailed on the *S.S. United States*, the fastest ship ever built. A birthday lunch was arranged for him on the ship at the captain's table. When we entered the harbor in New York, to great fanfare, Tom thought the celebration was for him. I'm sure that is what Mom told him. It would have been just like her to say something like that.

Once again, we were arriving somewhere on his birthday. This time it was on the opposite side of the world.

We had reached our destination, Saigon, the capital of South Vietnam. Our mother had somehow survived four kids squirming on and around her for three days straight. She was just about at the breaking point, however. As the plane doors opened, the heat from the tarmac hit me square in the chest. It seemed to suck my very insides out, breath and all. A mirage had settled on the runway blacktop: ribbon-like waves of heat rose from the tarmac, distorting the view. It was hot like you had stepped into a Dutch oven.

The planes landing nearby sounded like an approaching thunderstorm. Leaving our cocoon-like environment now was a shock. Deafening sounds along with a conglomeration of smells bombarded us. We were now in the Paris of the Orient. The Colonel had called it that.

Tân Sơn Nhứt airport was the main airport in Saigon at the time. Both military transports and civilian airlines utilized the runways. The French had built it in 1920. It was now 1960. Once we were in the terminal, the wait for our bags to be loaded into the baggage bins seemed interminable. Mom had attempted to get us changed into clean clothes on the last layover, but we were as wrinkled as kids could possibly get. The Colonel was dressed in his conservative brown military fatigues. Mom had put on a dress that was cooler than the one she had been wearing, having finally given in to the heat. The Colonel was moving back and forth, trying to coordinate things. Running the length of the terminal, we were like a pack of wild banshees. Standing to the side of the chaos, Mom was desperately trying to pull herself together at the far end of the terminal. I could see her with her compact and a tube of bright red lipstick in hand. When she pulled out that tube of red magic, it was best to stay far away from her if you knew what was good for you.

A big black government staff limousine and a military jeep were waiting for us. The drivers stood by the gate with signs reading "Lt. Col. Hanna." The jeep driver, named Chou, was to be the Colonel's official driver from this point on, he told us. He had a smile that knew no end. After finally corralling all the luggage, we were soon on our way. We had a lot of bags. Between all of us and the luggage, two vehicles were definitely needed. Bags that didn't fit in the limousine were put into the military jeep. We disheveled humans squashed into the limo. The Colonel sat up front with the driver, and Tom got to ride in the open jeep alone with Chou. Lucky stiff!

The two vehicles raced past the rice fields and water buffalo, down the Biên Hòa Highway toward downtown Saigon. Along paths that ran next to the paved highway, blurred images of Vietnamese men and women on their bikes flew by our windows. Peasants in black pajama-like clothing, walking with poles across their shoulders, appeared as dark, smeared shadows. Rows of eucalyptus and plain trees, metal huts, and white stucco walls all whirled by us. Shacks abounded, erected from every conceivable material imaginable, filling in the spaces between the buildings. At stoplights the crackling music of the cicadas roared in our ears. It was as though the entire city had crashed down upon us in a single moment. The smells were like nothing we had ever experienced before. The city basked in an aroma of fish sauce. We later came to know it as *nước mắm*. Our senses were being called to attention on every level. At the same time, it was extraordinary. I couldn't do anything but laugh. I was happy.

Exotic flowers were blooming everywhere, fuchsia bushes, flame trees, and forsythia creating an amazing new world of color around us. As we moved through the city, more and more shacks were visible down side lanes built against the walls of both modern and ancient French-style villas. These compound walls were covered with brilliant climbing crimson and purple bougainvillea. Tall eucalyptus trees lorded over the roadways from magical heights. My half-imagined exotic world began to fill in at a full Technicolor level. As we passed the downtown buildings, our vehicles passed under a welcoming gantry stating: "A Friendly Welcome to the American People."

A man with a bamboo hat stood in front of a cart on the side of the street banging two pieces of wood together to create a repetitive tune: *tap tok ticky toc*. He was selling noodles, and the sound he made indicated the dish of the day. *Phở*, we would find out, was a traditional rice noodle soup with varying ingredients. The pungent smell emanating from the cart man's tray was marvelous. In that single moment, I realized we had finally arrived. Our incredible new life in this Paris of the Orient had begun.

Having been whisked through the countryside surrounding the airport into a town of boulevards lined with tall trees, we finally reached the street where the American ambassador lived. A classic French villa with fading white-washed stucco walls had been assigned to our family as our new quarters. We were to live just a few doors down from the ambassador on a street named Đoàn Thị Điểm. Huge metal gates were swung open. Our shiny black limousine and overloaded jeep turned into the driveway of a compound surrounded by high concrete stucco-covered walls topped with barbed wire and broken glass. Before us stood a structure from another era, majestic and regal. Lush gardens in full bloom surrounded it. We had entered a world of luxury and splendor. Household servants stood at the door waiting to greet us and initiate us into a life that can only be described as opulent. I had to blink twice to be sure I was seeing what was before me. Standing two stories high, the villa had wide ornate entry doors, decorative tile pavers covering the driveway, and beautiful reliefs on the walls.

Amazing fragrances accosted us. The most prominent scent was that of jasmine. There was a riot of flora everywhere. Mango trees stood heavy with fruit for the picking. Two brilliantly colored peacocks sat on the wall watching the circus below. The eyes of their tail feathers were tucked up tightly behind them.

Although we were told that this was to be our home, it didn't really register. The presence of servants in black pajama pants and fitted white shirts standing on the patio in readiness left us kids a bit uneasy. We simply didn't know what we were supposed to do with them or even how we were to act with these strangers. Were they going to live with us?

Days of pent-up energy after the long plane ride had us on a short fuse. We were ready to explode. Our refuge was the basketball that my brother had clutched throughout the entire trip. Remaining in the garden feigning ease, we threw the ball back and forth, all the time just trying to get our bearings. Showing vulnerability was something BRATs didn't do. There were a lot of missed catches, running around, and calculated ignoring of anything else going on. Children find ways of coping that parents are not aware of. What is the saying? "Kids can adjust to anything"? I don't think that is true. I think they make a good show of it though.

As we entered this ancient villa through a large screen door, the temperature seemed to miraculously drop. There was a coolness to the space—coolness in terms of temperature, that is. Overhead fans whirled, and the marble floors that ran throughout were cool to the touch. This was a rambling house with a winding stairway. The ceilings were fourteen feet high and the spaces cavernous. White plaster walls lent a brightness to the space. Soft light filtered through the shuttered windows. The living room and dining room filled the entire first floor, furnished with bamboo furniture and glass tables. The kitchen was outside, part of a long row of servants' quarters at the back of the house. There were three large bedrooms upstairs and two bathrooms. We wandered through the space, relieved to be out of the narrow confines we'd been stuck in for the preceding days.

On the glass dining room table in the center of the room rested a sweating pitcher of icy French lemonade with glasses set around it. The essence of lemons hung in the air. This French concoction bore no resemblance to any American lemonade we had ever had, probably because Mom had always used an instant type. This French lemonade was different, made by squeezing fresh lemons over ice and piling in sugar, adding water, and stirring. Nothing had ever tasted so good! Our mouths puckered with the sourness of the first gulp.

Trudging up the winding marble staircase, we discovered our assigned rooms by recognizing our various pieces of luggage. The rooms were massive. Large French-style armoires were in each bedroom, with dressing mirrors as the door panels. Multiple days of travel had us completely and unknowingly exhausted. We fell upon our respective beds and literally passed out. It was the first of many afternoon siestas that we would give in to, an established tradition in this country to avoid the afternoon heat. The sounds of twittering birds lulled us to sleep.

When we surfaced from our jet-lag-induced slumber later that afternoon, we were told we would be starting school the next morning. Moaning, we lamented the injustice of this trick of fate to anyone who would listen. We didn't realize then that we'd have nearly six months of vacation when we returned to the United States. School in Vietnam let out in April because of the intense heat.

We were lined up and given a strict warning by the Colonel: "Do not drink any water out of any faucet or glass that has not been boiled in advance!" This warning extended to ice cubes too. A trip to the Army dispensary with cases of dysentery was guaranteed for anyone who did not follow this order, and he made it clear that he would feel no sympathy for any of us who did not follow his orders. Dysentery is diarrhea in civilian terms. The Colonel said it would just love to take revenge on any one of our intestinal tracks if given the chance. We listened intently to his instructions, accepted the immediate end to our summer vacation, and prepared ourselves as best we could for what was to come. Like all good military kids, we would settle into our surroundings, our school, and our new life with ease. That is what seasoned BRATs do. We adapt, and like good soldiers, immediately become part of the world around us.

CHAPTER 5:

THE AMERICAN COMMUNITY SCHOOL

Waking before everyone the next morning, I pushed the front screen door open to a world waiting to ignite. Explode. The garden was aglitter with dew in the early morning light, sparkling as the sun's rays spread across fragile green leaves and thorny stalks. The heat of the day hadn't taken possession yet, and the coolness of the morning still hung in the air. The sounds of exotic birds, the roll of a noodle cart on the roadway, the running water in the servants' quarters as they prepared for the day filled my ears. The smell of a forgotten city permeated the morning air. Sitting on the tiled half wall of the villa's front porch, it all filtered through me.

Beyond our ornate metal entry gates, a slightly bent elderly woman dressed in traditional attire, worn black pajama-like clothing and bamboo hat, was slowly passing by, singing a melodious tune. Over her shoulder was a bamboo pole with grass baskets on either end. Small birds inside these woven cages pressed small beaks through the openings. The wizardly sunken face turned to gaze into the world barred from the woman by the large gates of the compound. She moved further down the worn dirt path that paralleled our high walls, her shuffling feet taking her slowly toward her intended destination.

A large green school van was to pick us up early. We had been told that school started at 0700 (7 AM). Six people fighting for two bathrooms was an all-out war of first-come, first-served. Remembering not to brush our teeth using the water from the faucet was a trial. This mad schedule was to be the pattern of every day to come. The wake-up chaos eventually culminated in a quick run down the stairs to consume a breakfast of French crepes filled with jam, a full glass of freshly squeezed orange juice, and a sliced mango. A huge hunk of freshly baked French bread spread with rich, creamy butter was waiting in our school snack bags.

The driver honked as he pulled up outside the gate. Tom, Pati, and I piled inside the waiting vehicle. The driver was smoking gluttonously, filling the van with the acidic smell of cigarette smoke. The air conditioner was on full force. Other American kids were picked up at various stops. The Bingham family was our closest American neighbor, and the kids' ages were around ours; Janis was near my age, Patty was Pati's age, and Judy was Tom's age. We befriended them immediately. The route the van took headed us back in the direction of the airport to the American Community School (ACS).

Class was scheduled to run only until noon. The heat of the day restricted the time we could be in the classrooms, it seemed. I was beside myself, giddy you might say, at the announcement of this miraculously short school schedule.

The American Community School had its beginning in 1954, providing American-style schooling for the dependent children of Americans working for U.S. government organizations in Saigon. Students at the ACS were an assortment of military-dependent kids; children whose parents were in American construction companies and USAID (United States Agency for International Development) organizations, the State Department, the embassies; and a few Vietnamese kids whose parents wanted them there. I would learn many years later that there were a lot of Central Intelligence Agency (CIA) kids there too. I made a few friends quickly: one of the girls, Ann Peabody, had a father who was an aide to the commanding general, and another girl's father was a member of the USOM (United States Overseas Mission). Like all good transient gypsies, we met and decided what we liked about each other. We were friends in an instant.

The teaching staff at the school was recruited from the wives of the personnel who were stationed in Saigon for whatever reason, along with a few certified educators. The curriculum was sent from the States, defining requirements for each grade to assure school credit when students returned to America. The high school program was a correspondence course run by officers' wives conducted on the grounds of the ACS. This caused many parents to send their sons or daughters to a Catholic school north of the city, to the Brent School in the Philippines, or stateside to live with relatives.

The ACS building had French-style architecture, with open breezeways, an adobe tile floor, and satellite stucco buildings shooting off from the walkways. Shutter-like doors and windows helped keep the rooms cool, along with grinding overhead fans. Covered walkways led to rows of classrooms. There were two metal Quonset huts that had been erected in an open field just before the last row of classrooms. One was used as an auditorium, and the other a library.

I was entering the fifth grade, Pati the second grade, and Tom the eighth grade. The school had a revolving door of students. Overseas assignments for military families were usually for a two-year stay. There were only a few hundred kids at most. These kids qualified as BRATs simply by the very disruptiveness of their lives.

What interested me more than the school itself was what lay beyond the waist-high wall that surrounded the school: rice paddies. Vietnamese men and women worked in them standing knee high in the water with the bottoms of their pants rolled up. Bent over, they would plant thin rice stalks in the mud below the water. The familiar sloshing sound of water could be heard as the children peddled the water wheel like a bike, running it through bamboo troughs to irrigate the fields. Walls of dirt that had built up when the paddies were dug out held the water inside. Boards had been laid down on the dirt mounds, but not everywhere. Water buffalo were present and seemed to be treated like family, doing as much work throughout the day as their owners, if not more. Luckily, our shuttered classroom doors and windows kept this neighboring distraction from my view during classroom hours.

We arrived home less anxious and more grounded after our first day. Bob, my youngest brother, hadn't been with us. The ACS didn't have a kindergarten. He waited on the entry porch for our return, resentful, surrounded by a set of Matchbox cars. When he later realized that he got to sleep late and had our mother all to himself, he didn't mind our abandonment of him as much. Mom, in the meantime, had heard a rumor that younger children picked up languages faster than older ones. She was soon on the trail of information about a French Catholic school run by Vietnamese and

French nuns that had a kindergarten. Children spoke only French at this school. She registered him for class faster than you could say "*beaucoup dien cai dau*" (very crazy in the head)!

A Moment in History

In 1965 the ACS closed its doors with the evacuation of U.S. dependents. At the same time, the 3rd Field Hospital opened its doors in the same buildings. When the war ended, the buildings became a reforestation research facility, with a mission to revive the land that had been so decimated by the chemical deforestation of Agent Orange and bombings. Agent Orange was an experimental chemical that was sent to the Ordnance Corps to act as a defoliant around ammunition depots in the early '60s. The Airforce noticed the effectiveness of the defoliant and promptly requisitioned it to destroy everything that grew in this tropical landscape.

"The country and its people struggle to this day with the long-lasting effects of this destructive and debilitating chemical; deformities and cancer are its signature. By some estimates, forest cover in Vietnam declined by 50 percent between 1945 and 1980. During the Vietam War, U.S. forces sprayed 72 million liters of herbicides, including Agent Orange, on the Vietnamese countryside and dropped roughly 13 million tons of bombs, according to Jakarta-based forestry expert Chris Lang. Defloliants destroyed about 7,700 square miles of forests – six percent of Vietnam's land area."

—*Mike Ives,* In War-Scared Landscape, Vietnam Replants Its Forests, *November 4, 2010*

CHAPTER 6:

JE SUIS AMERICAN!

B ob's room was a small alcove set off from our parents' bedroom. Ludicrous shadow images flashed across his face and body at night from the fruit bats that soared in and hung outside his bedroom window. These were bats with five-foot-wide wingspans, gigantic as they canvased the night's blackness. They hung in rows along the roof over-hang of the house we lived in on Đoàn Thị Điểm. Bob lay still in the more-than-half dark, the whooshing sounds of the beating wings causing him a kind of furious annoyance. Most evenings he would just stay awake. It was his way of managing his fear. The bats were the last thing he'd see before going to sleep as premonitions of the dawn settled in the air. He'd wake up in sweaty wet cotton. Every night was like this for him. He'd stay awake as long as he could, finally falling asleep exhausted just as the rays of morning light began to break.

Bob had huge black circles under his eyes, which our mother attributed to poor eating habits. Sleep deprivation can cause the same thing. He never said anything about these nights of horror. He bore it and tolerated the terror each night. Although our parents slept in the room next to his, they never knew of his evening rituals. He'd get down on his knees and say his prayers as Mom sat next to him. She'd tuck him in on evenings whenever she was home. Those nights he felt better. His mother was near him, covering him with a clean white sheet and stroking his hair. She would press her cheek to his, kissing him on the forehead as she adjusted the sheets around him as she said goodnight. After she left, he would start praying again. For this little five-year-old, these prayers had mostly to do with bats.

L'Ecole des Enfants or some such name was to be Bob's new school. It was held in a beautiful white building with a large courtyard out front. It had a mix of children from prominent Vietnamese families and French children whose families remained in the country. Bob hated it. He wanted to be at the ACS, the school his sisters and brother were attending, not this one run by Catholic nuns. Each day, his snack was packed in a paper bag and he was sent off with one of the servants to what he clearly considered prison. She would drop him off and continue with her assigned shopping tasks for the day, picking him up later. After the first month or so of the same pat statement coming out of Bob's mouth when asked about school, it occurred to our mother to question him further. "What are you talking about? What tree?" She looked him straight in the eye and held him there to be sure they had a conversation. On that morning, she wasn't in a hurry and had time to follow up on this fantastic story.

"They tie me up to a tree," he said nonchalantly. He'd gotten used to saying this and no one responding.

"Who?" she drilled on.

"The nuns, those ladies in the white dresses and funny hats."

"Whatever for? Why would they want to do that, sweetie?" she said, now completely engaged.

"I fall asleep in class," he said, yawning. He was glad to finally have the chance to sleep unhindered by the thoughts and sounds of flapping wings.

"How often does this happen?" she asked.

"Oh, every day," he said without hesitation. "It's okay 'cause I want to be outside anyway. I told them I don't have to speak French. I'm American. That isn't what we speak in America." He was clear in his logic, and he knew it.

She seemed to weigh his words carefully. He had to get moving if he was going to be able to make it there on time. Anna, the only servant who seemed remotely to care about us, would take what was called a motorcyclo that day to make up for the delay. She knew Bob loved motorcyclos because they were a half of a motorbike on the back and a carriage on the front. They could go fast. They made a lot of noise. This was Bob's kind of ride.

Mom seemed preoccupied with her thoughts that morning and finally resolved to check out her son's story. Dressing in her best conservative outfit, a simple loose cotton dress, she set out in a taxi to go to the school for an unannounced visit. The blue-and-yellow Renault cab pulled up to the front of the school, and she got out. "*Merci*," she said to the driver. He watched her as she walked to the large gate that marked the entrance. She was a beautiful woman, as I've said, and she walked with an air of quiet confidence. She pulled up on the handle and the large metal gate swung open. Mom was to tell us the story of what happened later that day.

There in the center of the courtyard tied to a large banyan tree lay Bob, sound asleep. He was positioned between the big roots of the tree with his head resting on the tree trunk itself. The expression on his face was one of impish serenity. Rope was lashed around him so there wasn't any possible way of escape. His arms and ankles were twisted in the restricting rope so he couldn't get himself loose. He looked content, and even the sounds of children singing coming from inside the building didn't seem to disturb him.

I'm not sure what shade of red lipstick Mom had on that day, but her face must have matched its color. She moved toward her son and began to untie him. Bob stirred as he heard her muttering under her breath. I'm sure she was swearing, but she'd never admit to that, and Bob wasn't awake enough to confirm it later. A nun inside spotted her from a window and came out to greet her.

"What do you think you are doing?" Mom raged at the French nun before the woman even got her welcoming greeting out. Mom continued unraveling the rope. Bob simply remained quiet, staring up at his mother's giant presence.

"He is being punished," the Sister said without hesitation.

"For what? Falling asleep? Why haven't you let me know what was going on here?" Her voice was now rising by octaves.

"He won't learn French. He keeps saying he is American and doesn't have to. He won't stay awake. It is all very disruptive to the other children."

"Come!" Mom snapped when the last knot was released.

With this final command, our mother left L'Ecole des Enfants with Bob's hand tightly grasped in hers. I'd have loved to have seen the expression on Bob's face, because I am sure he wouldn't have held off sticking his tongue out at the nun who watched them leave. For her part, the nun was probably relieved to have him gone.

The next thing we knew, Mom was the new kindergarten teacher at a place that was in a different location than the American Community School. She hadn't wasted any time in getting this put together. It was in a garrison building in a restricted fenced area near the presidential Independence Palace, the Norodom Compound. She had never taught school before, but her experience running the daycare in Illinois was enough to assure her the job. Bob needed to go to kindergarten, and this was Mom's solution. She had surveyed the other women who had small children and found there were enough kids to justify the creation of one. The Colonel had run it by the upper brass. A classroom space and some funds to start it up were allocated. Each day, our mother and brother went off to school together. Bob couldn't have been happier.

"She's my mom," Bob one day proudly told another kid who was in the class.

"No, she isn't!" the kid snapped back. Kids like to think the teacher is theirs alone and belongs to no one else.

"Yes, she is!"

"What's the problem here?" Mom intervened.

"You're my mom, aren't you?" Bob said with a smirk as he looked at the other kid.

"No," she replied. "Never saw you before in my life."

When Mom told us this story later I had to wonder whatever possessed her to make this statement. It was a singular blow to this little boy who was already so displaced. He didn't like Vietnam. He wanted to be in America. To have this blow to his pride so easily done by his mother was hurtful. Although she apologized and corrected it later, he never did get over it. Mom had a playful, teasing nature, and I think she thought she was being cute. Who knows? But whatever she thought, it was damaging.

I was in my own world then and had no idea of how our environment was shaping any of us. Each of us children would come away from our time in Saigon different, with baggage we wouldn't even know we were carrying until years later. Then it would come at us like a freight train in the middle of the night. Fortunately, we wouldn't know about this until we were years older, scattered to the four winds across the United States and living separate lives. For now, we took each day as it came and adjusted accordingly.

A MOMENT IN HISTORY

"Until 1945, the Franco-indigenous school system oper-ated in parallel with the French educational system, serving the French children and selected children of Indo-Chi-nese elites (about twenty percent of enrollment). Most of the Vietnamese people could neither read nor write. Viet-namese nationalists could claim that ninety percent of the population was illiterate. However, despite such failings, the colonial educational system in Vietnam resulted in the emergence of a French-speaking or even Francophile elite—journalists, lawyers, doctors, scientists, business-people, landowners—many of whom became figures in the independence movement, in the name of the ideals of the French Republic they had been taught in school. After the end of World War II, the French hoped to reclaim their former colony but found that they could no longer rule

Vietnam as they had done before, since Vietnamese independence had been proclaimed by the Japanese in March 1945, and then by Hồ Chí Minh in September."

—Thuy-Phuong Nguyen "The Rivalry of the French and American Educational Missions During the Vietnam War," Paedagogica Historica: International Journal of the History of Education, *Paris Descartes University: Paris, France, April 2014*

CHAPTER 7:

LE CERCLE SPORTIF

Our strange new life was taking shape slowly, without difficulty, for both parents and kids. As BRATs, we had the ability to metamorphose into whatever was required to survive. Outside the screen door of the aged villa, butterflies congregated around the flowering plants and bushes that filled the garden. Butterflies, gliding erratically through the filtered light, landing ever so lightly on the brightly colored petals. Have you ever noticed that butterflies never fly on a straight course, but make choppy and sideways movements, sometimes just spinning? These butterflies would twirl and suddenly soar upward in a dance. It was intoxicating to watch them. For BRATs, this is what life is all about: erratic movements and responses to unpredictable gusts of wind. The Saigon wind was usually slight and hot. Just breathing in the air was like taking a long, slow, parched breath. It was like breathing in the air from an oven that had been set on high for some time. Our relief from it all was to be at the Cercle Sportif, a decadent former French refuge from the heat and everything else. It was a swim and tennis club located in downtown Saigon.

One day Pati, Bob, and I planned to go to the Cerc. More than planned at this point; we demanded it! The Colonel had gotten a family membership to the club within days of our arrival in Saigon. The waiting servant, the one assigned to take us there, was getting restless and wanted to get going so she could get back to her chores at the house. Adjusting to the intense heat of this tropical country wasn't easy. Finishing a huge glass of iced lemonade, we grabbed our swimsuits and headed toward the gate. We didn't know where anyone else was anymore and by now didn't care. The Colonel was most likely at work, but Mom had developed a habit of simply disappearing. The servants had their orders for the day from our mother, so we kids were herded in whatever direction they had been told to take us. Tom decided at the last minute to go with us, but usually he would make his own plans without us younger kids.

The Cercle Sportif was a welcome relief, something so strikingly different from the bustle of city life that was a shock to us. Built in 1896, it was a place to hide from the scorching heat of the day, an oasis. Located just behind Independence Palace, the home of the President Diệm and his family, it was one of many remaining monuments of the French era. Colonial in style, the Cerc maintained the traditions of correct etiquette and appropriate behavior. It was a cocoon of sorts, a club with foreigners dominating the membership, one that was limited. Vietnamese waiters and gardeners took care of the needs of the members. Although I saw tennis players dressed all in white on the grounds, I never tried to play tennis. There was a restaurant, but after having been served an extremely tough steak, the Colonel decided that in the future meals out would be taken at the Brinks BOQ (Bachelor Officers' Quarters). He kept saying he thought it was horse meat. He said this with dancing eyes. He was fully aware of the consternation it would cause his young children. Glancing over at Mom, he registered the effect he had made. So far, the Colonel was enjoying his life in Saigon. He liked his work and his Vietnamese associates, though he didn't disclose much to any of us of what he was up to. His orders stated that he was Chief of Ordnance Corps with MAAG (Military Assistance Advisory Group), and this position carried a great deal of responsibility. That much, the family knew.

The Cerc's swimming pool, gigantic and with multiple high diving boards, was divided into deep, medium, and shallow sections, along with a wading pool for babies and toddlers. I think the Cerc also had a library, where people could play chess, something my brother took up with a friend. From almost day one, we joined the club and were there practically three hundred sixty-five days a year. French, American and British: the Cerc was overrun with kids from every country, it seemed. The Vietnamese were few and far between, many choosing not to be seen in a place where so many Americans hung out for fear of government reprisals. President Diệm and his brother Nhu conducted spy activities on any Vietnamese socializing with Americans.

Pati and I were in awe in the girls' changing room at the Cerc. On our first day there, we went into a room with the word "Femmes" on the door. Girls of all ages were running around naked, dripping water and giggling. We were like two nuns huddled in a corner by some lockers we had found empty. Most of the young girls in swimsuits were topless.

I sat in horror. Our newly acquired Sears suits were one-piece. Only later that year did Mom break down and buy a two-piece for Pati, who was determined to try to fit in.

"They aren't wearing any tops," Pati said in complete amazement. I was holding both her hands so she wouldn't point. Mom had drilled into me long ago that pointing wasn't polite.

"Well, we aren't going to do that. Besides, our suits wouldn't let us unless we had some scissors nearby."

"Do you want me to see if I can get some?" she said, still transfixed by a girl her age who was sitting on the bench close by. Topless!

"No," I said in horror. This was truly a nightmare. Whatever lay beyond the door was now starting to perplex me.

We slid our suits on as the girls nearby watched us. They were trying to talk to us, but we were limited in our understanding of French then, so most of what we heard seemed like guttural nonsense.

A little girl about Pati's age was trying to engage her in conversation. "*J'aime beaucoup la natation. Et toi?*" She was smiling and hoping to make a new friend.

"Just smile and nod," I instructed Pati as we made a quick exit.

Tight-fitting Speedo swimsuits were on the foreign boys and men, their male members somewhat protruding under the stretched fabric. They seemed to have the same laissez-faire attitude as the girls and women. It was easy to tell the Americans from the French. The American boys had loose, boxy swim trunks, and the female children were in one-piece swimsuits. Some American teenage girls were sporting bikinis but not going topless.

The French paid no attention to any of it. It was simply natural to be either half naked or exposed. "Simply a fact of life," one of my French girlfriends would later tell me. What was all the fuss?

You would have thought the French were still in charge from the looks of the Cerc. There were very few Vietnamese present in any capacity at the Cerc, except as waiters and gardeners. It had that completely snobbish attitude so prevalent in countries under colonial rule, albeit former rule. I didn't think much about it until later. I was too grateful for the relief from the heat and the extraordinary pound cake they served at the pool bar. This pound cake was like Christmas on a plate. My ritual was to order a piece of it and a Coca-Cola with one ice cube. We could have an ice cube in our drink at the Cerc, a rare occurrence, after the Colonel confirmed that they boiled the water there. Life in Saigon came with many warnings.

Soaking up the sun and swimming, Pati and I fell into a comfortable tanning ritual. With tons of American suntan oil smeared all over us, we'd stretch out on our towels by the side of the pool. The chaises were taken up by the adults and teens, leaving us younger kids to compete for the space along the hot water-splashed pavement surrounding the pool.

Tom would drop Bob by the little kids' wading pool and tell us to keep an eye on him. Then he would go hang out with the kids his age. Bob was glad to stay in the shallow pool. He found kids to play with and was happy. Eventually, it would be time to catch a cyclo and return home. Tom would come with us to the club but then disappear. We didn't bother to look for him.

"*Đoàn Thị Điểm, s'il vous plaît,*" I would tell the cyclo driver, but immediately followed that with, "*Combien?*"

We'd been told to always ask how much before going anywhere in these vehicles. We had French classes at school, and I'd been working hard at getting the basics down, so I could attempt communication. English was not a prevalent language in Vietnam at the time. Most of the Vietnamese spoke French, the result of so many years of French domination and control of the school systems.

I'd completely given up trying to say anything in Vietnamese by now. It just got me in trouble. Because I used the wrong intonation, I seemed to always be offering an insult instead of a compliment. Inflection with any Vietnamese word can result in its having numerous meanings. Every word was like that in Vietnamese. It is like the English word "oh." Depending on how you say it, you could be asking a question or making a statement. Vietnamese was impossible for me, so I stuck with my piecemeal French. We would pool our wet and wadded-up piasters (the Vietnamese currency) together to pay the driver when we got to our destination. Mom was usually there waiting for us. On nights when she and the Colonel were going out, things moved rapidly from that point on. Homework, dinner, bed, no talking, and lights out were the drill.

Our life simply became an extension of what the French had established in Saigon. After all, we looked like them, learned to speak their language, and used their facilities. The Cercle Sportif was a lasting symbol of French colonial rule. We settled into this life of ease without another thought. The Cerc was a welcome sanctuary, as I mentioned, and we went there whenever we could get permission.

Mom was relentless in finding activities to fill our time with other than just school and the Cerc. She was tireless in her efforts to compensate for what she thought we kids were missing by not living in the United States. Right now, her focus was on her oldest son, Tom. She had big plans for him!

The Cercle Sportif was our escape from the oppressive heat of the day. My sister, Pati, was in awe of the French girls with their bikini bottom swimsuits.

CHAPTER 8:

CRICKETS IN
SHELTERED PLACES

"Chantilly Lace" by the Big Bopper blared loudly from the speakers. Tom had brilliantly assembled his music collection just before leaving the States. The Colonel's new reel-to-reel tape recorder made it possible for Tom to keep the music playing nonstop through the night, for the dance parties Mom created to give the eighth graders a place to go. She wanted them to be doing things they would be doing in the States. These parties would be held for Tom and his classmates once a month. Tom rose to the occasion, playing the role of DJ long before this concept was made popular decades later!

Vietnam represented a new start for Tom. It had been a difficult two years in the civilian town of our last assignment. Here in Saigon, the kids were like us: military dependents and government gypsies. Mom loved parties, and this was just the beginning of a full schedule she would organize during our stay. Mostly, she held cocktail parties for officers and their wives. Constant displacement had left me and my siblings somewhat shy. These were the types of social things our mother would organize throughout our lives in the hope of bringing us out of our self-made cocoons.

Our mother, with the blessing of every parent there, planned these youth shindigs at our house on Đoàn Thị Điểm. The parents were glad to have their teenagers under someone's supervision. The first dance was held on Friday, November 10, 1960. Kids showed up with Connie Francis hairdos or hair slicked back into what was called a ducktail, wearing short summer dresses or dragon shirts. They all looked older than their actual years.

The Postal Exchange (PX) was the place to get American goods. Brylcreem and Vaseline were hot sellers for sculpting that James Dean rebel look for the boys. Hairspray was more than available to this gaggle of adolescent girls, and their hair took on a voluminous scale. Kids sat around in clusters. The more popular ones hung together. The less popular youths clung to the sidelines hoping their moment would come. It was obvious, at least to me, that the girls who were developing faster were the ones getting more attention than the others. Unobserved in the driveway, kids would smoke. Smoking was the number-one activity, even though most of these kids were thirteen. This was a time for experimentation. Others sat on the porch out of sight listening to the music rather than having to face dancing with a member of the opposite sex.

In the beginning, Mom hired a Vietnamese dance instructor for the night. He was a singular vision. In his tight black pants, shiny pointed dance shoes, and greased-back hair, he attempted to instruct a group of doubting teenagers. He knew only the French dances of the time, and those time-honored steps weren't really in sync with the Bop. This was the dance that was becoming popular in the States and now in Saigon among these teens. He tried his best, but the kids, although polite, were less than enthusiastic.

"Gee, Tom," a girl named Cindy said one night. "This is great! If we could just get rid of the dance instructor, I'd be glad to show everyone some new dances going on in the States." Cindy had just arrived and was considered the one who was most up-to-date on everything stateside.

"No problem," Tom said, knowing he'd be able to get Mom to go along with it. He was basking in the moment. The most popular girl in school had just spoken to him. He was beaming.

After a few evenings like this, the dance instructor was no longer on the docket. With his dismissal, the kids were now in charge of the music and dance moves. Once a month, kids showed up using this party as an excuse to get out of their houses. They came in orchestrated waves. There were times when it was mostly girls, with the boys disappearing for extended periods of time. The dances didn't require partners, so the girls usually took over the floor, but some pairs attempted some of the slow dances. Mom kept herself busy bringing out pitchers of lemonade and sweets. She wanted these fetes to be successful. I watched from my perch on the dark stairway, hidden behind the spindles. Older boys scared me. I rarely ventured down except to make a run for the chocolate chip cookies and back. I wasn't welcomed. Tom would glare at me as if I'd suddenly contaminated the room. Mom always gave explicit directions to us younger children earlier on those nights that we were not to come downstairs. Tom added an extra warning that included the threat of death.

"If I catch any of you down here, I will kill you in your beds. It might not be tonight, but one of these nights I'll do it," he said, sneering. That was enough of a warning to keep Pati and Bob upstairs, but not me. I think Bob and Pati were fast asleep before the party was even half over. Mom eventually stationed herself near the stairway to keep me from making any more appearances.

As I sprawled on my bed staring at the ceiling that night, the sound of music pulsated and filled the room. I was thinking about how much more relaxed Tom was in the role of the evening DJ, not forced to dance. He was the master of the music, in control of it all. Back in the States when he was only eleven, he would have to dress up and wear gloves to go to the formal dance lessons Mom thought he should have. Although Tom knew how to dance, he preferred this new role.

As the music played on and on, the slow whirling sound of the overhead fan blended in with my brother's complete list of favorites. One by one, they were played. The tunes lilted upward. "I Wanna Be Cathy's Clown," "I'm a Travelin' Man," "Tell Laura I Love Her," Tom's playlist was extensive and included some of the best music of the day! At least he thought so. I think everyone at the party agreed with him. The Everly Brothers, Buddy Holly and the Crickets, The Big Bopper himself, the sweet-toned Johnny Mathis, a young Ricky Nelson, Richie Valens, Johnny Preston, Ray Peterson, the legendary Fats Domino, and dreamy Pat Boone were the favorites of these kids. "Splish Splash I Was Taking a Bath" had everyone on their feet moving to Bobby Darren's bopping music. I think even those kids who didn't know how to dance found ways to move to that one.

Once I was sure the younger kids were asleep, I'd watch the outdoor action from the upstairs screened-in porch, where I wouldn't be bothered. Kids would gather to smoke outside, trying to conceal themselves in the garden. Only the ends of smoldering cigarettes would be visible. I'd see a few of them sneak off to be alone and experiment with kissing. The shy ones would fade into the shadows just to watch.

This music was Tom's anchor, as it was for most of these Saigon teenagers. For these displaced American kids, it was their lifeline, something that tethered them in this strange world they found themselves in. I would never admit it to my all-knowing brother, but I liked the music too.

Older kids would show up at the entry gate, but Tom would tell them they couldn't come in. "Hound Dog Man" by the heartthrob Fabian would be droning in the background, and the kids' excited singing along with the music would roll out through the open doorway. I think my brother took pride in the fact that he could tell the older kids what to do. After so many years of his being bullied, especially when we were around civilian kids back in the States, this was now life on his terms. He relished it. They would leave muttering, but he didn't care. This was his party, and they could cry if they wanted.

The older ones who had been turned away hailed the motorcyclos passing on Đoàn Thị Điểm and left to find entertainment elsewhere. A lot of these boys went down to Rue Tu Do and Rue Catinat to drink *ba muoi ba*. The Vietnamese beer of choice was 33 Premium Export. A warning had recently circulated among all the kids, even the younger ones, about La Rue beer. It was generally known that this beer had formaldehyde in it, and it was subsequently known as "tiger piss." Our mother, thankfully, was oblivious to it all. She would stand on the sidelines making sure all was going well at the party as best she could. The Colonel made a point of being away, probably hanging out with his cronies at the Brinks BOQ (Bachelor Officer Quarters).

Tom surveyed everything while keeping a sentry position at the gate, occasionally running back inside to check on the state of things indoors. Eventually the party would end, and the kids would leave in small groups to share a cab or cyclo. There was never a question of a parent or servant's escorting them home. In 1960, they arrived on their own and left on their own. In Saigon, these kids had an independence that they would never again experience in their lives. It would all end when they returned to America. Adjusting to life in the United States would be a challenge for each and every one of them. Here, they were whatever they wanted to be. They could go wherever they wanted to go whenever they liked. The Vietnamese cab drivers would take them home without anyone's ever having to even say where they lived. In Saigon, everything was known. We were like crickets in sheltered places, merrily singing without any sense of any apparent danger. As described earlier, the next day, Novermber 11, 1960, we found ourselves in the middle of a military coup against the Diệm regime.

Being in a coup was certainly a strange experience, but I considered it our official rite of passage, our entry card to the real world that surrounded us instead of the glossed-over Americanized version our mother was so intent upon keeping us in. By the following day, after the coup, there was no evidence of any type of unrest. The markets were open. The people went about their lives, zipping from here to there on their bikes, motorcycles, pedicabs, carts, and in their cars. President Diệm forgave everyone, and the disgruntled officers returned to the fold. Although life continued as before, we all now had a new awareness about the world around us.

Our lives, those of American kids in Saigon, were a confused mix of Western ideas and those of a country set apart from us by its culture and beliefs, by its history. We knew nothing about what was going on around us. We lived in a sheltered world. Blissful. Ignorant.

A MOMENT IN HISTORY

"On November 11, 1960, a coup attempt against President Ngô Đình Diệm of South Vietnam was led by Lieutenant Colonel Vương Văn Đông and Colonel Nguyễn Chánh Thi of the Airborne Division of the Army of the Republic of Vietnam (ARVN). The rebels launched the coup in response to Diệm's autocratic rule and the negative political influence of his brother Ngô Đình Nhu and his sister-in-law Madame Nhu. They also bemoaned the politicization of the military, whereby regime loyalists who were members of the Ngô family's covert Cần Lao Party were readily promoted ahead of more competent officers who were not insiders. The coup caught the Ngô family completely off-guard, but it was also chaotically executed. The plotters neglected to seal the roads leading into the capital of Saigon to cut off loyalist reinforcements. They hesitated after gaining the initiative. The coup failed when the 5th and 7th Divisions of the ARVN entered Saigon and defeated the rebels. More than four hundred people—many of whom were civilian spectators—were killed in the ensuing battle."

—*Stanley Karnow,* Vietnam: A History, *Penguin Books, 1997*

CHAPTER 9:

RUE TU DO

Life in Saigon was an exotic whirlwind that never stopped, even when the sun had set and the night's magic unfolded. It was a full-scale theatrical production made up of trivial glitter against a black night. The painted ladies of Rue Tu Do in downtown Saigon were fascinating. Like shimmering candy, they seemed to be just children themselves made up as beautiful China dolls. Their skin was translucent, pale from the lack of sun and the heavy powders they applied. They sported lips as ripe as cherries. The áo dàis they wore were flamboyant, brightly colored, no longer tightly fastened around their necks in traditional style but more revealing. These redesigned traditional áo dais, now modernized by Madame Nhu, President Diệm's sister-in-law, had a new exposed neckline. The style had been readily adopted by these shimmering figures, even though so many of them didn't think well of her. Sometimes, an intricate beaded pattern crossed the tops of their lacquered two-tone high heels. Lounging in sidewalk cafes, they would sip the drink they were nursing as they lingered outside the streetside bars or sat in the faded wicker chairs fanning themselves. There was a deliberate ease about them.

They seemed like life's sideshow, holding the mysteries of an unknown and exotic world in their painted faces. They were compositions that had been drawn freehand with expressions that boasted that "All men are vulnerable."

The eucalyptus-lined boulevards of Saigon were thick with bicycles and taxis at all hours of the day and night. Rue Tu Do was no exception. Motor scooters transported whole families and young lovers sounding like a swarm of locusts. The high-pitched whine of these machines never stopped. The city never closed. People were everywhere. There weren't that many foreigners in 1960 in Saigon. The French had, by all accounts, left their colony—a colony not of citizens but, like most European conquests in the Orient, made up of subjects now no longer under their rule. Only a small number of French remained, ex-pats attempting to hold on to their comfortable life. Foreign diplomats, American military advisors, and USAID workers were becoming more prevalent, along with individuals from the CIA. Saigon was a city trying to maintain the income base it had garnered from the French, hopeful of having it replaced but without any imposed control by this new batch of American foreigners. Rue Tu Do was like a microcosm of the wold. Everyone eventually found their way there.

Mom had been quick to get me involved in the Girl Scouts in Saigon. This came with an even more impressive uniform than the Brownie outfit, one that was green. I'd made it through the Brownie stage while in the States. We were a small group of girls making up the Saigon troop, and I'd already started working on my Stamp badge. I'd go to the stamp store on Rue Tu Do and select new stamps each week. It was a solitary activity that suited my normally shy nature.

Afterward, I would wait under a tree canopy for the servant who had been assigned the task of getting me where I wanted to go and picking me up. It had been made clear to me that I was not to dump her, the servant, or all privileges would be removed permanently. As I waited outside the shop, I soon noticed the strange bubble of life that existed across the street from the shop. I would linger somewhat hidden by a peeling eucalyptus tree to watch the uniformed servicemen and the young Vietnamese men, with their greased-back hair and black attire, as they passed by or stopped. They were there to turn their piasters into every kind of known forgetfulness. Maybe it was women, opium, drink, or whatever that they hoped would deliver them from the past and the future, to leave them floating in the present moment.

Young American teenagers, with their pale expressions of expectancy, would often join the mix strolling by these precious flowers. Some of them I recognized from the ACS. They were the high school students. I'd hide behind the tree trunk so as not to be noticed by them. I never caught sight of my brother though. For many of them, it was so often their first foray into this exotic world of sex for hire. Their stories would be the ones they would tell years later. It would be the time of their lives when they were completely free and unsupervised, when they no longer felt like children. There was music somewhere at the heart of the hubbub. Throbbing American tunes filled the air, mixed with French love songs and the shrill notes of Vietnamese string instruments, so melodic and sensual. I was a voyeur of it all.

I bought stamps, not for their monetary value, but for their beauty. I had collected a series of stamps from the early days when Vietnam was part of French Indochina.

I had others that depicted fantastic colorful battles fought by men in traditional attire on top of elephants and water buffalo. The stamps depicting the life of Buddha were my favorite. These were like miniature paintings. I had a treasure that no one else had. The storekeeper got used to me. He knew to just put out lots of trays and let me go through them. He'd sit quietly reading his paper and wait for me to make my selections.

"*Merci*," I would say to the shop owner as I turned the door handle to leave.

"*À tout à l'heure*," he would answer, his sweet voice trailing me as the door closed behind me.

I bought a lot of stamps while in Saigon on Rue Tu Do, but mostly I stood back and watched the extraordinary parade before me on this world's stage. I became an observer of the observed, watching individuals in the first stages of experimentation. Age-weary older men were trying to find some comfort in a place they had come to without their families or girlfriends back home. I would sink back into the shade of a nearby tree or wall to continue watching after I had bought my stamps and left the shop.

This world I was a voyeur of made me uncomfortable. Being a female child in a military world is a singularly unique and weird experience. All my life, I'd always felt vulnerable on Army posts. These were places made up of enlisted men, officers, and adolescents mimicking their male-dominated society. Mom's constant warnings about staying away from strangers and not talking to anyone I didn't know somehow added to my fragile sense of well-being. Now, as I was living in this foreign country where light skin and blond hair created an immediate need for Vietnamese passersby to touch you and Americans away from home to hug you, my sense of being at risk was even greater.

A child's personal space is so easily violated, usually without his or her consent. I was at risk for what I still didn't know, but my self-preservation instinct made me aware of everything around me. No matter where I was, I scanned the world to be sure I was safe—and if my younger sister and brother were with me, that they were safe too. It wasn't a feeling of fear. It was just a general accounting for everything around me in short spurts. Combine this sense of vulnerability with a very cloudy and unclear understanding of some of the warnings my mother gave, and it didn't help things. In our early days in Saigon, Pati and I made our appearances more boy-like by getting our hair cut off, something we insisted Mom let us do. Dressed in boyish clothing, we were not bothered as much.

Our servant, Anna, would finally arrive to collect me from the stamp shop in a cyclo for the ride back to Đoàn Thị Điểm. I had questions that no one could answer for me. How could one get answers when there was no way of forming the questions? I looked at her and wondered whether she had any kind of life other than the one that seemed to devour her every moment: serving our family, living in the quarters behind our villa, getting one day a week off and receiving pay comparable to forty dollars a month.

Anna was in a hurry and it didn't seem a good time to embark on the many questions that filled my mind. Rue Tu Do was a hotbed of confusion for me. This parade of humanity in search of comfort and love on Rue Tu Do left me perplexed. It took me two years to put all the pieces together of what I saw on Rue Tu Do. My brother agreed to answer all my questions when I turned thirteen. When he did so, with obvious glee at my discomfort, I was horrified.

A MOMENT IN HISTORY

"Vietnam's national dress, the traditional áo dài (literally "long shirt"; pronounced "ow za" in the north and "ow yai" in the south) consists of two elements: a long tunic with a close-fitting bodice, a mandarin collar, raglan sleeves, and side slits that create front and back panels from the waist down; and wide-legged pants that are often cut on the bias. While in the past both men and women wore an áo dài, in the twenty-first century it is almost exclusively a woman's garment. Madame Nhu, the sister-in-law of President Ngô Đình Diệm, became notorious in the 1950s and 1960s for the skin-baring open necklines of her redesigned áo dài. The new áo dài was considered scandalous."

—*Wild Tussah,* History of the Vienamese Costume Áo Dài, *July 29, 2016*

CHAPTER 10:

MINE FIELDS, SCOUTING, AND BASEBALL

In Saigon, my mother's single-minded need to create American experiences for her children took many twists and turns. She saw this as her main responsibility as our parent. After her Friday-night youth dances for Tom became a success, she moved on to bigger and better things. She couldn't help it. It was just in her makeup to take charge and use her persuasive Southern ways to talk everyone else into whatever she had in mind. The other ladies in her group were one hundred percent on the same track and agreed to whatever she suggested. American movies and the Girl Scouts were high on her to-do list for me. My stamp collecting had met with enthusiastic approval when I suggested it. As far as Mom was concerned, we girls weren't going to be deprived of the advantages of an American upbringing. Not if she and her ladies could help it.

The mothers were determined to focus us girls on the task of earning Girl Scout badges. Lots of them! Mom chose the International Dance badge as the one we'd take on first as a group. She brought in her friends, mostly embassy wives, who could share a native dance for us to learn. Pulling costumes together for this was something they all put an inordinate amount of energy into. She had a Japanese friend who taught us a native fishing song. Dressed in traditional Japanese workers' blue-and-white kimonos, we pretended to pull in a harvest of fish as the lilting music played, keeping us in step and in tune as we sung along in Japanese. Yes, we had to learn the whole song in Japanese. For another dance, we were decked out in Thai headdresses, wrapped in colorful and flowing silks, as we attempted to bend our fingers back in the traditional Thai dance stance. Our feet were turned at impossible angles. An Indian friend of hers had us performing the mating ritual of the god Shiva. For this dance, we wore a number of bracelets, and brightly colored cloth was layered over us.

As the delighted ladies sat back with their red-tipped cigarettes and sweating glasses of iced whatever for our final performance, my sister was set on a glass table to represent Shiva. She was dressed in a traditional outfit with a flowing gown. Incense burned nearby, filling the air, and candles were lit throughout the house. Pati froze in a godlike pose complete with a flute prop, as our little troop of girls twirled around her in dervish hysteria. Suddenly, unexpectedly, Pati broke through the glass in slow motion. One minute she was on top. The next minute glass was everywhere, leaving her standing in the middle of it all. Everything came to a complete standstill, but Pati kept her Shiva stance throughout it all. She didn't even cry. She stayed miraculously still as the shattered pieces of glass lay in a jumble around her. Bob sat wide-eyed on the sofa with half of a chocolate chip cookie in his mouth. His eyes were as big as saucers. No blood. No death. Pati was picked

SANDY HANNA

straight up out of the bamboo frame and glass, examined, and released by the grimly smiling Colonel, who had been watching off in the wings.

I let out a relieved sigh, while at the same time muttering under my breath to the girls around me, "That should be enough of a finale for those ladies to sign off on our Dance badge." The girls followed me to the waiting refreshments, snickering quietly and shooting glances toward the clutch of women. The sound of glass being swept up behind us could be heard in the background. Anna, the maid, was watching Pati, probably in as much shock as her little charge was. As Pati came up to my side at the table, I looked at her still-shaken and startled face. "That was amazing!" I said, smiling. She looked up, and a grin slowly exploded on her face. I handed her a cookie.

Checking the appropriate boxes, the ladies signed the forms and sent them to the United States Girl Scouts officials for recognition. Badges were shipped to us from the Girl Scouts headquarters in America, and we sewed them on our uniform sashes. This could all be done in the comfort of our palm-shaded villas. The ladies weren't done with us, however.

What person in their right mind sends a Girl Scouts troop to a cleared-out minefield? Yes, that was the stranger-than-fiction idea that no doubt had its origin at a late-night cocktail party. God only knows what general these ladies got to agree to it. I'm sure they simply asked for everything they needed to create a day camp and the general came up with the location. I'd have loved to have been a fly on the wall, that's for sure!

The Biên Hòa Highway was the main road leading out of Saigon. This road was to take us to the designated campsite. Three lanes on either side flowed in two directions. Everything was pretty much up-for-grabs where lanes were concerned. Every type of vehicle and mode of transportation was visible as our muddy brown Army bus barreled down the road. The traffic was an exciting free-for-all. It felt like a game of chance, as vehicles seemed to be coming straight at us. I'd made the mistake of sitting in the front seat. I had white knuckles by the time we got to where we were going. Three-wheeled small delivery trucks, two-tone Renault taxis, bicycles with baskets tied on the back carrier, horses pulling carts piled high with furniture, and motor scooters with women who seemed glued to the backs of their drivers all roared in front, alongside, and behind us. Life moved down the Biên Hòa Highway *en masse*. Where they were going was always a wonder. Towering trees lined the road, shading the sides of the road. Villages just out of sight were fringed by bamboo groves, barely visible. A kind of wild, unkempt beauty surrounded us.

Now it was a known fact that all traffic was forbidden from dusk to dawn on this road. Vietnamese rebels hid behind the dense vegetation. The danger of sniper attacks was the stated reason. I had heard that many of the American teenagers, however, would play a game called 'Dodging the Bullet' sometimes at night on this road. They would ride along the highway on their motorbikes long after the sun had set, streaking through the night's blackness tempting fate, thinking nothing would happen to them. In those early days, there seemed to be an unspoken rule against any harm's coming to the children of the foreigners. This was the road we passed along for the daylong camp outing that only some disconnected, disoriented group of women could have organized. Where'd they think they were anyway?

We had loaded into the bus in front of the PX. This camouflaged vehicle with wire mesh on the windows and brownish-green seats transported us. We girls sang "Do Your Boobs Hang Low" and "Ninety-Nine Bottles of Beer on the Wall" as the bus jogged along. We sang them until all one could hope for was a contagious case of laryngitis for the entire group.

The trip took us out of the city, past the rice fields, forests, and former French plantations. Gazing through the wire mesh windows, we saw the majestic landscape unroll around us. Water buffalo tied to tills moved slowly back and forth as the rice paddies were being planted. Everything before me appeared as a beautiful small watercolor print. The little Brownie camera I had brought with me from the States never captured what my mind's eye saw. The film I mailed away to the States for processing would return with prints that were clearly uninspiring. I'd long since given up trying to preserve these images. A pinkish sky rested over an expanse of water. A man in a traditional bamboo hat in a birdlike form of river craft moved about his task with a long pole. Gates to massive plantation villas half smothered in bougainvillea appeared behind hedges of bamboo. All of this filled my blinking eyes as we sped through the open countryside. A single dark whiff of sound sometimes rose above the rollicking voices of the traveling girls, a sound that was so often unidentifiable. It was easy to be catapulted into the magical world that lay beyond the window.

We were driven to a cleared minefield complete with rolled barbed wire fencing surrounding it to make sure we knew the boundaries of where it was safe to venture. We girls were in complete agreement that this was the greatest leap of insanity ever on the part of our illustrious scout leaders. Several Vietnamese military personnel were present and were stationed as sentries of some kind. We were no longer in the supposed safety of the city; now we were in a countryside wavering between safe and unsafe at any given time.

After the drudgery of our setting up Army issued tents and getting a fire started with damp wood, the major activity was trying to cook our lunch in some lame-ass coffee cans that we all had brought with us. Sticking a carrot, a potato, and some piece of previously frozen hamburger meat in the can, we prayed we'd be able to eat the result. Crafts were big on the ladies' list, so we fell into making potholders with Popsicle sticks and braiding lanyards. The excitement of the outing quickly wore off once we realized we were confined within the boundaries of the barbed wire. Minefields and Girl Scouts—there was something wrong with this idea.

It was the rainy season, and the sky, full of cumulus clouds, suddenly became as black as night. A deluge of rain fell, drenching everything. We were like drowned rats that day. Then, just as quickly, the clouds and rain scattered and disappeared. When the sun came out, the humidity soared to a sweltering, unbearable high. I hungered for a thrilling flush of wind to suddenly start up.

My tent had a few of the friends in it whom I liked: Elizabeth Lopez from the Philippines, an embassy kid I think, and Peggy, another BRAT. It was a good-sized tent, one that could provide shade and protection from the rain for at least six girls. We had pretty much completed all the tasks the ladies had on their lists and were now wondering what we should do next. A large tree shaded our tent, so at least we weren't sweating like the other girls who hadn't anticipated the movement of the sun. If nothing else, I was practical!

On examining the area of our confinment we discovered a place in the fence that someone had dug a hole under. The security detail of soldiers that had been assigned to this little outing weren't paying attention to any of it or to us. Peggy, Elizabeth, and I scooted under the wire making our way down the adjoining dirt road. No one seemed to notice. As we rounded the bend, Peggy pulled out a cigarette and matches. Sometimes this eleven-year-old looked like a twenty-year old woman. We didn't get far.

The bus horn blared. The day had passed slowly, but now that we were leaving, we almost didn't want to go. The ride home was hot and dusty. There was no air conditioning in the bus. The French villas we'd be returning to didn't have air conditioning either, just air constantly circulated by the overhead fans. I stumbled into the house and lay sprawled on the cool marble floor directly under the fan until my body temperature dropped to something bearable.

Tom sat in a nearby chair, reading. He showed no pity at the sight of the sweaty mess before him. "Have fun?" He relished moments like this.

I earned a lot of Girl Scout badges while in Vietnam. When I returned to the United States, despite having earned my Tree Identification badge, I couldn't tell you one thing about any of the trees in America. I missed everything after we left. I missed my flame trees and the twilight smell of watered earth. I missed the reflection of me that was Saigon and the freedom I had in a country that was, in fact, fighting for its own freedom. I was a kid absorbed in the moment, not distinguishing one day from the next.

I had stopped trying to keep tabs on Tom. I could never figure out where he was going. He was out of the house as soon as he got the chance, leaving me behind, of course. One thing he couldn't get out of, however, was the Boy Scouts, which Mom signed him up for.

Tom's Boy Scout camping trip was even more bizarre than mine. His troop met at the Tân Sơn Nhứt airport. They were flown up-country to Đà Lạt in a military transport. There was a military base there. Issued surplus French Army gear, they picked out pup tents, backpacks, and any other items needed. These were old, mildewed, and basically filthy. Tom said the mold smell alone could knock you over. His troop leader was an Australian Special Forces guy. When they arrived in Đà Lạt, a platoon of Army of the Republic of Vietnam Special Forces soldiers accompanied the Boy Scouts as they marched five miles out to their assigned camping spot. The platoon took up positions surrounding the campers. They stayed in place all night.

Tom was assigned an Indian kid as his tent mate, most likely attached to the Indian embassy. They put up their tent, and Tom went off to check on everything else. He'd been given a semi in-charge position. When he returned, he found that the kid had covered their tent with nearby brush. "I've camouflaged it," he said proudly. Tom just shook his head and slid into his sleeping bag, hoping to fall asleep early. Unknown to either of them was that a nest of scorpions was in the vegetative debris the kid had disturbed. One had made its way into the tent and lay in wait in Tom's sleeping bag. He felt the sting from its poisonous tail. Throwing back the cover, he spotted the culprit. Shouting for help, he ran from the tent. The Australian Special Forces guy, the troop leader, snapped into action when Tom found him. With his knife in hand, he cut the reddening spot and immediately began to suck and spit out the bloody poison. What's the Boy Scout motto? "Be prepared"? I guess Special Forces guys must have the same motto. Tom quit the Boy Scouts as soon as the troop returned to Saigon.

While Mom focused on Scouts, the Colonel zeroed in on sports. After all, he had won letters in five different sports when in college at Texas A&M. It didn't occur to him that Tom wouldn't have any interest in the baseball team that had formed through the initiative of a priest named Father Crawford. A memorable man, the priest ran an orphanage for children suffering from polio in Saigon. Baseball is as American as you can get, so of course, it was a required activity for American teenage males in Saigon. The Colonel signed Tom up immediately when he found out there was such a program.

A MOMENT IN HISTORY

"On April 22, 1975, forty-two polio-stricken orphans, ages five to young adults, were airlifted out of war-torn Saigon on an unofficial flight under the supervision of four Daughters of Charity and Father Robert Crawford, a Vincentian priest. Father Crawford arranged for the rescue mission through Edward Daly, president and owner of World Airways, a commercial charter airline. It was a harrowing flight out of Saigon to the safety of the United States. At the time, fifty handicapped boys were under Father Crawford's care. Another one hundred girls, mostly polio vcitims, were under the care of the sisters. After receiving word, the Daughters collected the children and told them they were going on a picnic. The group bused through the unsafe

streets of Saigon to the Tan Son Nhut airport where a World Airways DC6 flight #803 awaited. Father Crawford and the Sisters of Charity quickly and quietly boarded all the children. It was nightfall when the plan departed. Fearing the unauthorized plane might be detected, the pilot kept all lights off during the take-off. The plane left Saigon just before the Viet-Cong overran the city."

—*Patricia Smith, Daughters of Charity Provincial Archives, "Escape from Saigon," April 22, 1975*

The cleared out mine field outside the city was to be our campsite for that day's Girl Scout activity. A small group of ARVN soldiers would accompany the group.

CHAPTER 11:

AN AFFAIR IN ĐÀ LẠT

Her black Mercedes passed by us as she exited through the metal gates of Independence Palace in downtown Saigon. The Colonel was taking photos of us kids next to the ornamental iron fence that surrounded the grounds. I wondered if the true subject he was focused on was us or the building behind us. His camera had a weird upward slant to it. When the film came back from processing, we appeared very low in the photos. His focal point lay beyond us, and in many of the images we were simply soft blurs. The Colonel didn't point his camera at the passing vehicle. Madame Nhu, President Diệm's sister-in-law, sat comfortably in the back seat of the sleek black sedan. Her chauffeured limousine took a right turn, sending her past us. The darkened windows were lowered, and I could see her profile through the glass. She wore her signature European-style dark sunglasses and was poised, upright, looking straight ahead. She held her head high, oblivious to anything around her. She paid no attention to the American officer and his four children standing near the gate, staring at her. Her attitude appeared to be one of contempt for all.

Something sparkled around her neck; a diamond crucifix caught the light in that shadowed car.

Madame Nhu was her name now that she was married to President Diệm's brother, Ngô Đình Nhu. She hadn't always been known by that name though. Her given name at birth, Trần Lệ Xuân, meant "beautiful spring." It was a name that was in great contrast to the title "Dragon Lady" that she was now earning for herself. She was originally from the North. Her Hanoi family had been very close with the French colonial administration, and her father had married into the ruling imperial dynasty. Her mother was a granddaughter of Emperor Đồng Khánh and a cousin of Emperor Bảo Đại. The rumor mill was alive and well in Southeast Asia, and it was rumored that her mother, Thân Thị Nam Trân, had a series of lovers. Among them was her future son-in-law Ngô Đình Nhu. When it came time to marry, for some reason Beautiful Spring insisted on Nhu, a man almost twice her age. She was eighteen years old when she married Nhu, who was thirty-two. She converted from Mahayana Buddhism to Catholicism, his religion. She couldn't write Vietnamese, which set her at odds with her countrymen. She spoke French instead. She was everything her country wasn't. Despite it all, she was now proving to be the power, if not the major influence, behind the current regime the American administration was backing—that of President Diệm, her brother-in-law.

I'd read the American press about her as part of our assignment in social studies class. I never met her; I just had this sighting that one day and other times when she made public appearances. She was someone who was always the source of so many conflicts and issues in South Vietnam. For some reason, she was intent upon conducting a reign of terror over the Buddhist priests. This seemed so confusing to me, since she had been raised a Buddhist. I kept track of her exploits as though I were reading an intricate mystery novel.

We didn't see much of the Colonel these days. Mom had full charge of us at this point, though she generally delegated us to the servants. My father had become consumed with the scope of the job he had in the Ordnance Corps with MAAG. Returning home from work after the first few days of our arrival, he had announced with relief that he had someone he could work with. His Vietnamese counterpart, Chief of Ordnance Colonel *Lê Văn Sâm*, was with the South Vietnamese Army. *Sâm* had a great deal of experience and an exemplary command of the English language. The Colonel bonded with the man the first time they met. He had an enormous amount of respect for Colonel *Sâm*, and a friendship quickly grew between the two. The months flew by, and they worked together on projects they both felt were critical to the success of their programs. This friendship and their work, however, were soon to be tested.

As in an ancient fable, the head of a dragon was to appear from out of nowhere to threaten those who knew of its lair. In this case, I am referring to Madame Nhu, the "Dragon Lady." When this dragon rose up and fired her heated breath, all around her collapsed. The "Dragon Lady" was in the process of singling out the *Sâm* family, and not with good intent. There would be no hiding from her destructive ways once she started her hunt.

It happened one hushed moon-filled night. A rare coolness filled the air that evening, something unusual in Saigon. Colonel *Sâm* arrived at the Đoàn Thị Điểm house unexpectedly. He entered quietly through the outside metal gate. We heard the ancient metal bolt sliding out of its holder, metal rubbing against metal. His shadow trailed him as he moved from the gate to the entry porch of the villa. The Colonel was sitting, reading, and nursing his last drink of the night. Soft music played in the background. I was still squirreled up on the bamboo sofa trying to finish the last of the homework assignment due the next day. Otherwise, the house was quiet. Colonel *Sâm* knocked gently on the screen door as he took the last puff of his cigarette. He crushed it out in the nearby planter. The Colonel bid him enter, happy at the thought of a pleasant distraction from his friend.

The appearance of our late-night visitor didn't surprise the Colonel. Colonel *Sâm* had shown up at other times in the night during the year to make him aware of some unrest that was brewing. *Sâm* once drove a tank around our block all night when there was the rumor of a coup brewing. He stood guard over the Hanna family until the early-morning light of the following day. Colonel *Sâm* was always a welcomed visitor. As he entered, the Colonel rose to grasp his hand in a warm handshake. They both sat down in the dim light of the illuminated lamps of the living room. *Sâm* began talking. He was unnerved and thoroughly shaken by something. He seemed unwilling or unable to stop. He threw a glance in my direction, and the Colonel motioned for me to leave. I politely said goodnight but quietly deposited myself in my favorite spy lookout, that single hard marble step halfway up the staircase. I had become proficient in spying on the Colonel from this angle. The two didn't seem to notice. I think everyone else had already gone to bed.

The two figures sat next to each other, deep in conversation. Their voices swerved upward like birds in midair toward my eager ears. None of it was making much sense to me, but I strained to hear every word. I could tell something was wrong. I lay curled up on the single step, my chin resting on the spindle ledge.

"I don't understand, *Sâm*. What's wrong?" The Colonel's voice had a low, puzzled tone.

"It is not so much what has happened but what is going to happen," *Sâm* said. Sitting on the edge of the nearby bamboo chair, he began a tale that spun into the dark shadows of the night. "Something has happened that will change everything for me and my family."

"My wife, Ngai, has just returned from a holiday in Đà Lạt with our children. She goes there often, as it is in the mountains and so much cooler than what we have here in Saigon. As a young girl, she had been in a convent there, and it gives her much happiness to return. She took our five children, but I was not able to join her this time. Đà Lạt has been a seasonal watering hole for Emperor Bảo Đại and his relatives for a long time. You were perhaps not aware that my wife is related to the emperor and is a cousin of Madame Nhu. It used to be a fashionable place for the French aristocracy in their day. It is an area that is currently under the command of Vietnamese General Đôn," he said, talking slowly and gaining more control of himself as he did.

"Madame Nhu had previously lived in Đà Lạt. It is here that she gave birth to her children. She lived there with her husband, Nhu, before helping her husband and his brothers, Cẩn and Bishop Thuc, form the current government in Saigon for Diệm. Mrs. *Sâm's* relatives come from that long line of wealthy aristocratic families that were originally from Hanoi, but she now lives the life of an officer's wife, as you know."

The Colonel was listening. *Sâm* seemed so upset. I thought the story rather uneventful so far and wasn't sure where it was going. There were no other sounds coming from inside the house. I watched as the Colonel pulled his pipe from his breast pocket and lit it, squinting, one eye closed. He settled back in his seat. He was going to let *Sâm* take all the time he needed. He offered *Sâm* a cigarette from the gold cigarette holder that resembled a car with a removable lid. Someone had given it to him, but for the life of me, I couldn't remember who. *Sâm* politely accepted one and proceeded to light it.

Colonel *Sâm's* story started slowly. It seemed that his wife had been alone, returning from a casual outing along a pathway that passed Madame Nhu's house. She spotted General Đôn entering Madame Nhu's boudoir through the side French doors. There had been rumors of this liaison, though nothing had ever been confirmed. Many tongues wagged that Madame Nhu and General Đôn liked to hang out at the King Bay piano bar in Đà Lạt together. There was a period in the past when Nhu had been transferred to the Tây Ninh jungle and was not accompanied by his family.

"Madame Nhu, she saw my wife just before the general entered her chambers. Madame Nhu just stood there looking at her. Ngai, she did not like the look that Madame Nhu gave her. She hurried away as fast as she could. She felt she needed to leave Đà Lạt quickly. She was much shaken. Packing up everything, she came back to Saigon with our children. Madame Nhu is not someone who likes you knowing things like this. She is a bad woman. Now, I have fear for myself and my family. Madame Nhu has become so powerful and uncontrollable these days. No one ever knows what to expect from her, especially if she feels threatened in any way." As he talked, *Sâm* began to pull a folder from the worn brown satchel he had arrived with.

"I have brought you something that I want to read to you," he said. "It is very important you understand now what is going on here in Vietnam. You must see what we suffer." *Sâm* seemed bitterly ashamed to have to speak in this manner. "I am giving this to you as protection for myself and my family. You must keep it secret until the right time or when something happens to me."

His voice floated toward me, reaching my stairway lookout. It was a strong, melodious voice full of passion. I sat quietly tucked in position, awake, wide-eyed, and straining to hear. One thing was clear: *Sâm's* family was in danger! He read from his written document as though revealing these confidences was like the edges of a wound being reexamined and now made real. Colonel *Sâm* told the Colonel that after his wife relayed to him what had happened, he had spent the rest of the day and night writing. He had filled page after page. Fearing retribution for what he and his wife now knew, *Sâm* had written what he called an exposé on the current Diệm regime.

I settled back on the stairway for a long, uncomfortable night. The stories seemed never-ending. There were so many names and places, most of them unfamiliar to me. He detailed the origins and political liaisons of the regime's members, giving the history of all the members of the South Vietnam regime the Americans currently supported. He unveiled the internal anti-American sentiment that was rampant in the regime and hinted at the eventual outcome of American involvement in Vietnam. He wanted the Colonel to know that the current regime was not pro-American! He warned about the involvement of both Mr. and Mrs. Nhu in their advisory role to President Diệm. On a table in front of the two men, sheets and sheets of thin onion-skin paper were spread out.

"I think something is going to happen to me and my family now. Hold on to these documents, Colonel, until I say it should be made public. Everything I say here is true. Everything I predict here will come true. Nhu and Diệm want the American resources but not the Americans. We have been too long under colonial rule. It is a complicated game," he said. He sat back now as though a weight had been taken off him. His burning cigarette lay in the ashtray untouched. Only falling embers remained. He picked up the first few pages, straightening them and holding them close to the light on the nearby side table, re-examining them.

His manner demonstrated a childlike concentration as he moved each page slowly. Colonel *Sâm* was a compact, handsome man in his forties. He had slicked-back black hair, a round face, and a complexion that would never disclose his age no matter how long he lived. At my young age, I had a bit of a crush on him.

He pulled another of the tissue-thin papers from the folder. This was the story of his own life. At times he read; at other times he simply spoke freely. He went all the way back to his birth and all the events that had occurred to bring him to this point in his life. I guess he thought that was the best place for him to begin so that the Colonel would understand his commitment to the struggle in Vietnam. The story he told about himself revealed an extraordinary life already lived. It was the life of a man who was committed to his country's independence. It showed the path he had traveled, as so many others had, in their efforts to free themselves from foreign rule and unite their country. This was a story that demonstrated the lengths to which so many Vietnamese had gone in their efforts to secure freedom from the French. Sitting in the dim light of the single bulb, *Sâm* had a determined look about him. His story stretched into the early-morning light. I was now wavering in and out of sleep.

Sâm stopped talking to look back down at his writing, more to be sure he hadn't left anything out than anything else. He glanced up at the Colonel to see if he was still listening. The Colonel sat riveted, leaning forward in his chair. I don't think he had known anything about Colonel *Sâm's* history. With this pause, he took the opportunity to rise to refill his drink, fix one for *Sâm*, and add a substantial amount of ice to both. The overhead fans continued to whirl away. The day's heat still lingered in the room, ever-present. The sounds of the evening rolled into the void, filling it with the buzz of the cicadas. Both men resumed their positions, and Colonel *Sâm* continued his story.

"We, Ngai and I, had fallen in love just two months before I was arrested by the French. I was a nationalist fighting against the French. After my release from the French prison, I went up to Đà Lạt to meet my wife. She was a teacher at the Catholic school named Convent des Oiseaux. The superior mother in this school had the idea to chase me back to Saigon. She told me, 'You are a fighter. Why you marry? You have trouble and you know we keep her like a princess.' At last, Ngai decided to go home with me, so we both took a special airplane from Đà Lạt to Huế. Our wedding was held in December 1947 at Hue. I was twenty-seven years old, and my wife was twenty-four." His love for his wife was clearly expressed in his face as he spoke.

"In 1951, my wife introduced me to Mr. Ngô Đình Cẩn, the younger brother of President Diệm. He became my Catholic godfather. My wife was also very happy, because she knew that I had been an orphan since I was born. In 1953, I was assigned to Saigon. Cẩn recommended me to Mr. Nhu. He was also poor like Mr. Cẩn, but he is much more intelligent than Mr. Cẩn. He was very happy with me; then President Diệm arrived in Vietnam. I sent seven soldiers to make sure Diệm was safe on his arrival at the Tân Sơn Nhứt airport.

I became Chief of Ordnance Corps at that time. I didn't have time to go see Mr. Nhu or Mr. Cẩn, because I worked very hard. I told Ordnance Corps officers we needed to learn with the Americans. 'Don't lose the time!' Some officers were qualified and used American systems. Each time I proposed them for promotion to the higher positions, I got surprise and shame that all of them were rejected. Unqualified officers were promoted from the list. It was unjust and continues even now. This is something you should know. It is why we have such a hard time getting anything done!" With that, he put everything back in the brown envelope.

Colonel *Sâm* now rose to leave. The sky was pale with the early-morning light. "I must go before anyone sees me," he said. The Colonel followed him out the door. Their voices now were muffled. They shook hands, and *Sâm* left as quietly as he'd arrived.

The Colonel found me at my sentry position. I pretended to be sound asleep. I didn't have time to pull myself up the steps before he started to climb them. Scooping me up in his arms, he laid me down on my bed next to Pati. Covering me with a thin sheet, he moved on to his own bedroom. His mind must have been full. The discovery of his daughter sleeping on the stairway didn't seem to concern him.

Whether we realized it or not, our landscape shifted that night, ever so slowly. My relatively uncomplicated life of school, swim club, menagerie of animals, and servants now had a second layer to it without my fully understanding anything. There was a life that ran beneath the surface of everything we saw and did, that was for sure. One thing I did grasp from *Sâm's* story was that the Nhus, especially Madame Nhu, were at the heart of it all.

A Moment in History

"When CIA Colonel Edward Lansdale arrived in Saigon in May 1954, he faced the task of building an alternative to the mosaic of religious armies and criminal gangs that had ruled South Vietnam in the later years of WWII. Ngô Đình Diệm's appointment as premier in July gave Lansdale the lever he needed. Handpicked by the Americans, Diệm was strongly anti-French and uncompromisingly anti-Communist. However, he had spent most of the previous last decade in exile and had few political supporters and almost no armed forces. Premier in name only, Diệm controlled only the few blocks of downtown Saigon surrounding the presidential palace. The French and their clients—ARVN, the Binh Xuyen (river pirates), and the armed religious sects Cao Dai and Hoa Hao—could easily mount an anti-Diệm coup if he threatened their interests. Lansdale proceeded to fragment his opposition's solid front and to build Diệm an effective military apparatus. By manipulating payments to the armed religious sects, neutralizing most of them, the Binh Xuyen were left as the only French pawn. The Binh

Xuyen financed themselves largely from their vice rackets, and their loyalty could not be manipulated through financial pressures. But deserted by ARVN and the religious sects, the Binh Xuyen were soon crushed."

—*Alfred McCoy,* The Politics of Heroin in Southeast Asia, *1972*

Colonel and Mrs. ***Lê Văn Sâm*** at our villa on Đoàn Thị Điểm. The Colonel's counterpart, as Chief of Ordnance ARVN, would be the target of the "Dragon Woman," Madame Nhu, because of what Mrs. *Sâm*, her cousin, had observed while on holiday in Đà Lạt. Older brother, Tom, and younger brother, Bob, are seen in the background.

CHAPTER 12:

LITTLE BROTHER NGÔ ĐÌNH NHU

Unbeknownst to me, the Colonel had asked *Sâm* to return the next night. It had become too late the evening before for them to finish their discussion. I think the Colonel wanted to hear more and to ask questions. The next evening, *Sâm* appeared again. Mom kept an eye on me that night, making sure I went to bed and stayed there. The Colonel must have told her about finding me on the stairway the night before. Under such strict supervision, I finally gave up and fell asleep.

I woke up unexpectedly, hearing the faint sounds of my father's voice breaking the darkness of silence that surrounded me. The door to the bedroom wasn't completely closed. Muffled sounds made their way into the room. A soft light radiated from the doorway. It didn't sound like he was talking to himself, something he often had occasion to do. I slid off the bed that Pati and I shared and tiptoed over to the big double door. Mom's bedroom door was open, but I could hear her deep breathing. The door was a monster of a thing and took great skill to open quietly. Once I had opened it, I closed it without letting the latch click shut. I knew that my sister wouldn't stir; once in bed, she never moved. The marble floor felt cool against my bare feet. I slid, one step at a time, down the stairway on my bottom until I'd reached the place where I could clearly see through the spindles.

Colonel *Sâm* seemed calmer than the night before. As *Sâm* went through the other documents, this night's discussion was about who did what to whom and who was in good with the Nhus; who got what positions without any experience and who was paying off whom with graft. The names flew up the stairs one after the other, but I missed most of what was being said. I heard General To, Lieutenant Colonel Nhan, Lieutenant Colonel Duong, Colonel Guang, Presidential Minister Thuan, Colonel Vinh, Lieutenant Colonel Liem, Lieutenant Colonel Chau, General Khanh, General Ty, Major Thong, and Major Toam. One of the stories was about General Chieu. It seemed that General Chieu had been involved in the 1960 coup d'état against Diệm while he was head of national security. I remembered the flier that the Colonel had read to us after the coup we kids had been in, the one that my siblings and I thought was a parade. The Colonel had read the announcement at that time that "all would be forgiven" by Diệm. This instigator, General Chieu, hadn't been dismissed. It was a complex political web here in Saigon that made no sense to me.

"Because I support the training the Americans give the Vietnamese Army through MAAG, it makes many problems for me," he said. "I am labeled as being pro-American. This isn't something viewed positively by the Diệm regime. You will see. Something is going to happen!"

Sâm seemed to be finished reading through the reams of paper. He looked up at the Colonel in a singular kind of tearless detachment. "They put people in prison if they think you know anything or say anything against them, the Nhus."

"What do you mean by that?" The Colonel was now standing, walking up and down as he pondered everything he had heard. "Is that what you think is going to happen to you?"

"In these prisons now, there are teachers, students, anti-Diệm intellectuals, Việt Minh, Buddhist priests, nationalists. Only crime is that they speak out about corrupt regime. Americans don't understand what happens here. Americans think everyone is Communist, but it is not true. I am afraid for myself and my family now," *Sâm* stated.

"You should know that Mr. Nhu has organized all restaurants, shops, and places that are often visited by Americans," he continued. "Those men working for him report to Tuyen. He is placing any Vietnamese officers' names that are gotten by these people into 'black records,' because they were together with Americans in these places. Three months ago, Madame Nhu was sick at Huế. Our family doctor examined her, and she said, 'Please help me. I need to only live two years.' Nhu has a two-year plan. Also, a month ago, she confided her secret sentiments to a top Catholic Mother, saying, 'We do not leave. We stay here. President was stupid and incapable to challenge the Americans. Now President Diệm is disenchanted and trusts Mr. Nhu more than ever. You going to see with two more years Nhu wins and America down!'" *Sâm* said this last statement robustly, in a voice meant more to reassure himself than related to what he was saying.

He pulled out the page he had written about Nhu. "You will see when I tell this story about Nhu that what I just said is true. Mr. Nhu was nobody before Diệm came back from France. In fact, it was his brothers Cẩn and Nhu who orchestrated the entire political juggling that brought Diệm from Paris to Vietnam. Let me tell you this," he said, sitting back now to begin yet another monologue, this time about Ngô Đình Nhu, President Diệm's youngest brother.

"Everything is at cross purpose here in Saigon," Colonel *Sâm* said. He dug one more paper from his stack and proceeded now with the story of Mr. Nhu. "Understanding grows slowly. You will see how it will be for you."

"Mr. Nhu was unknown before World War II. Mr. Nhu is the one who formed the government for his brother Ngô Đình Diệm. He had a lot of contact with nationalist leaders like Hoang-Chan, sects like *Bình Xuyên*, and religious groups, like *Hòa Hảo* and *Cao Dai*. All these groups were fighting for control. He said there was only one way, and it was to persuade their leaders and rally other parties so his brother Ngô Đình Diệm would come back to Vietnam from France to rule the country. He told them that if they showed Diệm too much complexity, he would go back to Paris and never come back again. Nhu's remedy was to form a provisional government, but every party and religious sect disagreed, because each one wanted to seize an important department. The same story continued and lasted until two weeks before Ngô Đình Diệm arrived Saigon Tân Sơn Nhứt airport. Mr. Nhu received a message from Diệm in Paris that Premier Minister Ngô Đình Diệm will arrive Saigon Tân Sơn Nhứt airport by Air France that evening six o'clock. Nhu was puzzled, because the last message he'd received said Diệm wouldn't be there for another week. I drove him to meet people. When he talked to them, I hear him saying to everyone, 'You must take it. If not, he will go back.' They agreed, and our government was born. Mr. Nhu, before 1954, had very few members working with him." Colonel *Sâm* paused to gauge how the Colonel was receiving this information. His story was starting to bounce around from one thing to the other.

"Mr. Cẩn, Nhu's brother, is no longer in favor. He secretly ordered the arrest of Madame Nhu several years ago, and Mr. Nhu now is against him. There is more. Mrs. Dung, wife of Lieutenant Colonel Dung, has now become foe of Madame Nhu, and Mr. Dung also foe of Mr. Nhu because of the love affair of Madame Nhu with General Đôn in her Đà Lạt house. Mrs. Dung knew about this, like Mrs. *Sâm* now knows and did not tell story to Mr. Nhu. She might tell him now." *Sâm* shifted in his chair as he turned the page to another piece of information he thought was important for the Colonel to hear. "There is much corruption with Mr. Nhu. Nhu is also running the secret police."

I thought about all these stories about the "Dragon Lady" and her husband, Nhu. They were becoming more and more incredible. These were people who idealized the past and misconceived the present. The Nhus weren't just insecure and defensive with Americans; they were the same with their constituency, the Vietnamese people.

The Colonel quietly listened. He didn't comment, letting *Sâm* talk. His response during the readings was simply profound sighs of sympathy for his friend's distress. "All right, I understand," the Colonel said. "We'll figure something out if anything happens; don't worry. It's my business now," he concluded. The mood was dangerously intense.

All that could be heard outside now was the sound of the ever-present gecko hanging on the wall of the front porch. Hours had gone by in what seemed like seconds. *Sâm* moved toward the door slowly. He said his goodbye suddenly, quietly shaking hands with the Colonel. His feet running at full speed, fast, lightly, in the warm rain could be heard.

The Colonel passed through his children's bedroom not long afterward, closing his door quietly. I had crawled up to my bed before this, not wanting to get caught again. I pulled the sheet up high over my thin legs, cotton nightgown, skinny arms, and head.

The town had drained itself of life. The morning rays were gently easing the new day into existence. I thought about the life *Sâm* had lived from what I'd been able to understand. Although I couldn't make sense of it all, I knew that whatever these documents were that *Sâm* had given the Colonel, they were important. Something was going to happen. There was a drama unfolding.

A Moment in History

Commenting on President Ngô Đình Diệm's role in Asia, the *Hindustan Standard* in its November 4, 1957, issue described President Ngô Đình Diệm as not only "a champion of resurgent Asia but a philosopher who could guide Asia to attain economic progress without sacrificing essential human liberties." It could not have been further from the truth in 1960 as the country began its free fall. Anyone not supporting the current regime and its corrupt practices would be imprisoned and persecuted. American involvement in Vietnam was kept at arm's length, and only financial aid, military supplies, and consultants were permitted a role. Visiting politicians were humored but not given any hold on the country.

President Diệm, in his signature white suit, walks the length of a military review area.

CHAPTER 13:

THE 704TH DEPOT

It wasn't long after these late-night rendezvous with the Colonel that Colonel *Lê Văn Sâm* was suddenly relieved of his command as ARVN Chief of Ordinance and imprisoned. Colonel *Sâm's* demotion and imprisonment came without warning. Theft in the 704th demolition depot was being cited as the cause for dismissal. He was immediately replaced by a crony of the Ngô brothers. The promotion of the officer to *Sâm's* position was gained because of his loyalty to Diệm; he was not necessarily qualified for the position. That's what the Colonel said as he stormed into the villa that evening.

In response to the accusations against Colonel *Sâm*, the Colonel ordered every depot in South Vietnam to be inventoried. Depots are repositories of munitions and equipment. All the depots in South Vietnam were under the command of the ARVN Ordinance Division, with MAAG Ordnance Corps advisors attached to them. Nothing was found missing. The Colonel now spearheaded a smart piece of work to get *Sâm* out of prison. With a flurry of memos sent around to his superiors, he lobbied for *Sâm's* freedom. No evidence of theft had been uncovered.

With Colonel *Sâm's* removal, there were sudden changes throughout the entire Ordnance Corps. The ARVN Corps started to unravel, as chaos began to wag its slinky lizard tail. The Colonel was getting copied on things that were starting to undermine the thread of the MAAG Ordnance Corps program in South Vietnam. His nightly tirades at the dinner table let all of us know what was happening. It was as *Sâm* had said. Promotions and replacements for individuals created a swinging door that made it impossible to assure any progress with what the American advisors were trying to achieve. Lack of progress was something the Colonel just could not abide by. He had recently been sent a report from one of the senior advisors.

Captain Glen Wilts of Ordnance Corps C detailed in his senior advisor's report the individuals who had been removed or replaced and the absolute chaos that had erupted within the Ordnance Corps after Colonel *Sâm's* removal. All these individuals were relatives or deemed to be supporters of Diệm.

The Colonel was greatly relieved when *Sâm* was finally released from prison. He now pressed on his superiors the fact that the allegations against Colonel *Sâm* were false and that *Sâm* should be reinstated to his former position. Getting Colonel *Sâm* reinstated to his previous position as Chief of Ordnance Corps in the South Vietnamese Army after his release was another matter entirely. It was proving to be impossible. The Colonel had just received the last disappointing response to his memos from those in command and was planning his next round of attacks. Our evenings were now filled with the Colonel either talking to himself or Mom, reading aloud the memos he was working on.

One night, there were several typed memos marked "Confidential" sitting on the coffee table next to the Colonel. He'd read them silently for the fourth time as he sipped his watered-down whisky. Taking time to relight his packed pipe, he scanned the documents once more.

The Colonel held Deputy Chief MAAG JB Lampert's confidential memos in his hand. He read item number three from Lampert's brief several times aloud: "'We cannot make strong efforts to have Colonel *Sâm* reinstated.'" This paragraph seemed to irritate him the most. He had been seated for some time, and the day had moved into a moonless dusk. He was still busy with the problem at hand, and the tone of his voice was now one of anger. It boomed and rolled through the silent room like a sudden wave of water, rippling as it just as suddenly died down. Keeping remarkably quiet, we were all ignoring him for the most part. We didn't think this anger was focused on any of us, so it was nothing to be worried about.

"Nothing is going to be done about *Sâm*. Incredible! There might be 'valid reasons for his dismissal'...bullshit! Don't the powers that be know what kind of signal this sends? It says that we have no power with this government at all if they are permitted to discard the one good officer they have. Now there will be no stopping them." Irresolutely pacing, the Colonel eventually sat down.

"Okay. Let's see what they do with this information!" He took up pencil and paper once again, turning the tablet pages until he came to a clean sheet. "This is bigger than Colonel *Sâm*. It is about an unwelcomed truth," he said quietly. The document he now wrote supported the exposé that *Sâm* had given him. He spoke out loud as he wrote.

28 September, 1960
To: Chief MAAG
Subject: Colonel Le Van Sam,
Former ARVN Chief of Ordinance

1. *Reference previous DF dated 14 Sept. Subject Col. Sam and DF dated 22 Sept. Subj. alleged demolition storage 704 depot.*

2. *In referenced DF's, it was pointed out that one of the principal cause for Colonel Sam's removal from his job as Ordinance officer was his pro-American sympathies and close cooperation with MAAG Ordinance Fr. and other MAAG advisors.*

3. *Since submitting the previous DF's the following information to support this accusation has been developed:*

    a. <u>*An anti-American group exists headed by General Chien, Chief of Staff, ARVN*</u>

    b. *Other active members are:*

        1. *General Ty, C/JS*
        2. *General To, DCS/Log, ARVN*
        3. *General Guang, ARVN G-4*
        4. *Lt. Col. Nhan, ARVN, Chief of Ord.*
        5. *Major Clan, Exec. For Lt. Col. Khoi, DOD*
        6. *Lt. Col Chau, Chief of Psycho. Warfare*
        7. *Major Duong (Works for Mr. Nhu) brother of President*
        8. *Five Ordnance Officers who formed a group to serve and pass on information on Colonel Sam's weak points. This group consists of:*
            a. *Maj Toan, CO 100th Ord. BN and former CO of the 701st Ord. Br.*

    b. *Maj. Thong, III Corps Ord. Officer*

    c. *Capt. Khuong, instructed at Guang Trung Training Center*

    d. *Capt. Hoa, Exec Officer 2nd Ord. DS. Br.*

    e. *Information of this list was given to me by Colonel Le Van Sam in strictest confidence.*

4. *Lt. Sand, Office Chief of Ordinance, confirmed the existence of the Ordnance group listed in 3b (8) above during a discussion separate and distinct from those held with Colonel Sam. Lt. Sand stated this secret group was called: PHONG TRAO CACH MANG QUOC GIA (Believed to be a group within CAN LAO).*

5. *Unconfirmed information has also been received that General Chieu is strongly influenced by Bishop Le Huu TU, of Guinhon. I am told that Bishop TU, kept General Chien for 10 years sometime during his childhood. Bishop TU is known for his opposition to certain activities of Diem.*

6. *Col. Sam stated that he believes Mr. Dung, Asst. Sec. of State for Defense is aware of some of the above information.*

7. <u>*It is pointed out here that the anti-American group is becoming bolder now that they have managed to remove Sam.*</u> *Friendly counterparts in Ordnance are afraid to cooperate with advisors from Ordnance Branch Sâm, MAAG, without clearing with Lt. Col Nhan, OCO. In turn Col. Nhan must clear with G/S.*

8. *The personnel listed in paragraph 3 are all members of the Can Lao party but from the Hanoi group.*

9. *I am told also that Mr. Dung is still waiting for MAAG's opinion of Colonel Sam's removal and the causes therefore.*

George T. Hanna
Lt. Col Ord. C
Ch, Ord, Br., Log Div, CATO[2]

His attention now turned to the stack of *Sâm's* papers. He reviewed the many pages spread before him. He sat back in his chair slowly. A new resonance seemed to spring from him as he attached pages from *Sâm's* exposé to his written document. His drink was now almost completely water. Rising to dump the remains, he added ice and poured more of his favorite Kentucky bourbon into the glass.

Mom was already herding us kids up the stairs to listen to the American-language overseas radio broadcast for the night. Without television, this served as our connection to America. Outside the villa windows, the rustle of leaves whirling in the wind was the only audible sound.

We would find out that, despite all the memos and positive support the Colonel gave Colonel *Sâm*, Lieutenant General McGarr was to follow the advice of Lampert, sending a memo that didn't demand any action on the part of anyone. It attempted to make the Ordnance theft issue a nonconcern. Too many people would "lose face" was the justification for nothing stronger. Colonel *Sâm* would not be reinstated to his previous position, but he would remain in the Army, at least for now. This and the fact that *Sâm* was no longer in prison were of some relief to us all.

Later that year the Colonel carried this information, the exposé, with him on an unannounced trip back to the

States. Mom told us children that he was in the Philippines, having had an appendicitis attack, and was in the hospital. Our Texas cousins said he stayed with them in Texas during a stateside trip and was on his way to Washington, D.C. One of our cousins said she had seen him with a briefcase locked to his wrist. My brother, however, said he did have an appendicitis operation in Manila. What is true remains a mystery. I have no way to confirm any of this now. What is clear is that nothing was what it seemed in Southeast Asia. Politics in both the United States and Vietnam were slowly becoming untenable.

A MOMENT IN HISTORY

In July 1960, Lieutenant Colonel George T. Hanna was put under the command of Lieutenant General Samuel T. Williams, MAAG Vietnam commander. The General was fondly referred to by his subordinates as "Hanging Sam Williams." Williams was in charge from November 1955 to September 1960. Lieutenant General Lionel C. McGarr replaced him and was in charge from September 1960 to July 1962.

"In September 1960, McGarr was named Commander of Military Assistance Advisory Group (MAAG). He served at this post until July 1962 when, against McGarr's advice, U.S. military escalation began. He was succeeded by General Paul Harkins, who commanded MAAG-V's successor unit, Military Assistance Command—Vietnam."

—Ruben Grosbe and Stephanie Tavares, "Gunning for the Globe: Giles Gunn," The Daily Nexus, *November 4, 2003*

The Ordnance Corps in Vietnam was responsible for maintaining control of the ammunition depots that were spread throughout south Vietnam. This team was made up of Vietnamese officers from ARVN with American advisors assigned to them to create supply systems and training. Colonel *Lê Văn Sâm*, Chief of Ordnance ARVN in 1960, to the left of an American advisor.

CHAPTER 14:

THE ELECTION
(NOVEMBER 8, 1960)

It was a guttural curse. A clean and simple swear job on my part. "Goddammit!" I was sitting on the top step of the staircase muttering this word like a chant. I was feeling happy. It seemed like a word that had expression, at least when I'd heard it used. Anyway, I thought it appropriate for the moment. I'm not even sure what had set me off. The 1960 United States presidential election results were being broadcast, and we'd been listening to it in English on the radio. The American overseas radio broadcasts were now available to us in Saigon. We were like starved children relishing the sound of American voices blaring over the radio waves. We kids had all piled onto our parents' bed to listen, happy to be sharing time with them and not at odds particularly with each other for a change. Where Tom was at the time, I'm not sure.

The energy in the room was alarming, probably because the Colonel was a devout Republican and a Democrat had just won the United States presidential election. I ran out of the bedroom to sit on the steps of the stairway by myself. I was excited by the words I'd heard from John F. Kennedy and his passion. I didn't have any idea what the swear word I was muttering meant; I only knew people said it when excited. When said many times, it kind of sounded like music to me. Bob, who had followed me, slid down the steps next to me and started saying it too. It was fun! We got louder and louder, both of us laughing as we said it, our feeling of elation rising along with our voices. Jumping up, who knows why, Bob suddenly ran back into our parents' room.

"Goddammit, Goddammit," Bob yelled at the top of his lungs, running around our parents and the bed, laughing.

Suddenly, his glittering smile transformed to one of alarm. The Colonel had grabbed him by the arm and thrown him onto the bed.

"Where did you hear that?"

"Sandy!" He whined as his eyes began to turn upward into his skull, whimpering, a child suddenly overcome with terror and self-pity.

As I sat on the steps, I became aware of a sudden change in the surrounding atmosphere, kind of like when a plane goes into an unexpected free fall.

"Sandy, you get in here *now!*" I heard the Colonel yell. In desperation, I said a prayer under my breath. I only knew one: "Now I lay me down to sleep...." It probably wasn't appropriate, but I thought it might help.

He pulled out the belt that was hanging in the armoire, a sure sign that things were bad. It wasn't going to be a parade down to the kitchen sink for a bar of Ivory soap this time, Mom's method of punishment.

"Did Bob learn this from you?" he demanded.

"Yes. I was saying it out there on the stairway."

"Whatever for?" he said angrily.

"I was feeling happy."

"Sandy, that makes no sense at all. Where in the world did you hear it?" he continued.

"From you," I said as quietly as I could. A pin could have dropped, it became so quiet. Silence. I watched the Colonel's lips become pale. Not a good sign.

Now I don't know why he proceeded to strap Bob, since I was the one at fault, but I can tell you that the guilt I felt at Bob's getting the whipping instead of me bothered me more than if I'd gotten it. We were all confused by the Colonel's reaction. Mom told me later when I asked about it. She said he was afraid he'd hurt the girls and wasn't afraid of hurting the boys. Boys were supposed to be tough. The Colonel never did acknowledge his part in this drama, but I think he knew he was completely out of line. The three of us were whimpering more from the shock of the Colonel's sudden change in behavior than anything else. Bob, however, had the welts to say otherwise. I waited for when I could quietly sneak out of the room. I burst into guttural sobs when I was far enough away not to be heard.

"*Merde*," I mumbled under my breath. I knew the meaning of that word, and they were probably worse than the one we'd gotten in trouble over. I shot defiant looks back toward my parents' bedroom. "I hate you! I hate you!" I whispered defiantly. I was mad!

We'd had times like this before, when the Colonel's actions were baffling to us kids and his anger seemed misplaced. We would find ourselves in these types of situations throughout our young lives with him. How could a beautiful sunny day like this one turn so ugly in a matter of moments? From that point on, Bob looked at me with a deep distrust that never would be repaired in our lifetime. The

Colonel never accepted his responsibility and continued to remain a mystery to me. This was one thing I could count on.

The Colonel was a self-made man with an unbelievable amount of drive, almost inhuman. He expected the same of his family and wouldn't accept less. He came from an era and upbringing that promoted "you make your own luck." He had been raised to believe the world was his for the making and it would not be handed to him. He worked hard throughout his life to create the opportunities that formed his life. This is what he tried to instill in his children. It didn't involve coddling of any sort. He believed that he had to be hard on the boys to make them capable of taking care of themselves in the world. He didn't apply the same standards to the girls. He expected less from us. I think his exposure to the horrors of WWII left him feeling he had to raise all his kids to be tough, though he looked at his sons with the expectation that they should be able to do better than he had done. This was an impossible require-ment, especially for young children who could not possibly understand any of these unreachable demands. Despite it all, we looked up to our father, us kids. We were completely in awe of him.

Being General Patton's Ordnance officer in WWII, he was the guy who kept things going when supplies had been cut off from the general. He'd fill up water trucks with French cognac and wine he had found hidden by the Germans and would trade them to supply sergeants for tank treads. He'd create false requisition orders for tanks coming off ships so that Patton could have them. He was a can-do man, and his Texas horse-trading skills were put to good use in the war. He expected a lot from everyone, mainly because he expected it of himself.

It was hardest for my older brother having this old bull of war as a father. He was so very young to be treated like a recruit instead of being given the gentleness needed by a sensitive child. In Tom's way of thinking, there would never be anything he could do that would please "the old man"; nothing would ever be good enough. Tom's face used to flush when the "old man" started in on him about this or that in what appeared to be some weird form of humiliation. I doubt the Colonel would have acknowledged it as that. Tom would fight back the tears that would come to his eyes. His pride never allowed him to let the Colonel see them. Sometimes I think we are born to love those who are most able to wound us. It must have been a lonely place for Tom. I wasn't much of a friend to him either, caught up in my own struggle for survival and recognition.

"He just can't resist the old pointed-finger, thumping-on-the-chest thing," Tom said as he pulled on his baseball uniform for yet another day of torture on the baseball field. The Colonel had just spent time telling him what he was supposed to achieve in that day's game. Tom's sport, one he loved, was basketball, and this baseball thing was purely the Colonel's idea.

"Well, why don't you tell him you don't want to play baseball anymore?" I said.

"Yah! You tell him and see what happens. It's some kind of male-bonding thing with him and the other fathers, his pals. Don't ask me; I'm just a pawn in this thing." He put on the tennis shoes that had been special-ordered from the United States and dragged himself out of the room. We would all soon be loaded into the station wagon and driven to the baseball field located near the ACS.

The baseball field, known as Pershing Field, was a cleared section of land that was near the Golf Club de Saigon, which was south of the Tân Sơn Nhứt airport. In the field near the baseball diamond, Vietnamese children would play soccer. To my way of thinking, we Americans should have been trying to learn that sport so we could play with them. We should have been trying to understand their world and be a part of it instead of trying to make everything have an American identity in this foreign environment.

There is a photo of my brother's baseball team in the 1960–61 *Gecko*, our Saigon ACS yearbook. It shows a group of young boys together, squinting in the blinding sunlight. The expression on Tom's face is one of resignation. He would have to play baseball whether he liked it or not. Humiliation. That is what the Colonel would heap down upon my older brother for his inadequacy in playing sports. It was shame that covered him, not to be easily washed away. How does a child get rid of that bottomless indignation that fills all aspects of his life? I think one must emotionally shut down to survive. That is the look that the camera captured on his face.

We attended the afternoon game traveling in the family station wagon and eventually made it back home. The Colonel settled in downstairs with his late-afternoon cocktail. Drinking wasn't a punishment or pleasure, just a habit. He would usually have only one of them before dinner and one after. Do that for your entire adult life and you will most likely be an alcoholic when you reach a ripe old age. Our mother was a social drinker, nursing one gin and tonic for an entire party; otherwise she abstained. It was a sign of the times; everyone drank socially.

My parents were sitting in the living room talking. Dusk was settling over the city. Colors that resembled fractured light through a prism filtered into the room. The Colonel had recently returned from upcountry, where he and Colonel *Sâm* had been trying to refit a rifle manufacturing plant that the Japanese had put in place during WWII. It was antiquated but workable, he had told us over dinner that day. It seemed that both men had their hands full trying to secure qualified officers to oversee the work. Colonel *Sâm* was at least working with the Colonel again, just not in a command position.

Colonel *Sâm* showed up later that evening. He and the Colonel were reviewing the latest trip details. Both men were telling Mom about how impossible things were becoming. Pati, Bob, and I were spread about on the floor doing homework. Eavesdropping was my major occupation these days, so I was disappointed when we eventually were herded up to bed, leaving the adults to continue their discussion.

A few days later, an unexpected thing happened. A bombing. "Oh, my God! Did you hear? You must have if you are here in the middle of the day!" Mom said to the Colonel when he unexpectedly arrived home. He wanted to be sure that Mom was not at the Golf Club de Saigon. She had told him that morning she had a golf game scheduled. That was where the bomb had gone off.

"I was supposed to play golf today, but I canceled at the last minute. Thank God!" she stated, visibly shaken. She knew not to get hysterical. That wouldn't do for an officer's wife at all.

It was December 6, 1960. Rebels dynamited the kitchen at the Golf Club de Saigon, killing a Vietnamese kitchen helper and injuring two Vietnamese cooks. Small incidents like this one were intended to terrorize and show everyone's vulnerability, especially that of Americans. These types of things were becoming more and more frequent throughout the country. Highly motivated, willing to take great risks, operating in either urban or rural areas they knew well, the rebel groups could strike virtually anywhere, at any time. The Colonel and Mom stood embracing for some time. She let her head fall against his chest, silent. "I gotta go," he said.

During this first year in South Vietnam, we all had our established routines. We lived a carefree and enjoyable French-style life complete with villas, solicitous domestics, and chauffeurs. Half a day of school, a menagerie of animals of every sort to play with, and leisurely afternoons soaking in still blue water at the Cercle Sportif had us living a decadent lifestyle. We attended baseball games and went to just about every American movie that shown and reshown at "the underground theater," an American military facility. In the coming months, we would soon find that our Asian life was to become very complex.

Creeping slowly out of the mire, rearing its ugly head, a dramatic shift was to take place in life for the Colonel and subsequently for all of us. He would be wrestling with an insolvable problem: the reality of Vietnam and America's involvement.

A Moment in History

On February 10, 1964, *The New York Times* reported:

"Two Americans Dead in Saigon Bombing; Stadium Blasts Laid to Reds Injure 20, All from U.S. – More Attacks Feared – Two United States servicemen were killed here tonight and more than 20 other Americans were injured by two explosions under the bleachers of a stadium during a softball game (at Pershing Field, Saigon.) The blasts were atributed to Communist terrorist.... The explosions demolished a section of the bleechers. Authorities believe they were caused by two American made 20 pound aerial fragmentation bombs planted 20 feet apart."

This signaled a change in attitude and in America's relationship with the Vietnamese.

PART II

*"We support this government
until it fails."*

—AMBASSADOR ELBRIDGE DURBROW

CHAPTER 15:

THE UNDERGROUND
THEATER

The jaunty redheaded boy swaggered down the steps of the Postal Exchange (PX) toward us. We BRATs were all waiting for the movie bus by the roadside curb. The sergeant's son lived above the PX, a two-story white stucco building. He was a bully, a self-proclaimed one at that. Always wearing a smartass cheeky grin, he dressed in a haphazard fashion. He'd wear a striped shirt with plaid pants and always seemed to have mismatched socks, a fashion faux pas even then. His long, deceitful face surveyed the crowd. As he circled our small group, his squinty eyes came to rest on me. Little did he realize that this day was just not the day to be messing with me. Let us just say I'd gotten up on the wrong side of the bed that morning, and thus far nothing had gone right. Knowing we would most likely see another showing of the same movie we had seen the last time our mother had shipped us off to the theater, I wasn't in the best of moods. This was becoming a regular thing now that Lieutenant General McGarr was away a lot more on reconnaissance upcountry. The staff didn't change the movie until he'd seen it, and at this point there was no telling when they were going to do that. I was thinking about what my alternative could be to this repeat performance when the boy quickly slipped up to me, quietly whispering in my ear.

"I don't know what makes you such a cow, but you are," he said, snickering.

The heat rose immediately in my face. I turned bright red. To top it off, the "crazy siren" in me went off then and there. This was what my siblings called it when I lost my self-control. It wasn't my fault. He made me do it!

"Take it back, you idiot, or you'll be sorry!"

Pati and Bob quickly moved away from me. Out of the corner of my eye, I saw them position themselves next to this kid's completely embarrassed sister. She was in my grade but wasn't taking sides in any of this.

"You're a jerk!" I screamed, shaking with rage, the veins bulging in my neck.

He couldn't have been more delighted. He'd gotten a reaction. He began to mimic me. "You're a jerk. You're a jerk," he crowed, a smirk on his face. His lips were drawn back over grody yellowish teeth. He was enjoying the whole thing.

The death match that ensued sent our spit flying into each other's faces. Insults spewed from our mouths. A wild revulsion had taken hold of me. Even I knew my anger was out of control. His being grossly entertained by it all just fueled my rage. I wasn't going to back down, that was for sure. Sides were beginning to be drawn by the kids who were waiting with us. My side was growing faster than his, probably the result of his having bullied almost every kid there. The boys who were watching were no doubt thinking it was beneath this guy to be fighting with a mere girl.

Pati and Bob stood nearby, ready to support me if things got bad. It was like having two sneering pit bulls ready to lunge and jump into the mix if needed. I was confident that Tom would be my ultimate weapon if it went too far. He wasn't paying attention to any of it though, leafing through a magazine he'd just gotten. He sat by himself on the lower steps leading to the PX, reading. He always appeared to be disinterested in anything going on with us younger kids.

Then, just as bizarrely as it had all started, the sergeant's kid became silent. Turning and casually ambling by me, letting it roll off his lizard tongue, he whispered, "You're all losers." He said it with a Cheshire Cat–like smile plastered across his mouth. He moved past me toward the nearby high whitewashed wall. Leaning back against it, some distance away from the group, he busied himself picking at his teeth with a toothpick he'd had squirreled in his pocket. As I spun around to keep an eye on him, I saw a tall figure emerging from the gates of the PX. It was his father. The sergeant!

The PX was located on Phan Đình Phùng. It was housed in a compound of white buildings surrounded by a high wall with barbed wire running on top of its entire length. This was a complex that had other service facilities that were found on most military posts: the commissary, the dispensary, and even some housing for military families above some of the buildings. Established to provide services from the United States to the small group of American military folks in Saigon at the time, this complex was where we waited for our ride downtown to "the underground theater." We called the theater that because, inside, it resembled a bomb bunker made of concrete. The PX would be our last chance to stock up on candy and other items while we waited for a military transport to pick us up. During our stay in Saigon, we could tell the mounting number of American members of the military posted there by the increase in goods being offered for sale at the PX. You had to have your military identifications cards to get past the military police (MPs) stationed at the gate. Each of us kids had our own ID, so gaining entry was never a problem. These same IDs gave us entry to all U.S. military bases around the world. It was the magic card that let us kids go where others couldn't.

Pati, Bob, and I now moved as far away as we could get from the bully. The bus doors opened just as the wave of exhaust fumes from the back hit us. Tom made it on first. Pati, Bob, and I moved as one, climbing the high steps, rushing for the nearest seat. The sergeant's kid made a quick dash, cornering me as I made it to the last step. I had to repress an impulse to turn and kick him in the balls, something Tom had told me to do if I was ever in trouble with a boy.

"Do you know about 'the birds and the bees?'" He said as loud as he could muster, moving close to me. I could feel the heat rising in my face again. I didn't answer. "Does she know about 'the birds and the bees?'" he said, hurling the question at Tom, who had already moved to the back of the bus. My brother was hoping to get seated so no one else would sit next to him. Pati and Bob had sat down toward the front. I squeezed in with them.

"Haven't you told her yet?" the sergeant's kid continued loudly, swaggering back to the end of the bus, where Tom sat buried deep in the pages of his latest *Mad* magazine.

Raising his eyes to gaze curiously at this freckled, slightly heavy redheaded boy now standing over him in such a confrontational manner, Tom paused to consider the situation. Tom was bigger and older than the kid, but he didn't like being involved in conflicts. He preferred to manipulate others into things and be the observer of whatever he had managed to create. Tom's only recourse now, however, to keep some level of self-respect, was to answer. "I've taken care of that. She knows," he muttered softly, dropping his eyes back to the page he'd been reading.

The kid looked disappointed, left with only a ludicrous blink as a response. He hadn't expected Tom's seeming support of his younger sister. After all, I was just a girl. The kid's self-assurance was fleeting as he fired back, "Yah! I've told my sister too." He sunk down in a nearby seat and was quiet the rest of the trip. I was somewhat surprised at Tom's coming to my defense in this way. I got up and moved to a seat closer to him in case this barrage was to continue. Tom gained immeasurably that day in my estimation. I felt I'd been saved, but from what I wasn't sure.

The movie theater showings were unpredictable. As usual, we didn't know if it would be a new film that day or one we'd already seen. The problem with the movie schedule, as I mentioned, had to do with the acting general at the time, Lieutenant General McGarr. Every night, his servant would set up the projector and screen in the study of the library in his villa and run the film he'd received whether the general was there or not. The film aired to an empty room nightly. I had a good friend at the time, Ann Peabody, whose father was the aide to General McGarr. When the general was away, we'd slip in through the side door of the library with our freshly popped popcorn to watch whatever was playing. The movie didn't get shown to the rest of the Saigon contingent until the general came back from whatever trip he was on. Like clockwork, however, it ran every night until then. This was true for the movie theater as well. Until the general had released it, we were destined to see the last film he'd seen.

An empty storefront with a metal gate half open, somewhere in downtown Saigon, masked the location of the underground concrete bunker that had become a movie theater. It was complete with a stage and balcony seating. I'm not sure when it was built, but it was inconspicuous. Our theater showed whatever movie made its way to this foreign outpost for both matinee and evening runs. The facility was for military only, I think, and it wasn't until years later that I learned there were other theaters that American kids went to. One was called Alhambra. Our theater might have been called the Kinh Do Theater, but I knew it only as the "underground theater."

When the bus finally pulled up to the storefront, we got off *en masse*, hurrying through the half-open sliding metal gates. It was an empty space. Wide. Open. Narrow. We ran through it to the back. Someone was selling tickets, and a kid had set up a makeshift candy stand with his mother. We three kids rushed by everyone, going down the concrete ramp into the theater, so we could sit in the front row. We'd be so close to the screen, we could pretend we were part of the movie. That was my intention anyway. Sitting up front, legs stretched out, slumped down in the seat, we were ready for the magical image that would soon be projected onto the big screen in front of us.

Before showing the film, however, the military organizers often scheduled a USO (United Service Organizations) performance of sorts. This wacky form of entertainment generally reduced us kids to peals of laughter. We couldn't help it. It consisted most often of a bimbette, usually a blond, outfitted in skimpy clothing. The military men in the theater, as well as the teenager boys, were usually very appreciative. I think the applause and whistles were meant to bolster her spirits. I could predict within five seconds when that baton would be dropped and when those 'ta-tas' were going to be given their day. She would stand front and center twirling her baton and doing leg lifts, keeping time to the music. When she dropped the baton, she was nearly eye level with three somewhat forlorn-looking American children in the front row. Without any sympathy, we would stare back at her as she bent to pick it up. There were times when her low-riding top would get pulled down a little too far and her breasts would nearly dangle out. God, it must have felt like the end of the world for her. For us, we already knew we were at the end of the world, so it didn't matter.

The movie would start soon after this patriotic homage to all things American. As was usually the case, the movie was a repeat of the film we'd seen the last time we were there. This month's continually repeating movie was *The World of Suzie Wong*. I said prayers each night for the general's safe return so this infernal movie might change.

I had watched *The World of Suzie Wong* at least twenty-one times. I might be exaggerating, but it seemed like I'd watched this film forever. The movie was about a lady of ill repute in the guise of a love story between an American man and a Chinese girl.

I will remember one particular movie day forever. Maybe it was my brother Bob's jumping up and running to the bathroom, where he proceeded to hurl the bag of popcorn, candy, and Coke he had managed to put into his small stomach in such an amazingly short time. It was no wonder it had been rejected. He didn't make it to the toilet and spewed it all throughout the men's bathroom. For whatever reason, this was the moment I suddenly realized that Tom had not been visible inside the theater for weeks.

Tom used to go to the balcony section along with all the other kids his age. We weren't allowed to join him there, of course. Once we three younger kids had entered the theater, walked down the cement ramp, and sat in our front-row seats, we didn't pay much attention to where he was. He'd been with us at the PX and on the bus, but I realized now I wasn't sure whether he had come into the storefront with us at all. He was always the last one off the bus when we arrived, and he barely had time to climb on the bus at the end of the movie before the doors closed and it left for home. Of that I was sure. A light bulb went off in my tiny brain. Tom was AWOL (absent without leave). Turning around to survey the balcony and the seats below it, I searched for confirmation. Right! No Tom. I sat smiling even though Bob had returned and needed to be taken into the women's bathroom to be washed down from his lack of control with projectile vomit. Pati and I marched him in and re-emerged with a nearly soaked Bob. As we returned to our seats, my mind was racing. The seed of a plan was slowly being hatched. Wherever Tom was going, I would be going too! Watching *The World of Suzie Wong* that day now wasn't so bad, because I was convinced I'd never have to sit through it again. The movie finished, and we once again climbed onto the waiting military transport. Through the bus window, I caught sight of Tom running toward the bus. He was coming from the big circle across the street from the storefront. He stood on the other side of the traffic circle, caught up trying to get across.

As we had all learned during our time in Vietnam, to get across a traffic circle in Saigon, you had to become one with the undulating flow of bikes, motorcycles, cyclos, and cars, not to mention the horse-drawn carts and taxis. You had to simply see yourself as part of the traffic wave and begin to walk across. No looking right or left, no stopping no matter what, just keeping a defined consistent pace that had you think that you were walking on water from one shore to the next. You could be run over at any moment if you stopped, changed pace, or hesitated for any reason. It was quite simple when you discovered the secret. It might have been our only real initiation into an Asian way of thinking. The older American kids in Saigon called it "Zenning."

Tom was moving across the circle, through the mass of vehicles, trying not to change pace. Finally making it across to the other side, he made a mad dash for the bus. I yelled at the driver not to close the doors. As Tom rolled into the bus, the driver pulled the door lever. The doors closed. With the sound of grinding gears, we were on our way. I could tell he'd been drinking. He was thirteen and had already developed a fond taste for the local *ba muoi ba*, 33 Premium Export beer. He smelled of cigarettes and was busy ripping the paper off the gum he carried in his shirt pocket. He flung himself across the seat in the back of the bus and didn't say a word. Pulling out of his back pocket the *Mad* magazine he'd been reading earlier, he settled in for the ride. This was my moment! I got up from my seat and moved to the one opposite him at the back of the bus.

"I'll tell Dad what you are doing if you don't get me out of going to the movies! I know you aren't seeing any of these films. Do you know how many times I've seen *The World of Suzie Wong*? I think I can recite the entire movie by heart. I don't know what you are doing, but from now on you need to take me with you or else I'll tell, and you know I will!" I stated my case and waited with arms crossed for the storm.

"Yeah, but how long will you keep it a secret?" he said, looking at me doubtfully but very calm. "You know I can't trust you, right? You always blurt things out to save your own skin. If I let you in on this, how do I know you won't blow everything?"

"You're right. I don't have a good track record. Make me part of whatever you are doing, and I can't tell because I'll be in just as much trouble as you," I said confidently, knowing this made a lot of sense and was very logical.

"Okay. But I need to think about this and plan it out. What about Pati and Bob?" he said, shooting a glance in their direction.

"No problem. I'll just tell them we'll sell them if they don't do what we say. Besides, we can bribe them with candy. What are you doing anyway?" I said, feeling that at long last Tom and I might be partners in something. He never knew it, but I looked up to him. This was something I would never tell him. No way!

"I'll let you know later. I just need to figure out what I want to do now. Having another person helping might not be so bad. But if you tell, I swear I'll kill you!" He said it with conviction, so I knew he wasn't kidding on this point.

The future was starting to look bright. I didn't know what it held, but it had to be better than the prospect of another viewing of *The World of Suzie Wong*. The possibility of not having to be the designated babysitter of my younger brother and sister was a bonus.

When we arrived home, we found a huge cardboard box sitting on the floor in the dining room. "Sears Roebuck! It's finally here!" we all screamed gleefully. The Sears Roebuck catalog was our lifeline to all things American. We kids would scour through the colorful pages of the catalog dreaming of the toys we wanted for Christmas. We'd mark the pages by turning the corners down to be sure we'd be able to find the objects of our desire again, but more important so that Mom might notice what we were thinking about. Mom usually just focused on clothes and shoes. Her way of getting the correct shoe size for us was to place our feet on pieces of paper and outline them by drawing around each foot. She'd staple them together in the hope that they wouldn't get mixed up. Months later a huge cardboard box would arrive, shipped from the Sears distribution center to an APO box that all military personnel had in Saigon.

This shipment had the new Keds sneakers that had been ordered several months earlier. We truly believed they made us run faster. As soon as they were on our feet, we sped out of the room and started running "loop de loop" around the villa until we were exhausted. Tom had no interest in this; besides, he had ordered loafers and was sitting with his feet propped up on the glass coffee table admiring them. These shoes had white lightning bolts on their sides, and I must say were very cool! I had ordered red tennis shoes and couldn't imagine a better pair of shoes anywhere in the world. I would wear these until they were nearly falling off my feet. Luckily Mom would have already mailed in the orders for more Sears Roebuck treasures just in time. Later that day, Tom told me what plans he now had for me and about the secret life he was living.

A MOMENT IN HISTORY

On February 17, 1964, two years after the Hanna family left Saigon, the Capitol Kinh Do Theater was bombed. *The New York Times* reported:

"3 Americans Die in Blast at Saigon Movie Theater – A terrorist bomb exploded in the lobby of a movie theater of the American community here last night. Three American's were killed and 50 injured."

CHAPTER 16:

BABY POWDER AND HERSHEY BARS

"I'll tell" always worked where Tom was concerned, though he was usually skeptical as to how long I'd hold out before I'd sacrifice the truth to save my skin if cornered. What an untrustworthy brat I was! I'll admit to that, and I mean it in the truest sense of the word. Maybe the sergeant's kid was right. I was a jerk. I saw it all as simply an effort to survive, however. As the oldest female child in my family, I was always fighting for attention from the Colonel whatever the cost to anyone else. After we had ridden back to the PX on that fortuitous day at the movie theater and finally gotten home, Tom let me in on the fact that he had a black market business going with items he'd purchase at the PX before we got on the bus. He would have preferred buying American cigarettes, but you had to be eighteen and have a cigarette ration card. American cigs were highly desirable. Other than that, no one cared what this young kid was buying. The PX wasn't well-supervised. The cashiers could care less what was bought.

The plan was simple. Buy baby powder and Hershey bars in quantity. Take them to the black market. Make money! Now Tom had no idea what this meant for me. It wasn't just that we'd be working together, it meant my future as far as I could see. My dream had always been to get a horse and go to the Olympics. Could this be the way I could do it? I was beside my self with excitement, but I tried to not show it. We started purchasing hefty supplies of this contraband. Tom had some money from his earlier exploits that we used. We broke up our purchases at the register so that all four of us kids were approaching the checkout at different times. We would bring some of the woven plastic bags that the Vietnamese seemed to carry everything in so we could carry the loot. I'd pilfered a few from our cook's kitchen. Once outside the PX, we packed them full of our contraband.

The movie bus was painted in that awful Army green-brown, a shade that you'd get if you mixed peas and dirt together. It was a huge moving monument compared to the compact Renaults and pedicabs that dominated the streets of Saigon. This giant vehicle carefully entered the flow of traffic and headed to the underground theater for the round trip it would make that day. Today was the day! I was now to be a part of what would turn out to be a very profitable business venture with my older brother. The younger children were to have the worst part of the deal. We threatened them into silent obedience. We told them we'd sell them if they came out before the movie was over or if they told. We meant it, or at least I did. They were little and cute. They didn't trust me anyway and took my words seriously, following our instructions to the letter.

Once the bus had dropped us in front of the theater and we were sure the little ones were safely inside, Tom and I slipped around the bus unseen. We then Zenned our way across the circle. This was a completely knee-shaking experience for me. Reaching the opposite side, we proceeded to the market's large entryway. Old men sat sipping coffee on benches that were propped up against the fading stucco of a massive building from another era. It was a huge old colonial-style structure with a giant vaulted opening and high ceilings. It looked like a warehouse from the outside, and the aged stucco walls told the story of its decline. Inside the building, a village of tented stalls sheltered hundreds of merchants displaying and selling their goods. The earthen floors were hard and worn. The windows, dirty from years of gritty buildup, allowed a muted and soft light inside. It was a shock to enter the market from the stark daylight brightness. Single bulbs hung inside each stall. It took time for my eyes to adjust. Most of the stalls were surrounded by mesh metal structures that would allow the vendors to lock up when they were not there. In places, merchants had vacated, leaving only a bare square of earth where they had once been. We would be using one of these spaces.

Tom had made a deal with the guy who had the stall next door. He'd negotiated a set price as a form of rental, even though the man probably had no real claim on the space. A Coca-Cola crate and grass mat were hidden behind the stall from Tom's previous visits. He pulled out the box and unrolled the mat. Think about it! I was a skinny ten-year-old girl, blond and blue-eyed, sitting on a mat with a crate in front of me, with my thirteen-year-old brother barking orders. On top and all around me we displayed the baby powder and Hersey bars. It was a weird experience, but I was motivated. I had great plans. I needed to buy a horse. I wanted to go to the Olympics! Never mind that I'd never ridden a horse at this point. This was a small, insignificant fact as far as I was concerned. I had, as civil rights advocate Martin Luther King Jr. would so poetically articulate in later years, a dream.

A short, faded little Vietnamese man stopped to watch us. Tom and I were removing the last of our stash of PX contraband from the woven plastic bags we had carried it in that day. This small, drab man smelled of spirits and stood smoking the last of a rank cigarette. The smoke was acidic, and I breathed in the plume that drifted toward me. His eyes were slits devoid of meaning, unblinking. He was wearing ill-cut clothing, as though he'd recently lost a great deal of weight. He moved into the shadow of the stall across from us, disappearing into a small walkway. Unconsciously, I memorized everything about him without being fully aware of the fact. Although unnerving at first, it was not a look of malice, more the appearance of involuntary boredom. I wondered if this man had somehow been assigned to us. I thought of what I'd heard Colonel *Sâm* say about spies keeping an eye on Americans. I decided not to say anything to Tom about it. No way was I going to tell the Colonel either. Whatever the reason, the man simply stayed there for the entire time, smoking one cigarette after the next. All around me was the bustle of people in a place that smelled ruinously of dust, blocked drains, and fish oil.

I believed at that time, and still do to this day, that everything in life lies in the act of acceptance, and I was ready to accept anything that was going to happen from this point on. I'll admit that the start was a bit of a nail-biter, however. I was glad Tom was sticking with me. Well, that was until he announced he was off to the bar to play pool. He'd put in enough time with me for training, he figured. Besides, the money in his pocket was burning a hole. He would soon be betting the young Vietnamese men in the pool halls with it. He stressed the fact that my responsibility was now to be increased exponentially.

"Take over!" These were his parting words.

"What do I do?" I cried out as Tom walked away.

"Have fun. Make money! I'll be back for you before the bus comes." He was smiling as he exited the market.

With that and a wave, he left the market to continue his life of leisure at the nearby bar; drinking his *ba muoi ba*, playing pool, and betting the men who populated the game rooms. His gait was confident. He had found his place in Saigon, one that he felt comfortable in. He was independent. Here, there was no one putting him down or demoralizing him. He was happy.

Despite my fears and revulsion, I now concentrated on the task in front of me. When I raised my eyes, having spent some time rearranging my goods on top of my wooden Coke crate and bamboo mat, I had an audience curiously hovering over me. I had tried learning Vietnamese from the moment we arrived in Saigon, but I hadn't been very successful. I had resorted to pidgin French and had gotten by fine so far. Hand expressions were also helpful. In my broken French, I would explain to my customers that my white skin and blond hair were the result of the baby powder. I was petted and touched as my prospective buyers attempted to see what the result of the baby powder was. I suspect they just wanted to see if the feeling of my hair and skin was much different from their own. Some seemed to just want to buy the baby powder untested. I wouldn't have been surprised if they had plans to use it for something other than their skin. When the French ruled Vietnam as one of their colonies, opium was a major part of the Vietnamese economy, something I had learned from Tom. These customers were a bit shady looking. The Hershey bars sold without a routine. I'd break up a bar or two to give candy samples to any hesitant shoppers.

That day, I made a good thousand piasters. This wad of Vietnamese bills bulged in my pocket. I was well out of supplies to sell by the time Tom returned. He had done well in the pool hall. He too had money stuffed in his pockets. Tom said we couldn't divide up the money until later when we were somewhere safe. I don't need to tell you that it wasn't a fifty-fifty split and I wouldn't be sharing any of the pool hall winnings. I knew it was an unequal division. He said something about management fees. It wasn't fair, but then again, I felt lucky to be part of the thing. We packed our wares and crossed the circle just in time to get on the bus. We missed it only once and had to take a motorcyclo to beat the bus back to the PX. A bewildered Pati and Bob stepped down from the bus as our motorcyclo slid into the parking space in front of the transport.

School was the only real structure my siblings and I had. I think the term "feral" is an accurate description of us and all the other third-culture children who were living in Vietnam. Tom and I had a lucrative business in Saigon that first year, before he was sent away in July to the Brent private school in Baguio, Philippines, to start high school. Our partnership had ripened as the money flowed. Our sibling rivalry had been put on the back shelf.

Life for all of us went on as usual, with an occasional bizarre side show to provide variety to the unending hot days and humid nights. There was something singularly unconscious about our life as we moved through the city's human limbs and ancestral ruins. However, Saigon was a place where, for the present, plotting and conniving actions lay just outside our immediate scope.

CHAPTER 17:

NO GOOD GIRL

No longer bothering to look at the mesmerizing world outside the stamp shop window on Rue Tu Do, I tried to keep my mind simply on my collecting when there. My world had returned to a seemingly easy and uncomplicated cocoon. I went about each day like a seasoned pro. The black market business was booming. The baby powder and Hershey bars were moving at a good pace. Pati and Bob were keeping their mouths shut.

Unexpectedly, as with all our family moves, we were told we were relocating to a different house. The owner of the villa on Đoàn Thị Điểm no longer wanted to rent to Americans. Our family went in search of a new house. We found a fantastic villa in a different part of the city. This second house was located on Phan Thanh Giàn. It was 1961. This move took place in the beginning of our second year in Saigon. As was the custom of the day, different servants came with the different houses. We were no longer to have Anna with us. We moved; they stayed. This seemed a little weird, but in hindsight it was perhaps the best way. Their lives weren't disrupted.

I don't remember the names of the other servants in the first house very well, the ones on Đoàn Thị Điểm. French people had lived in that house before us. I think these servants preferred the French to us. As Americans, we were unfamiliar with being waited on, and I think they viewed us as a bit pedestrian. Little effort was made to befriend us children. In that first house, we had a male cook who was stealing and watering down the liquor. That made fast work of him—touch the Colonel's alcohol and it was curtains. I often wondered if it was the cook or my brother who was doing it. Anyway, the servants we had in the first house changed a lot. They seemed to lack personality, or perhaps they just didn't have much interest in us kids. The second house was different. They were wonderful. They liked kids. They even liked us.

Thi Ba, Thi Tu, and Lucy made up the help at this second house, along with a part-time gardener, though Lucy wasn't officially a servant. She was a university student and lived with her mother in the servants' quarters that were part of the property. Thi Ba and Thi Tu were the main staff, and I spent countless hours just hanging out with them. They both spoke English and French, though Thi Ba's English was not as good as her French. Thi Ba was our cook; a short, jolly robust person in her early forties. Thi Tu was the official maid of the house, and her English was much better. She was a wonderful housekeeper. Tall, thin, and very proper, she was probably in her early thirties. She wasn't married, and her life seemed to revolve solely around her work. I said a silent thank-you daily to the gods above for her. She relieved me of bed making, picking up clothes, and baby-sitting chores. They too had been serving French people before us. We were their first Americans. Thi Ba's daughter

Lucy was the one who helped me to communicate. She had studied English in school. In her early twenties, modern in her appearance and very smart, she was a pretty woman with a perky personality. Through her came my real understanding of the contrast between Western ways and those of the Vietnamese or even the French. I came to depend on Lucy for what I considered my informal education while in Saigon.

The second house was not on such a posh street as Đoàn Thị Điểm. It was, as mentioned, on Phan Thanh Giàn, named after a Vietnamese notable. It was just a few blocks away from a hospital. The road in front of the villa was a busy thoroughfare compared to the relatively quiet, majestic eucalyptus-tree-lined Đoàn Thị Điểm. The blare of the ambulance sirens as they raced down the street could be heard day and night. The main watering hole for the entire area sat just outside our walled compound. This free-flowing water spigot ran day and night. It was alive with children at play and woman collecting water in cans to carry back to their homes, and generally, was a social gathering place for everyone. Their lives seemed ones of austere toil, yet there was also a feeling of harmless joy surrounding the place. The inequality of fortune confronted us every day as we went to and from the villa.

This city location wasn't quiet, but I liked this house better than the first house because it had a separate fenced area where I could keep all my animals. Bamboo and banana trees abounded, and we could handle even more animals here. I had collected a menagerie of animals while living at the first house that were welcoming gifts for the Colonel from various Vietnamese officers. Mom brought home a baby blue-bellied monkey one day from one of her bridge games. Her name was Mou Hou Lui, which means "no good girl" in Chinese. When we moved to the new villa, my menagerie of animals blossomed. Besides the cat, dog, monkey, and rabbits that we had brought with us, we were given a stork, three turkeys, and a red rooster by various other Vietnamese officers, most likely with the idea that they would be eaten. We found that if we put a bucket of water out for the stork, he would stand in it all day on one foot. This became his complete world, this small bucket of water in the bamboo grove. A poodle-shepherd mix dog was given to us too. That was probably the stupidest animal I've ever owned.

Our feline population grew exponentially too, as Momma Cat had one litter after the next. Later that year, a baby elephant joined the ranks. We didn't keep it for long, however. It was part of an elephant rescue program, and several American homes had been given them to take care of until they could be relocated. I think bringing it into the house one too many times had Mom finally putting her foot down.

"Sandy, if you don't get that elephant out of the living room now, there won't be enough soap bars in South Vietnam left when I get through with you! Do you understand, young lady?" The elephant's stay was short. The vast amount of sugar cane it required was becoming a chore too. We weren't too sad to see it leave.

A tiled driveway wrapped around the whole house. It had a portico overhang, creating a carport of sorts in front of the big double screen doors that led into the living room. The servants' quarters ran along the back in a row with shuttered doors and windows. They connected to an open garage, where the Ford station wagon we'd brought with us from the States spent most of its life. The monkey cage was housed there as well. The kitchen was separate from the house, with an outdoor adobe-tile-roofed walkway connected to the main building. A lush tree-filled garden surrounded the property, and like at the first house, jasmine was everywhere—a scent one never forgets in a lifetime.

This new home was much more modern in design than our first villa. Built during the last generation of French rule, it was pleasant and open. The floors were marble and the rooms spacious, with whirling fans overhead. We didn't have to pass through each other's bedrooms here, but as there were only three bedrooms, Pati, Bob, and I shared one, while Tom had his own room with a private entrance. Our parents' room was separate but had two doorways, one connecting to the children's room and the other leading out to the hallway. Instead of huge armoires, some of these rooms had proper built-in closets. The ceilings were still high, ranging around fourteen feet, and the walls were white stucco. Air conditioning units rested in the windows of the bedrooms. The day we moved in, we made an interesting discovery on the second floor.

"Hey! You guys, come look at this!" Bob yelled as he hung on to the door frame of the upstairs bathroom.

"What'ja find?" Pati said excitedly as she and I tore up the stairs to join him.

"I don't know. I think this is the bathroom. Right?" he said, somewhat puzzled. We all stared into a relatively large tiled open room.

"Wow. This is definitely a real French bathroom," I said, scanning what only the French could have come up with. Inside the bathroom on the floor were two metal raised flat foot holders with a hole between them and a metal water tank attached high up on the wall behind it. A pull chain hung from it. This was a French toilet. The foot holders and hole had us completely confused at first. Learning how to use it was a gymnastic feat at best. You didn't sit. You squatted.

On top of the building was a glorious roof garden where we could see over the wall and watch the world pass by. The hum of human voices swirled upward. We had felt isolated in our first house, apart from everything around us, alone in our private cocoon. Here, we could look at Saigon life from high above. Many days were spent lounging, curled up on the chair cushions reading, tucked under the shade of a sprawling potted palm. We would listen to its wind-caressed clicking leaves, hidden from the sun's burning rays. The *clip-clop* of horse hoofs, the chugging of an engine, the squeals of children playing and splashing water created a stored-up constellation of moments for me. This medley of sounds rose from the street to meet me in my up-on-high world.

The new house was the perfect place for throwing cock-tail parties, and our mother didn't hold back. It became the refuge for so many of the Americans who had come without family to Saigon. The Colonel had a grill that sizzled steaks from the commissary that he ordered in special. They were shipped frozen and held at the commissary for him. He was afraid of getting horse meat if he tried to get red meat in Saigon. The bar was always open, and I had become quite adept at making gin and tonics, rum and Cokes, and other such mixes. They placed me on a crate behind the bar so I could be tall enough to pour the drinks. I'd later be replaced by someone else as the party got into full swing and I was told to go to bed. It would already be dark when I was dismissed.

I must admit that the women all looked beautiful. The ladies were in their newly tailored raw silk dresses, sleeveless, cinched at the waist, sporting hemlines hovering just above the knees. Most had them tailored in Cholon, having shared with each other their discoveries of good shops in this Chinese section of the city. Many of the ladies had also been taking advantage of easy trips to Hong Kong to buy fabrics. They'd use the latest fashion pictures torn out of magazines they'd gotten at the PX to be copied. Mom would avoid the problem of only bringing fabric back to Saigon, by simply having the clothes made overnight when she and the Colonel went to Hong Kong for rest and relaxation. The Chinese seamstresses could turn anything around within twenty-four hours. Having taken an almost empty bag with her when she left Saigon, Mom would have it filled to the brink by the time she was ready to come home.

At our cocktail parties, the women would have all been to beauty parlors that day, and the amount of hairspray in the living room could have set off a small explosion. The officers didn't wear their uniforms but rather would be in embroidered Vietnamese or Philippine-style white shirts. They weren't the colorful embroidered dragon shirts Tom had started to wear, but subtle without additional colors. They wore the shirts outside the pants, not tucked in, as they had side slits. The shirts had short sleeves and were more casual than what they would no doubt wear back home, and everyone appeared comfortable in the still sweltering heat of early evening.

The ceiling fans would run on full throttle all night. The American civilians working on various government projects and other military consultants would arrive one by one or in small groups. The ratio of men to women was probably ten to one. Gin and tonic with a lime twist over ice was the drink of the day. While the men congregated around the front of the bar, the women stood in small bunches, holding sweaty drinks in hand, puffing on cigarettes and talking. Everyone would be in high spirits, and laughter could be heard over the buzz of conversation. The servants moved about the room with trays of canapés and finger sandwiches. Sometimes Mom simply set up the dining room table with her famous barbecued ham in a warming tray. This was to be put on the nearby small warmed buns. This dish was quite popular, and she had a reputation as a great hostess who served good food. I think the fact that she used American recipes made her food even more welcomed.

One night, I was moody and restless after my bar shift. It was a raucous evening with no moon, just what was needed to set off a bored child. I was feeling particularly mischievous. Why that night had to be the night I would sink into complete anarchy, I'll never know. I didn't see it coming. I had snuck back down the stairway and out the side door, having initially mounted the steps earlier to go to my room. Once outside, I reached Mou Hou's cage, where my crazy blue-bellied monkey excitedly shrieked a greeting at my arrival. I unhitched the cage door and put her on my shoulder. I peered around the corner of the building into the party room, being neither seen nor heard by anyone inside. Insanity had never been a factor that I knew of in my family, but I suspect there must have been some in me that night.

Pati's voice sounded at my elbow. "What are you doing?" Where that munchkin had come from, I didn't know, but she always wanted to be a part of things. She must have seen me turn around at the top of the steps. She and Bob had been confined to the upstairs bedrooms after being allowed to be at the party earlier in the evening. Bob now made an appearance as well.

"What are we doing?" he said in complete innocence.

Pati always knew when something out of the ordinary was going to happen, and she followed behind me as I moved toward the screen doors of the living room, monkey in hand. Bob fell in line behind her. These were big doors that opened out to the tiled driveway portico. Everyone was inside, the result of an earlier sudden rain shower. The room was thick with people, smoke, and conversation.

Mou Hou was quietly picking through my hair. I lowered her down off my shoulder and quietly slipped her through the double screened door.

"You're crazy!" Pati said in a barely audible whisper. Her eyes were as big as saucers. Bob started to giggle.

The three of us watched silently from our hiding place as Mou Hou, once released into the room, stood upright and walked on her hind legs. The space was crowded. It wasn't likely that anyone could spot a small blue-bellied monkey walking among them. For her, their legs were more like a forest that she was maneuvering. She moved around without any hindrance or notice. More than anything, Mou Hou loved legs with silk stockings on them. All around her now were these coveted things. She began to survey her choices.

"Oh, my God! She's going to do it!" I said, knowing full well that the moment was coming when all hell was going to break loose.

In one swift premeditated move, Mou Hou grabbed hold of a high-heeled leg close to her. With lightning speed, she shimmied up toward the top of the leg. Clutching with both arms, she took hold of the thigh. Describing the scream that was heard is almost impossible. As soon as the little monkey arms attached to that leg, the woman started to jump and spin around, batting at the unknown thing under her skirt that was holding on for dear life. Mou Hou rode her leg like a seasoned rodeo rider! Eventually the battering was too much for her. She jumped for freedom. Running now on all fours with her lips curled in a sort of demented smile, almost an expression of happy mockery, she made for the door. She headed straight for us three kids hiding in the wings. The sound of my mother's voice rose above it all. "Sandy!" Her eyes were glued on the monkey as it escaped.

I quickly opened the door as soon as Mou Hou reached it and grabbed her. With her arms waving, I put both hands around her waist and catapulted her upward. Our feet were hardly touching the ground as we ran toward the only place that seemed to make sense: heaven. The roof garden had an outside stairway, and we flew up it hoping to hide behind the large potted palm trees for the rest of our lives.

"She's going to kill us! She is going to kill all of us," Pati said, whimpering. Bob had already started to cry and had tears welling up in his eyes.

"Quiet!" I said, pulling them in behind me.

We quickly crouched down behind the ornamental pots holding decorative palm trees in the corner of the roof garden. Mou Hou, however, became interested in the stiff, bristling leaves of the nearby plants and, despite all of us trying to keep her still, kept moving the branches of the palms. Mom made it to the top of the outer stairway breathless and fuming. She made a beeline toward our hideout, holding in her right hand a leafless switch. When she had time to grab that was a mystery. I was impressed.

"What were you thinking?" Mom said, towering above us. It was a voice that made me think she was counting internally to calm herself.

I couldn't say what I had been thinking. I had no idea. It just seemed like a good idea at the time.

After the spanking, a right usually reserved for the Colonel, came the apology made to a very traumatized junior officer's wife. I was restricted to quarters for the rest of the weekend, deprived of any sort of allowance for weeks, and generally treated like a leper by the servants. Mou Hou had her privileges revoked too and was caged for some amount of time. Pati and Bob were assumed to have been innocent bystanders. They got off scot-free. The black market business was to be put on hold.

Downstairs the party went on late into the night and flowed over into early morning. The Colonel liked to offer steak and eggs to any early-morning hangers-on. The servants would be fast asleep by then, but he'd persuade Mom to go into the kitchen and whip something up. She'd serve up a complete breakfast with piping-hot coffee American-style, laying it out on the table for everyone to help themselves.

Eventually, I'd hear the metal gate to the driveway open and the few remaining partygoers attempt to find transportation home. Our parents would give us strict instructions not to be bothered, and we knew better than to enter their room until they made the first move. That wouldn't be until well into the afternoon. Sunday was their day of rest.

The CIA (Central Intelligence Agency) already had operatives in Saigon during these early days. The Colonel had become friends with a few of them. They were often a part of these parties. I'd sometimes see the Colonel quietly discussing something with one of them alone and off from the group. The Colonel, as mentioned, was the Chief of Ordnance Corps, and he was the person the Army war college would send experimental things to; a defoliant that kept the jungle from engulfing his network of supply depots was one such item. It worked great and was soon noticed by the Air Force higher-ups. It would later be known as Agent Orange. The Air Force commandeered the stuff when it discovered its capability. Scrap metal embedded in a plastic explosive was another item sent to the Colonel as an experiment, later to be discovered and copied later by the Việt Cong for use on the pathways running through the jungles. Of course, we Americans were the ones who laid it down on those jungle paths first.

The Colonel would tell me years later that one of the men at the party had asked him for a weapon that could be easily transported, then quickly buried and disposed of if necessary. He was looking for something with some fire-power. The Colonel requisitioned some bazookas for him. The man told him that he was taking them upcountry to create a disturbance along the Cambodian border that could be blamed on the North Vietnamese. This CIA operative had a makeshift office at the Brink's BOQ.

Parties were Mom's second favorite thing to shopping and she held some of the best gatherings of their day in Saigon. As children, we would be allowed to mingle with the guests, usually bringing in several of our favorite animals, monkey included. Ruby Nell pictured in photo with Pati, Sandy, and Tom.

CHAPTER 18:

LADY BYRD AND THE TEXAN (MAY 1961)

The Colonel was becoming more and more removed from our lives. Work now took up most of his time. Much to his relief, Colonel *Sâm* was still working with him. The two men had recently taken a trip up north. Photos of the two of them sitting astride ancient horse statues in front of a temple in Huế documented their visit there. Nothing more had developed with Madame Nhu and the Đà Lạt affair. Colonel *Sâm* still worked in the Ordnance Corps, but in a lower position; he was no longer in charge.

The Colonel was now the one having problems. A run-in with the higher-ups in Washington was to be his next challenge. It had to do with a bid for the purchase of twenty-five hundred jeeps. The contract was to be awarded to the company that met defined military specifications for the order. He followed the specs, awarding the bid to Toyota as opposed to an American company. Willys, a big supplier of military equipment, was the other company vying for the contract. It was an American company already gaining a lot of the military contracts in Vietnam at the time.

One day after my father awarded the contract to Toyota, the salesman for Willys stood in the office of the Colonel's boss, along with the assistant American ambassador. They were both demanding an explanation as to why he hadn't given the contract to the American company.

"They had the better vehicle and the better price, as was detailed in the guidelines of the bid specs," the Colonel said calmly in response.

Wonder who was paying off whom for these contracts? Someone needed Willys to be awarded the bid. Some lobbyist must have been pissed off. When he returned to the United States, the Colonel was dragged before some congressional committee to justify his decision. He said at the hearing, "I didn't know we were still at war with Japan." What is the saying? Follow the money and you will understand everything.

Things were beginning to heat up in Vietnam; we were no longer allowed to go anywhere without a maid or an adult. Tom and I continued with our undiscovered life at the black market, however. There was no way I was going to give this business up now. Our trips to the movie theater went on as usual. The younger children kept their mouths shut, happy no doubt at not having us around in the theater. The piasters we took in from our sales were mounting. I was busy relocating my stash of cash so it wouldn't be found.

One particular day, however, there was to be a change in the schedule: without much notice, we were told we were to meet Vice President Lyndon Johnson and his wife, Lady Byrd. The location was to be disclosed at the last minute. The date was Friday, May 12, 1961. Johnson was coming to Saigon in some official capacity, to look over American involvement and go back with a report no doubt. We were told he'd spent the day meeting with South Vietnamese President Ngô Đình Diệm. He later called Diệm "the Winston Churchill of Asia" when confronted by the press back home. Johnson had encouraged Diệm to see himself as indispensable to the United States; Johnson promising additional military aid to assist the Saigon government in fighting the Communists.

The Colonel had been emphatic that we dress nicely and be on our best behavior. Tom was AWOL (Absent Without Leave) and had somehow managed to disappear before my parents could nab him. The rest of us kids weren't sure what we were going to see—there is always something peculiar about official government visits—but everyone else seemed excited to be on a family outing, all of us going together. This was a rare thing at that time. We were even going over to the event in the family car. The Ford station wagon was just plain excessive in this country. For good reason, the car sat most of the time unused in the garage. It took up most of the roadway and required a great deal of time to get anywhere. It couldn't easily pass the carts, bicycles, cyclos, and small French Renault cabs that dominated the roadway.

Orders were issued for the day. Pulling ourselves out of our sluggish and lethargic state, we climbed the stairway to dress. I hated getting dressed up. I was a tomboy, and those dang dresses blew in the wind and could so easily show your underpants. They made me feel vulnerable. I'd sneak a pair of shorts under them without the folks' knowing whenever possible. I also didn't want to miss a chance to climb a tree if the opportunity presented itself.

Lyndon Johnson was chosen as President John F. Kennedy's vice president in 1960. Like most vice presidents, he did the traveling in those days to foreign lands as the representative of President Kennedy. His job was to assess various situations around the globe. Both he and Lady Byrd were going to be making a speech behind the horse stables at the Cercle Sportif. In true Vietnamese fashion, subtly reflective of the present regime's real attitude toward Americans, a wooden stage had been built over the manure pile that was there. I doubt the Johnsons or even most of the Americans knew about it, but all of us kids were snickering on the sidelines knowing what lay beneath. There were some government officials along with military personnel and their dependents in attendance. It was not a large group but was very heavily guarded. Johnson said he had come on a fact-finding mission, and of course he made the usual "thanks for being here" speech. Fact finding? In retrospect, he obviously didn't get the facts right.

"Who is he?" Pati asked. We were sitting in the grassy area to the right of the stage waiting for whatever was going to happen.

"Vice President Johnson of the United States," I said.

"He looks like everyone else," she mumbled, her attention turning to other kids who had moved away from the gathering to play.

That, he did! He was dressed in a beautifully cut suit. Lady Byrd was in a simple but stylish summer dress. He was tall, but then all adults seem tall to children. She had been given the traditional long-stemmed red gladiolus from an exotic Vietnamese woman as she stood on the stage. These ladies were always dressed in traditional Vietnamese attire with too much makeup and lip coloring. Much too red. Both Johnsons had Southern accents, Texan accents to be specific.

Lady Byrd's hair was dark, perfectly curled and styled. His was wispy and thin. Their complexions were light, not having been in the Saigon sun to get that deep tan that so many Americans were now sporting. They seemed tired. The flight to Vietnam is not an easy one, and jet lag takes time to get over. They reminded me of some of my Texas relatives with their mannerisms and speech patterns. I scrunched down on a nearby bench to see if I could make out what this was all about. I listened to his speech.

"President Diệm, a man with a deep religious heart, here to save the people from the agonizing prospect of Communist rule; the man who has halted the red tide of Communist Asia," Johnson said. I moved closer to see what his eyes said. Did he believe what he was stating so emphatically or was this just theater? It was hard to tell. Texans are like that: good poker faces! I'd learned that from watching the Colonel.

I think Johnson believed what he was saying. Lucy, Thi Ba's daughter, had been trying whenever we got together to help me understand what Americans thought they were doing in Vietnam. Her view wasn't one of a global ideology; it was a simple one that understood her Vietnam. This country's desire was that of being a whole nation without foreign intervention. After all, the Vietnamese had been fighting China, Communism, and foreign rule for centuries. I now listened, hoping I'd gain some new understanding from Vice President Johnson.

It was a warm day with a slight breeze. Grand old flame and eucalyptus trees towered above, giving us much-appreciated shade from the midday sun. The stables lay just beyond the stage, and the occasional neigh of a horse could be heard. I was probably the only one who noticed.

The adults were clustered in front of the stage. Most of the children were running around playing tag and ignoring the event altogether.

The family got back to our house that day after another long and slow winding crawl through the streets of Saigon in our gargantuan car. The Colonel was in an irritable mood. He sat down, and Mom handed him a much stiffer drink than the usual daytime gin and tonic. We stayed out of the way. There was a storm brewing, and it was best that we were nowhere to be found. The Johnsons left Saigon later that afternoon.

The Colonel's view of the situation in Vietnam those days wasn't the same as it had been when we had arrived. He didn't like the shift taking place in which the involvement of politicians was starting to mean the removal of the MAAG heads from decision making. Saigon was now becoming a political football, seemingly no longer under the direction of the military. The advisors felt they weren't being heard. "Nothing is going to come of that visit that matters; same crap, different day, not a clue," the Colonel mumbled in a voice that was cynical and despairing. He swallowed the last of his drink. The ice in the glass clinked as he set it on the table and left the room. To his way of thinking, things were changing, but not in the way he thought they should.

The Vietnam situation was not understood at all by Americans. It was a complex mixture of culture, history, and beliefs in a country foreign to Americans. It was all in direct contrast to the cultural strategy the United States was trying to impose, one of capitalism and democracy. The two were like night and day. My real understanding of the country came through my encounters with the servants and, more specifically, the lessons Lucy attempted with me. She was determined someone would understand!

A Moment in History

Upon his return home, Johnson echoed domino theorists, saying that the loss of Vietnam would compel the United States to fight "on the beaches of Waikiki" and eventually on "our own shores." With the assassination of President John F. Kennedy in November 1963, Johnson became president. He chose to go against Kennedy's earlier evaluation to order American withdrawal from South Vietnam. As top-secret papers have been released from the Library of Congress, it should be noted that Kennedy had been planning to remove 1000 American military personnel starting in 1963 and the remaining 16,700 would be withdrawn by 1965. He had made the announcement to his staff two weeks before he was assassinated but did not make it public. The order was National Security Advisory Memorandum (NSAM) 263. Johnson reversed this order with modification to it in NSAM 273. "The Joint Chief of Staff and MACV responded to Kennedy's withdrawal plan by telling the truth about the failing war effort at the 20 November SECDEF Conference in Honolulu. The chiefs had no intention of letting JFK pull out of Vietnam in a winning scenario and wanted to diminish his chances of winning the 1964 election. This marked the end of false optimism the military had begun in February 1962."

—Library of Congress

—John M. Newman, History in the Making Essential New Work

Vice President Johnson and his wife, Lady Byrd, visited
Saigon in 1961, giving a speech to Americans in Saigon.
Held at the back of the palace stables, everyone was
unaware of what lay beneath the platform stage.

CHAPTER 19:

REST AND RELAXATION

O ur mother and the Colonel made great use of the
opportunities available to them for standby military
transport trips to Hong Kong, Bangkok, Japan, India, and
the Philippines. Mom delighted in shopping excursions
in these countries and loved haggling in the stalls for the
goods that she bought. She would return from her travels
with rugs from China, porcelain lotus lamps from Japan,
and beautiful silks from Bangkok. It was easy for my folks
to claim available seats on military planes and take off on
the spur of the moment. We kids were generally left behind
with the servants, but in the summer of 1961, they finally
decided to take us along on one of these junkets. We were
all going to visit India together. I imagined a mysterious
and exotic place. I conjured up pictures of elephants and
Brahma bulls, holy men and exotic silk-wrapped women
with dots on their foreheads. I was beside myself.

The MATS plane stood in the middle of the tarmac with
its engines turning as we rushed up the steps and found empty
seats. The plane's interior had the usual uncomfortable hard
benches and otherwise was relatively bare. We had come
to expect this as our mode of travel. The flight originated

in Saigon at the Tân Sơn Nhứt airport with a stopover in Bangkok. We eventually landed in New Delhi, India.

The Colonel was working with a sergeant at the time who was from India. He was part of the British Army, a contingent assigned to South Vietnam working with American military advisors. In conversation one day, the Colonel mentioned that he might like to take his family to see India. Snapping into action, this fellow immediately arranged for our entire family to stay at a hotel that his cousin managed.

With so many of us, we were generally on a budget for family vacations. We weren't expecting much in terms of our housing possibilities. The pedicabs that transported all of us from the airport merged with the flowing stream of humanity, eventually coming to a stop in front of the palatial entry to the New Delhi Grand Hotel. Dumbfounded, we stared in disbelief at what stood before us. The structure was massive and magnificent, gigantic and with ornamental designs everywhere. We entered the main hall as attendants swarmed around us to grab our bags and welcome us. Inside, the ceiling height was unfathomable. Huge chandeliers hung everywhere. It oozed British dominance from every pore. The staff was magnificently dressed in classic Indian garb. After checking in, we were graciously escorted to our suites. Not one room that we'd all have to find a way to fit into, but three large suites, each with a living room and two dressing rooms. Incredible lavish meals were served in the hotel, and room service was available at any time. This was all included in the price my folks had been given. In true Texas style, the Colonel couldn't get enough of the spicy curry dishes, and I couldn't get enough of the "high tea" confectionary trays. Tom stuffed himself with grilled steak every meal.

The streets of New Delhi were filled with women adorned in incredible saris: flowing material wrapped around their bodies in miraculous ways. Beggars were everywhere, and children showed no shyness about coming at people *en masse* asking for money. White Brahma bulls leisurely wandered the streets unattended, considered sacred and honored. Everywhere, ancient buildings with intricate tile reliefs and archways tied the city together. Manicured gardens were everywhere, and frangipani bushes outlined squares. The hotel made travel arrangements for the family, packing extravagant lunches for us to take along on daily outings.

Transported to the train station, we found that the train was packed with everything. Goats and chickens were in the seats next to us, and there were as many travelers on the train car roofs as inside. It was literally bursting with life inside and out. We traveled to Agra to see the Taj Mahal, the king and queen's architecturally unique resting place. We also visited Red Fort, an incredible massive structure with secret passages and gem-encrusted walls where the royal couple had resided.

The fashion of the day in Saigon among us American girls was Bermuda shorts and short-sleeved shirts. I had packed my bag with several outfits that matched. Pati had done the same. I was soon to learn that it was forbidden for females to show knees. It was an insult to the gods, it seemed. At every turn, someone was trying to tie dirty rags around both Pati's and my knees. Entering the Taj was no different: shoes off and rags around our knees. I think our snickering brothers looked forward to its happening to us every time. Boys could show all the knee they wanted. I spent most of my time in India angry at the injustice of it all. I hadn't packed anything but shorts, so I had no way of blocking this daily interaction with every beggar that lined the street.

Our mother went in search of a sari, a traditional form of dress for Indian women. She had no intention of saving Pati and I by buying us new clothes. We all went to the Kamal Silk Emporium, 17/A Grover Mansion, Asaf Ali Road, New Delhi; an address no doubt passed on by a friend. This was a place that manufactured and exported Banaras saris. Beautiful ladies at the place demonstrated the proper way to arrange the fabric. It was a marvel to watch a single piece of fabric get wrapped and folded in such a way as to produce what appeared to be an exotic dress. After a bit of practice mastering the art of the fold, we moved on to Old Delhi. There Mom proceeded to buy a prayer rug and everything brass she saw: trays, candleholders, ash trays, and punch bowls with goblets.

We whirled through the city, a place where fabric was dyed and dried in the open, revealing bright reds, blues, and yellows. The scents of musky incense and spicy cooking battled for dominance. The nearby slaughterhouse had buzzards lined up side by side on the roof. Poverty screamed out from every corner. Beggars and dirty, ragged children were everywhere. Escorted by our guides, we were taken to the nicer parts of the city, avoiding the massive slums that abounded. History was all around us, and my parents focused our attention on historical things. There was an incredible iron pillar in Delhi's Qutb complex that stood twenty-three feet high, notable for its rust resistance thanks to the metals used in its construction. Being an engineer, the Colonel was very intrigued by this marvel. As in Saigon, the heat of the day was almost intolerable, and we'd arrive back at the hotel grateful for a reprieve from it.

We were treated like we were VIPs. I don't know what this sergeant had told his cousin, but they didn't hold back and our bill was minimal. The Colonel was more than pleased. Mom couldn't stop talking about the trip to her friends when she got back to Saigon. She went on and on about how inexpensive and grand the place was. Impressed, her friends booked the same accommodations. They didn't get the special deal we'd had when they went there.

After we got back from India, school was to start soon, and we were told that Tom would be going away. Far away! He would no longer be part of our world except on holidays and summer vacations. He would start his high school education in the Philippines. Pati, Bob, and I were in shock.

CHAPTER 20:

BLACK MARKET DAZE

G oing to the Philippines for school was not Tom's decision. It was July and the school year was starting up again. He was being sent away to the Brent School in Baguio, a private school that boasted the attendance of sons of officers and presidents as its students. He was starting ninth grade, his freshman year of high school. The family accompanied him to Baguio for the first week, staying at nearby Camp John Hay, named after a former secretary of state. The Colonel decided before we were to depart that it was time to talk to Tom about the "facts of life." Pulling him aside in the school bathroom, the Colonel laid it all out to his already distressed fourteen-year-old son, who was soon to face abandonment by his family in this completely foreign country.

"About time for you and me to have a man-to-man talk. You know how this works, right?" he asked, not waiting for his son's response. "Good. Always wear a rubber." With that the Colonel turned and left. Tom stood watching him in complete disbelief. This was a story Tom later told and retold to me, probably because of the absolute absurdity of the encounter. The family would all return to Saigon riding standby on a military transport. Tom, in turn, was left to deal with this new life of isolation and complete separation from his family.

Tom was gone and I was on my own. I missed having him around. I'd never admit it to him of course, but I depended on him and appreciated any direction he could give me. I am sure he felt like he'd been ripped out of his life and dropped into oblivion. But as I said, he didn't have a choice in the matter. The Colonel wanted to be sure Tom got a good education and didn't think the high school correspondence course the ACS offered would be adequate. He had goals for his oldest son, whether he communicated what they were or not.

In my brother's absence, I continued to run the black market business we had set up. I don't think my brother even knew that fact until years later. I gleefully now kept all the profits, except what I had to pay out to my adjoining stall mate as rent.

The days and weeks passed. Business went on as usual at the market. I'd started to have my regulars, and the stall keepers had come to accept me as a familiar fixture. There were greetings shouted across the stalls, but I couldn't help thinking they were simply humored by my presence. At the end of my shift, usually when I'd run out of product, I'd fold up the mat and move my crate behind my neighbor's stall for safekeeping. He always nodded. I always made sure to say "*merci beaucoup*" as I paid him the day's rent. If there was extra time before the bus arrived in front of the theater for our pickup, I'd wander through the market with my now empty bag slung over my shoulder. It was a veritable highway of life—noisy, and everyone was haggling and bargaining for goods. Everyone's technique was different. There were the shouters, the nodders, the whisperers, the fist shakers, the squealers, and then there was me, the voyeur with bright eyes, smiling. It was expected, this heated form of interaction. In fact, it was the most fun part of the whole thing. This lively repartee went on at my makeshift stall too.

"I give you two piasters," my customer would say in French, a language they seemed to all know. I think they thought I was French. After all, the French had dominated that country for decades. We even looked like the French, being Caucasian.

"For this, you only offer me two piasters. It is an insult," I'd volley back in the same language.

In the end, we'd agree on something, as long as it wasn't less than what I'd paid, and hopefully some profit would be made.

"How do you expect me to feed my children?" I'd conclude.

This always set off a volley of laughter, and we'd part ways with big smiles on all our faces. I liked the people I met. They were kind. Shop owners would offer me food and drink, which I would respectfully decline unless it was a hot cooked item or a drink with an unopened lid still on it. I didn't want to be rude, but I didn't want to get sick either. I'd had enough of that, and I wasn't up for the interrogation I'd have to go through from Mom trying to identify the source of the nasty amoeba. Besides, I wasn't keen on trying to find a toilet at the market to use. If I'd had a good day, I'd save a few candy bars and give them to the surrounding shop owners as a thank-you for keeping an eye on me and being kind.

That strange Vietnamese man with the stale cigarettes still appeared on a regular basis, standing in the shadows for the length of my stay. The occasional expiring of a match in the dark walkway would remind me of his presence. He never said anything. I'd see him leave before I was completely packed up.

Wandering around the network of stalls, I'd eventually end up at my favorite vendor. This was a vendor with hand-carved animals made of both wood and ivory. He was always sitting at the very back of his stall. I loved the things he had and bought from him regularly.

"Bonjour, ma petite fille. Comment vas-tu?" he'd say, talking to me in a tone I'm sure he must have used when speaking with his own daughter.

"Bien, et toi?" I would answer, looking around to see if he had any new stock. One day I spotted a lovely carved wooden fan that exploded with the scent of sandalwood when opened. *"Combien vous dois-je?"* I was always mixing up the *tu* and *vous* pronouns, the personal and the formal.

"Dix-sept piasters," he said, smiling. He knew full well he was asking too much and was ready for the bargaining that would now ensue. The skin around his eyes crinkled when he was happy, and so we began.

"Vous demandez trop!" I said, putting the fan down for emphasis and laughing. We eventually settled on eight piasters and were both pleased.

His French was about as good as mine, so we'd stumble through our negotiations, but inevitably I'd buy something after a volley of dialogue on the price. It was always this way. I bought things at his stall just because he was so nice to me and seemed to enjoy it so much. It might be a deer carved in light wood, a large cricket carved out of ivory, a wooden fisherman in traditional attire wearing a bamboo hat and holding a fishing pole or a wooden music instrument. These were my treasures, and every purchase made me feel rich. It gave me a heady feeling of independence.

"*C'est épatant! J'aime beaucoup*," I'd say of my purchases, holding them close as I left, yelling back to him. "*À tout à l'heure.*"

The floors of the market were tamped dirt, and the smells covered a full range of things that could assault your senses, good and bad. There were always strong smells of urine mixed with intense aromas coming from the area where the food vendors prepared every sort of dish imaginable. As usual, there was the smell of fish sauce, *nước mắm*, something one could never get away from. Whiffs of richly spiced dishes with meat filled the market. The smell clung to your clothing long after you left the building and walked into the hot breath that infiltrated the town. The spice stalls were fantastic, with colors I'd never seen, at least not in Mom's kitchen. These aromas often seemed acidic: orange cumin, red cayenne pepper, ocher curry powder, beige ginger, maroon saffron. Stalls were packed with every sort of fruit or vegetable. My child's imagination ran wild in this exotic buzzing world.

I can't say I'd let my guard down when I was there alone. I was aware of everything going on around me. I'd developed this habit after our earlier indoctrinating and unexpected coup experience in Saigon. I'd worked out several escape plans, just in case they were ever needed. Just because I was blond didn't make me dumb! Being alone, however, was somehow comfortable for me. I didn't have to take care of anyone. It was just me. I luxuriated in my sense of independence even though I was moving through a thoroughfare of undulating humanity.

Zen. I think in many ways I achieved it in Saigon. I read somewhere that Zen is just a reminder to stay alive and awake. Zen is about appreciating your life in the moment. My reality was the here and now. As a child in Saigon, there was no other way to be really. Buddhist temples were everywhere throughout Saigon and the shaven heads of the monks with their colorful robes could be seen throughout the city. The beauty of the temples with their red orange coloring and strong smell of incense was enticing. I loved to peer into their entries as we road pass them. Huge golden Buddha statues sat above the alters. There seemed an utter peacefulness to the place. On a whim, I visited one close to the market. Walking up the steps to the pagoda's opened entrance, I took off my shoes. I entered along the back wall to sit and watch as the faithful came to bring offerings, light incense sticks and candles in front of the golden statue and pray. How different from the backwoods religious approach with all its fire and brimstone. This calm silence and beauty was in such sharp contrast. Nearby monks chanted. It was a calming and rhythmic sound that entered my very soul. I wondered if I could adopt this religion as my own. To a religious country, all religions are one, I think.

It was time to get back to the theater storefront. The movies, the newsreel, the USO show, cartoons, and feature presentation could usually be counted on for a good three-hour run. That was enough time to devote to my makeshift retail profession and still have time to make it back before the bus arrived. Usually, when I'd exit the market I'd be blinded by the intensity of the afternoon light. I'd gotten used to the muted light of the market with its few trembling yellow electric light bulbs and the dirty-window-filtered light. I'd make my way back to the bus across the buzzing circle, amazed each time that I got to the other side without being killed.

As the younger kids exited the storefront, I'd slide in between them. If I got back early, I'd burn up any extra time in the neighboring shop trying to stay out of sight. Pati and Bob were always glad to see me but didn't relax until they were safely on the bus. They didn't trust me not to carry out my early threat of selling them. Like I said before, I wasn't trustworthy.

"Okay. What was the movie today?" I asked them as we boarded the bus.

"It was weird! About a white girl whose mom was a Negro and a maid. I didn't understand it at all. The girl was pretending to be white, and her Mom was really sad because when she was older, the girl pretended the lady wasn't her mom," Pati said. "Bob and I didn't like it!"

"Well, if you can't remember the name of it, we can at least tell them that story if anyone asks," I said, sitting on a bus seat. I found out later it was called *Imitation of Life*—not a movie that children should have been watching. There weren't any servants present to collect us when we arrived back at the PX. I waved down a cyclo driver as he passed. Getting in, I gave directions.

"*Traversez la route et prenez la première à droite. Je veux descendre à Phan Thanh Giàn,*" I said, more comfortable with my French then. The black market encounters had given me the opportunity to practice it.

Bob had wanted us to take a motorcyclo, but I didn't feel we could escape easily if needed. A cyclo isn't like a rickshaw, with someone pulling a cart from the front. A cyclo is the back end of a bicycle with peddles pushing a carriage in front. A motorcyclo is the same idea but with the back end of a motorcycle instead. Motorcyclos were fun and fast, but I'd already had to jump and run from a cyclo once when the driver wouldn't go the way I wanted, and I couldn't imagine how I'd be able to do it again if needed in something going faster. Even if I could get out, how would I get the two younger kids out too? Not with the speed that a motorcyclo could go. Bob was disappointed.

"Arrêtez," I called out as we reached the villa. *"C'est tout ce que j'ai,"* I said, handing him a twenty-piaster note. I waited for change while Pati and Bob piled out of the carriage. No one was there except the servants. The younger kids marched upstairs as I snuck out the back door to stash my recently ill-gotten gains in the cigar box in my make-shift science lab in the servants' quarters. As we gathered for dinner, it was easy to see that the Colonel was out of sorts. We kept quiet, letting him talk, making sure we didn't become the object of his attention. Safer that way.

"I can't believe the lengths these people will go to!" He was addressing our mother and seemed oblivious to our presence. The Colonel was in full-blown steam mode at this point. His patience was worn thin.

It seemed that another effort to discredit and hopefully remove the Colonel from his position as Chief of Ordnance Corps was in the works. It was being orchestrated in the same manner as had been done with Colonel *Sâm.* It was being carried out by a civilian, a tech rep with the Vinnell Corporation of California. The Vinnell Corporation was an international private military company based in the United States specializing in military training, logistics, and support in the form of weapon systems maintenance and management consultancy. He had been sent to Vietnam as an advisor assigned to the Ordnance branch of MAAG in Saigon. A retired major, he had been contracted by a privately-owned civilian corporation. The Vinnell Corporation was an international private military company based in the United States. Money was to be made, and Vinnell wanted a foothold. The retired Major Eugene A. Peterson had written a report about ordnance conditions of stock control and supply at the 601 Ordnance Corps of ARVN, advising the chief of storage on problems he saw. Peterson was ripe for the picking by the ARVN officials who had already sabotaged Colonel *Sâm*. It was being carried out by a civilian, a tech rep with the Vinnell Corporation of California, similar to what happened to *Sâm* with an unfounded issue of the supply depot. They were at it again, but this time with the Colonel. His unwavering support of Colonel *Sâm* made him a target. Peterson had no idea what he had been pulled into when he addressed his report to Lieutenant General J.H. Hinrichs, Chief of Ordnance, the Pentagon, Washington, D.C., on April 1, 1961. He would, unfortunately, suffer the consequences for this naive action. His letter in part read as follows:

General Hinrichs, I am not in a position to be critical of anyone or anything. My only reason for writing to you of these conditions is that you should be made aware of exactly what Ordnance's position is here in order for you to be in a position to better evaluate a course of action.

As I have no capacity here except that of tech rep, I have tried to make Lt. Col. Hanna, the senior

*Ordnance officer here aware of the magnitude of the
problem. As he is very inexperienced in supply and
maintenance he seems unable to grasp the magnitude of the condition and seems unable to foresee
the seriousness of the problem.*[3]

His report listed some number of small arms stock
numbers and quantities. His report went on and on about
stockpiles of munitions that were creating an oversupply to
the depots throughout South Vietnam.

"Inexperienced! This coming from a former major tied
to a private corporation that is no doubt interested in getting
more federal contracts. Undermining any person in charge
is the strategy they are using to get a foothold. How else
can he justify his position? Right? Who was the fellow who
kept General Patton's Third Army going in World War II?
Me! Who was the guy that handled all supply and maintenance then? Me!" The Colonel was venting his frustration
to our mother, but he knew he was going to have to take
this up with someone higher. I think he was venting so he'd
be more controlled when he had that meeting. He had an
advocate in his boss and made contact immediately the
next day. Deputy Chief Colonel Parsons, Logistics Division, CATO wasn't about to have this civilian get away
with anything so transparent with one of his best officers.
He had a great deal of respect for the Colonel and acted
immediately. These civilian contractors were itching for a
war. They wanted as much involvement in the affairs of this
little country halfway across the world as they could get.
There was money to be made, a lot of it.

LOGISTICS DIVISION, CATO,

MILITARY ASSISTANCE ADVISORY GROUP, VIETNAM

Lt. General J.H. Hinrichs
Chief of Ordnance
The Pentagon
Washington 25, DC

Dear General Hinrichs:

This refers to the letter written to you by a retired Ordnance Major, Eugene A. Peterson on 1 April 1961, concerned with the problem of excess material in the Ordnance system of the Vietnamese Army. General Thorlin left a copy of the letter here and I had the opportunity to discuss it very briefly with him. Because the nature of the allegations raised by Mr. Peterson involves the whole MAAG, I believe a short explanation to you is appropriate.

The problem of disposal of excess stocks here is not restricted to Ordnance. We have excess in virtually all of our Technical Service Branches. There are many difficulties attending the out shipment of such material, but much progress has been made and is being made under the CINPAC "Clean Sweep" programs. That we would like to move more rapidly is true, but with the complicating factors of having to deal with the problem through use of indigenous facilities and manpower, speed of action can be achieved only in relative terms. Despite all the problems, there has been considerable progress made in the field. The CINPAC Inspection Team which recently completed a two week visit here praised the results of MAAG Vietnam's efforts during the "Clean Sweep" operation.

There is an unfortunate tendency on Mr. Peterson's part in his letter to grossly overstate the amount of excess in existence. He mentioned a figure of "80% of all stocks" as applying to the depot in which he worked. This is not the case. Our excesses across the board in all Technical Service would not approach a 25% figure and in Ordnance, the figure would be considerably lower except in specific commodity groups.

Mr. Peterson made some derogatory comments concerning Lt. Col. George T. Hanna, the Chief of Ordnance Branch here. From a command standpoint, we could not permit these comments to stand. Lt. Col Hanna has a very complicated and responsible assignment here and he is doing a very commendable job. He is highly regarded by the Command element of MAAG as his efficiency reports will attest.

We intend to take no further action on the matter here. Ret. Major Peterson has been discharged by the Vinnell Corporation and is returning to the States. I understand the letter he wrote was partially the cause of his short stay here although he was an object of concern because of a series of other, varied incidents.

Fred Thorlin mentioned that you thought of paying a visit here at one time soon. I believe it would be worthwhile if you could come. I unfortunately am not able to spend much time with Ordnance as I would like but from the several field inspections and trips around the country which I have made, it is obvious that our Ordnance people have done a fine job of training the Vietnamese. The base shops and depots are just about as good as can be found in any Army.

Sincerely,
WM J. PARSONS
Colonel, GS
Dept Chief, Log Div, CATO[4]

This letter did the trick. The complaining major was sent back to Washington. The Colonel continued with his assignments and was left alone, for now anyway. This wouldn't be the end of this thing though.

Tom was no longer part of the black market business he'd
introduced me to; instead he was being sent back and
forth on military planes to school in the Philippines.

CHAPTER 21:

SOUTH OF THE CLOUDS

The city was overflowing with papaya, mango, coconut, jackfruit, soursop, and exotic fruit of every kind. The rich soil of the Mekong Delta supplied almost half of this produce. It had always been the heart of Vietnam, the Mekong. Its bounty flowed into the markets of Saigon. It was known as "the rice bowl" of Southeast Asia.

Walking through the back alley off Rue Pasteur on a sultry one-hundred-degree afternoon one day was without doubt a singular moment for me. I was sweating. Sweating was something I usually didn't do. On that day, it seemed impossible to find refuge from the heat. I was on Rue Pasteur with Thi Ba. She was running her many errands. Rue Pasteur, named by the French of course, was one of the many places we frequented during these shopping trips. The sweaty faces of the shoppers passed by, like us, intent upon completing their tasks and getting out of the heat. Thi Ba was to go home to her family's hamlet for a funeral that week, and we were picking up the supplies she needed.

Thi Ba cooked the entire rest of the day, preparing dishes to take with her as offerings for the feast that would be held in honor of her family member. She and Thi Tu sat in the courtyard preparing the many packages that she and Lucy would be taking with them. Watching and listening, Pati, Bob, and I got the chance to taste some of the many things they made. Sprinkled with the Vietnamese combinations of herbs and spices, the flavors were exquisite. It was a rare treat.

Absorbed in the food preparation, we weren't paying attention to Mou Hou, my crazy monkey, who was screeching and jumping around inside her nearby cage. Unnoticed, she began furiously working on the twisted wire that kept her cage closed. Her little hands reached through the holes in the chicken wire, turning the wire until she had it unfastened. Mou Hou passed quietly by the group and entered the kitchen. Leaping up onto the counter opposite the stove, she settled down to wait.

Needing more rice for the banana leaf stuffing, Thi Ba and I got up and headed toward the kitchen. Pushing the screen door open, Thi Ba moved over to the stove to refill the bowls she was carrying. As she turned around, full bowls of rice in hand, one stacked on top of the other, Mou Hou made her move. She stood straight up with arms spread wide and let out a shrill hair-raising screech. Her little teeth clinched, Mou Hou's monkey squeal hit its highest note as the bowls of rice became airborne. Thi Ba's scream matched that of Mou Hou's as Thi Ba barreled by me. Mou Hou was now squatting contentedly by the pile of white rice covering the floor. She was stuffing her cheeks with the white stuff. Thi Ba was completely frazzled. After a good scolding and demanding that I clean up the mess and remove the little monster from her domain, she went to her room for the remainder of the afternoon.

Lucy told me that her uncle would be buried in the rice field of her village. "The Vietnamese don't believe in death in the same way you do in the Western world. They believe there is no end. By being buried in the rice field, they believe he will continue to sustain his family," she said. "The body of this man's flesh will become soil. All things are in harmony. There is a succession of life even after death." She said that her uncle's sons, her cousins, would now be the ones to do what their father had done, in the same way that he had done with his father.

They were up early the next day for their journey. I so wanted to go with them to this funeral, but Lucy explained that this was a very personal family event. It was not appropriate for me to be there.

"I know you would be good, but it wouldn't be right for you," Lucy said.

"I believe in spirits. I really do!" I said, still hoping to convince them.

"This is a world that is not a part of your understanding. We are going south of the clouds. Just look in that direction if you miss us. Do not fret, little sister; we will return in a few days," she said, patting me gently on the head and looking skyward. She and Thi Ba made their way down the driveway and out the gate.

I watched them leave with the feeling of being caught between two worlds. As a child, I was more than influenced by their thoughts and the stories they told me. My view of the world was changing, becoming a mixture of Eastern and Western beliefs. Lucy was also helping me to understand the different religions in Asia. Those and the damning prediction of my going to hell by that preacher in Kentucky were like night and day. I would later find I was to carry aspects of these Asian beliefs with me for the rest of my life.

We did not accompany Thi Ba and Lucy for this visit to their village. The celebration was one to honor their ancestors, and they were going to participate in the burial rites. The place was hidden in a bamboo curtain of dense foliage. Autonomous and anonymous, it was a world hidden from sight and removed from the rest of the world. We had been there on a previous visit. Rice fields spread out on all sides. Frightened pigs ran between huts. Chickens lazily scratched for treasures in the dry, dusty earth. This life of the village had the certainty of repetition; each day was simply a continuation of the day before. These villagers lived lives that were fully extended by day, and every night they returned home exhausted.

As I sat alone on the one step near the door under the portico, the world behind the bamboo hedge loomed in my mind. How different we Americans view the world of death and the obligations of family. Our Western views are like a reversed mirror image of theirs. I would be buried and that would be the end of it when I died. That thumping, blustering minister in Kentucky said my soul would go to heaven or hell. Everything ended there. Not so in the beliefs of the Vietnamese.

As time went by, I found that the Vietnamese had more ways to celebrate the dead than I could keep track of. If it wasn't a personal death in the family, it was a celebration of the dead in general. It seemed like the dead were always being considered, and with that came one holiday after the next in a celebration of them. Another holiday rolled around, and the servants asked for the day off and were given it. Our alternative to Mom getting in the kitchen to prepare dinner, something she had avoided since arriving in Saigon, was to pack up the entire family and join the American officers at the Brinks BOQ.

The Brink's BOQ, in downtown Saigon, had a roof garden bar and restaurant. There was a parking garage under the building that we could easily enter and park in, and then take an elevator up to the rooftop. We'd been told to dress appropriately and be on our best behavior. Despite the season, there was a cooling breeze even though the temperature was still high. It came across the rooftops from the Saigon River. Here, the smell of city life mingled and contrasted with the strong aroma of steaks grilling that came from the rooftop. The smell of charcoal-grilled meat caused our nostrils to flare and our mouths to salivate. It was wonderful!

The foreign men of war gathered on top of this towering structure appeared to be a pretense of normalcy. They could have been anywhere in the world. Officers stood with sweaty drinks in hand under colored paper lanterns that hung the entire length of the open rooftop. A full bar ran along one of the walls under an extended part of the roof. Awnings hung stiffly over other areas for daytime shade. American music played in the background.

It was the night of the lunar moon. With it came a traditional Vietnamese feast of celebration. The sound of fireworks exploding in Cholon, the Chinese section of Saigon, and throughout the city could be heard. It was Wandering Souls Day, Trung Nguyen, held in August on the fifteenth day of the seventh moon. This is the second-largest festival of the year after Tet. Offerings of food and gifts are given to the wandering souls of the forgotten dead. The streets below were alive with activity.

"This is Wandering Souls Day, the day the forgotten dead return," I announced with a slight trill in my voice, hopeful of setting the mood with my younger siblings.

"Huh?" they both responded, then dead silence. They knew to be suspicious of me when I was telling them something about dead people. Their eyes were wide.

"You just want to scare us," Bob said defiantly.

"Lucy says that families offer food and gifts on this day to the ones that have been forgotten, the dead," I said, feeling like I could draw this story out a bit more and get them scared. Bob was right. I did want to frighten them. After all, it's a big sister's right!

"Maybe we should put something out for them. We don't want them to get mad because we didn't do anything," Pati said, taking off to collect some of the food she spotted that was left on discarded plates, and a few half-filled glasses of something.

Bob and I collected some candles already lit inside their red glass encasements and swiped some shiny ashtrays to make our offering appear richer. Our makeshift altar seemed shabby and forlorn in comparison to the Buddhist temples we'd seen. Pati found some red napkins, and she draped them across a small side table. We stood back to admire our work.

We leaned over the railing again and looked far out to where the river meandered below us. "See that light on the river?" I said, pointing in the direction I was indicating. "They put floating candles in the river at night to guide the lost souls to nirvana. I guess nirvana is sort of like heaven."

We all decided it was a good time to put in a prayer or two. We had the altar, and it couldn't hurt. I wondered if those people who had gotten killed around us in the coup would make use of this day to get home. I hoped so. I thought about them often. Our time in Vietnam had left each of us feeling that anything could happen at any time to any one of us.

I looked back toward the adults and could see the Colonel and Mom together. They were smiling at each other, as if sharing a private joke. They sparkled with affection for each other. They made a splendid couple, envied, like people trained to work together since childhood. Instinctively responding to each other's unspoken words and desires, they moved throughout the crowd, supporting one another with their smiles. I saw eyes watching them. I felt proud of who my parents were, how they looked. They were both strikingly attractive. I wondered how they had ever ended up with me. I was sure I'd been adopted and no one was telling me.

A delicious evening coolness suddenly came from nowhere, bringing with it a wave of relief. The day of the wandering dead was almost over. From what I could understand, if the Vietnamese didn't get these souls put to bed, back in their rightful family graves, today, they had a whole other Holiday of the Dead, Thanh Minh, in April that would take care of deceased relatives. It seemed like a very good way to deal with this ghost thing. The Vietnamese, as I mentioned, had all sorts of days for remembering the dead. Tet Doan Ngô (Summer Solstice Day) in June sees the burning of human effigies to satisfy the need for souls to serve in the "God of Death's" army. In the United States, we just leave the souls of our dead to wander, and maybe if we have time, we visit their graves. It just didn't seem right. The Vietnamese never forget their dead. We could learn a lot from them about this, I thought.

A Moment in History

A supreme error on the part of both Diệm and the Americans after 1962 was the implementation of The Strategic Hamlet Program.

"The Ngo brothers had from the beginning favored the new program in the expectation that it would give them more control over the village...and were willing to commit once they knew how much money the Americans were willing to commit. Without a clear understanding of the culture and the importance of the ancestral burial grounds, the United States launched into this counteroffensive with the Diệm regime. It was described as a pacification effort to separate and protect the rural population of South Vietnam from the Viet Cong. Villagers were moved into hamlets protected by police and security forces in fenced-in compounds fortified by a ditch, bamboo spikes, and barbed wire. Once security had been established, social and economic initiatives were supposed to be implemented to compensate the resettled villagers and win popular support for the government of Vietnam. However, in practice these vital socioeconomic aspects of the program were often lacking. Villagers were in fact being put into camps and taken away from their ancestral lands and family members. More damage was done to the rural population's perception of Diệm and the Americans through this program than can possibly be imagined. "

—*Frances FitzGerald,* Fire in the Lake: The Vietnamese and the Americans in Vietnam, *1972*

Thi Ba, our cook, and Lucy, her daughter, patiently put up with the antics of us children. Lucy became my confidant and an appointed teacher of all things Vietnamese.

CHAPTER 22

DIỆM'S BIRTHDAY PARADE

When and where the celebration of President Diệm's birthday happened is a bit of a blur for me, though history has recorded it as being on January 3, 1961. What I remember most about this celebration is the large ornate floats passing the Congressional Hall in downtown Saigon. These floats had huge placards with images of Diệm towering above the moving vehicles. Women and men in traditional attire were positioned on the floats next to these huge billboards. Music blared from huge speakers set up on the vehicles as they passed. As I looked around, I was surprised that there were very few Vietnamese present for this elaborate display. Vietnamese people who should have normally been lining the street to watch this colorful parade pass and join in the celebration were absent. It was a parade in honor of Diệm's birthday, but the route was completely barricaded off so that very few people could come close. It seemed to be more of a publicity thing for the benefit of the foreigners, including the Americans, and the press.

The paranoia of those in the current regime had reached new heights, and they weren't going to create an opportunity that might turn on them. Only foreign officials and those seen as loyal to Diệm were allowed on the parade route and grounds. The Vietnamese population was not. Palace guards were the primary security force, as distrust of Diệm's own military was growing. Floats passed by the review stand supposedly honoring the man.

Diệm was wearing his traditional white suit along with his signature sunglasses. A short, round man with a full face, pleasant in appearance, he sat with his shiny black hair glistening in the afternoon light. His brother and confidant, Nhu and Madame Nhu, were seated on either side of him. Other trusted officials sat behind.

Nhu was much older than his wife, as I mentioned earlier, and his face wore the strain of years of the political intrigue he was orchestrating. Recent bad times seemed to have left their mark on his weathered face. Madame Nhu, on the other hand, appeared exuberant as she sat uncharacteristically demure next to the two men. She was paying attention to President Diệm, making sure he had everything he needed. She occasionally would lean over to say something in his ear. Madame Nhu was seated in a position that would indicate she was the pseudo First Lady. President Diệm was a bachelor and had sworn an oath of chastity, so his sister-in-law had taken on the role without hesitation.

Madame Nhu was sporting her newly designed áo dài, one that the older Vietnamese were constantly discussing as being sexually suggestive. Many people did not appreciate her imposing her values on their lives and found her to be a hypocrite due to the now widespread rumors of her infidelity. What was even more brazen on her part was that she had been active during Diệm's presidency pushing for the passing of morality laws. This included outlawing abortion, adultery, divorce, contraceptives, dance halls, beauty pageants, boxing matches, and animal fighting. She was closing the brothels and opium dens as well. People viewed her ban on divorce as tied to her attempt to keep her sister's husband from divorcing his wife because the sister had a French lover. Her sister's husband was extremely wealthy, and the Ngô family would lose highly valuable assets if there were a divorce. There were many contradictions in the Ngô family that were all too obvious to the Vietnamese people. Madame Nhu represented them all.

Madame Nhu was very petite. Looking at her that day, it was hard for me to match her image with the names she had been recently given. Names like "Dragon Lady" as well as "Lucretia Borgia" and "Queen Bee" were becoming names all too familiar for this tiny woman with the beehive hairdo and risqué áo dài. This was a woman who, as time went by, became mocked for her ostentatious flaunting of power. Like so many things in Vietnam, she was not what she seemed.

I had been reading a lot about her in newspapers and magazines assigned for my social studies class. The press was having a field day with her. She exerted influence wherever possible with her fiery attitude, often abusing Diệm and Nhu, who bowed to her angry tirades. She once said, "Power is wonderful. Total power is totally wonderful." She told a group of American congressmen, "I'm not exactly afraid of death. I love power, and in the next life I have a chance to be even more powerful than I am." This was an insane thing to say. Perhaps she was insane. She was certainly power-hungry!

On the day of the parade, I was much more interested in watching Madame Nhu than the parade itself. She was a curiosity to me. As far as I was concerned, I just didn't like her! Colonel *Sâm's* removal from his position in the military had me dead set against her. I was sure she'd had something to do with it!

At the birthday parade, we three younger children were under strict orders not to wander away from where our parents were. "Stay in the general vicinity and be visible at all times" was the command. My sincere hope was that there wasn't going to be another coup attempt in which we would be scrambling to get out of the way of gunfire. Dancers with huge traditional dragon heads and flowing fabric moved down the parade, lunging toward spectators behind the barricades. Traditional patriotic songs were piped through the speakers affixed to the wagons. Madame Nhu's Vichy-style troop of young women marched by in their gray uniforms, carrying weapons. "Why don't we get to carry guns like them?" Pati asked. She thought this was great.

"Are you nuts? We don't want to be carrying guns, because then someone might shoot us!" I answered.

"Does this mean they will get killed?" Pati was persistent if nothing else.

"No, it is just for the parade today." I moved closer to the fence and turned my attention back to the passing floats.

"Will they shoot people then?" She looked nervous.

"No!" I said trying to reassure her we were safe. I didn't think we'd be in a coup, but then again who knew these days? An undercurrent of unrest was flowing through the country.

When the parade was finally over, our family moved back toward where the Colonel had parked the monster station wagon. He had parked it in a restricted area. It would be slow going back to Phan Thanh Giàn. Unaware of anything other than our small world, we tormented each other in the back seat. We had purchased a papier-mâché head resembling Diệm at the parade and were making mock speeches in the back seat, trying to grab it off any head it was resting on and, of course, squealing at the top of our lungs. By now the Colonel should have taken a swat at one of us and used his Colonel voice to threaten confinement in our rooms for the rest of our lives. Instead, he just stared at the mob of people and vehicles in front of us as we meandered down the streets of Saigon.

We moved past beautiful white buildings and narrow abandoned alleys of dirt and mud. Eventually, with the sun moving westward, we arrived home. The gates of the villa opened. We were once again safe in our sanctuary on Phan Thanh Giàn.

In hindsight, so much was taking place in front of us at that parade that we weren't aware of. Perhaps the Colonel had an inkling that day; I'm not sure. The "Mandate of Heaven" had changed, that was for sure. At the time, we Americans were in the dark about what would soon unfold. The torture of the Buddhists and students went on in the background unbeknown to most. Support by the South Vietnamese population for the Diệm regime was dwindling. The government was at odds with the people and its own military. All this was in plain sight, but none of us could see it.

We children continued with our daily schedules. I was in the sixth grade now, along with the other BRATs my age. We were a tough group, and this year was beginning to have its challenges, mostly for our teachers. Let me just say, we were not an easy group to manage.

A MOMENT IN HISTORY

"In their support of the Diệm regime, Americans had no real understanding of the belief system that was at the core of the Vietnamese people's perception of their rulers. This belief ruled supreme among the Vietnamese: whoever ruled the country had been chosen by the Mandate of Heaven (Chinese: 天命*; pinyin: tiānmìng—literally, "heaven decree"). This was an ancient Chinese belief and philosophical idea that tiān (heaven) granted emperors the right to rule based on their ability to govern well and fairly. The mandate was revoked for unjust rulers. A country could turn overnight if it was believed that the Mandate of Heaven had changed."* When a Buddhist priest set himself on fire in 1963 in protest of the Diệm regime's persecution of Buddhists, the country turned overnight.

—*Frances FitzGerald,* Fire on the Lake: The Vietnamese and Americans in Vietnam, *1972*

Massive floats and marching military were brought out to
celebrate Diệm's birthday, but the Vietnamese populace
was strikingly absent from the sidelines.

CHAPTER 23:

THE REDHEAD

I was always amazed at how short our school day was. It ran from only 7 AM to 12 PM. We'd have a snack break in the middle of the morning, when we were allowed to take the bagged treats we'd brought from home to sit outside, along the corridors, or in the field at the back of the school. In the open field, we could watch and listen to the jets that were breaking the sound barrier above us. The breaking made an odd booming sound. They'd fly high, these completely black planes, over the field.

During the snack break, the teachers tried to encourage some type of physical activity. I usually snuck away and propped myself up on the half wall, sitting with my back against a support column. I loved to watch the show that was unfolding before me in the adjoining field. Under a celadon sky with its puffy white clouds, the progress of the rice growth was a marvel to watch. The thin shoots would grow and gain strength until they were finally ready to harvest. Fields were planted at different times so that there was never any downtime. The rice paddies were always being worked by the family.

Lucy had told me about how the villages and farms worked, what they believed in. She enjoyed being able to speak about things she knew. It also gave her a good opportunity to practice her English. She was always trying to get me to understand her Vietnam.

"In Vietnam, there is not so much good land; it is limited. Not like you have in America, where they say it goes on forever. The Vietnamese live in their villages always doing the same thing over and over, sowing and reaping of rice. We honor our ancestors this way. We believe it is through them that we have our life, our fortunes, and our civilization. Everything is passed from one generation to the next. We say, 'People flow over the land like water for all the generations to come,'" she recited.

After I'd been told about her uncle being buried in the rice paddy, I looked at the rice fields differently. I wondered how many bodies had been buried in the fields in front of me. Maybe Lucy was pulling my leg. At first, it had seemed kind of gross thinking that bodies were in the rice paddies. I was greatly relieved when I heard they cremated the bodies. The ashes were spread in the rice fields. I had imagined whole bodies surfacing at any given time until Lucy cleared up my confusion. Did that mean all rice was made up of dead bodies? I decided not to bring this up with the younger kids, or they might never eat rice again.

We'd gone through a lot of teachers already that year. We were now beyond the middle of the school year. The Tet holiday had already passed. My sixth-grade class was notorious for its cruelty to new teachers. Those unfortunate individuals who had hoped to inspire knowledge in us didn't last long. Our teachers changed every two weeks or so. One day, the poor Philippine woman who had been there only one week had been reduced to tears. We were expecting the principal to be conducting the class after the snack break. Her goal was simply to keep us quiet and in our seats. The boys in our class were congratulating themselves for having gotten this poor woman out in only one week. It was a new record.

Military kids take control in order to feel their world is not out of control. Imagine moving every two years and never having any idea where you are going next. Orders came in, and usually there was no time to say goodbyes to any attachments you might have made. We are nomadic by nature. We Saigon kids tested everyone to see if we could trust the individual to be in control so that we could let down our guard. Our survival instinct controlled our needs. It was unfortunate to see so many teachers leave. I liked all of them. They had been sweet, a surefire recipe for failure with this ragtag crew.

Within a week, our sixth-grade class was told we would have a new teacher taking over and that she was from New York. Not that this little tidbit of information meant anything to us, but the way the principal said it, the smile that was on her face, should have given us pause. My class took the information in as one would when getting ready for the next assault. We weren't worried. As it turned out, however, we should have been. A true force of nature would soon be entering our lives.

As the students slid into their seats at the sound of the bell that fateful day, a few of our more colorful fellows held their places where they stood, leaning against the back wall. A tall figure came into the doorway silhouetted by the glaring light that filtered through from that direction in the morning. It was the silhouette of a woman, a shapely one, in a relatively tight-fitting dress and high heels.

"Class be seated. Now!" was all she had to say. It was a voice that came with a cloud of knowing.

She wore red high-heeled shoes. I mean very red with really high spikes! The dress was a short red summer dress that matched the heels perfectly. Her hair was red and was piled on top of her head in the beehive fashion of the day. Her lips were perfectly colored in the reddest of red lipsticks. The class sat silent, not something that ever happened. We were in awe. The lingering 'wall boys' melted into their seats, amazingly without any protest. She was most certainly a vision. The boys were gaga and without any sense, it seemed. There was no fear in her eyes, no indication of weakness. She wasn't looking like she'd be sweet. No, this was a different animal altogether. She slowly moved to her desk, put her purse and books down, turned, and began to write her name on the blackboard. Mrs. Sheldon. The room was silent.

"The Redhead," as I referred to her, was most definitely from New York. That meant there was no room for any kind of misbehavior. I now came to understand the phrase "tough New Yorker" thoroughly. Amazingly enough, no one tried anything. It was almost like it was understood without anything having to happen to establish that fact. It was just implied with everything she did and every gesture she made that there would be no questioning her directives. We immediately settled into the structured programs of the day that she put in place. It was a relief to be able to relax and let her be in charge. We all learned a lot that year. There was nothing to do but work hard and study. We were all anxious to please her. Despite the tough exterior BRATs display, ultimately, we just want to feel safe and liked. It became almost a mission on everyone's part to try to win her favor. This was not an easy thing to do.

The subject I loved most in class was social studies. I went to great lengths on assigned projects. I would buy notebooks at the little Vietnamese shops in downtown Saigon that had the most beautifully illustrated covers: watercolor pictures of animals—tigers and monkeys—and beautiful women with long hair in flower gardens. Each one was more interesting than the next. I had mastered excellent penmanship in Hinsdale, Illinois, under the watchful eye of my beloved fourth-grade teacher, Mrs. Hibdon. I treated each page as though it had to be a work of art. The Redhead had us write reports on various countries. Using an illustrated encyclopedia set that the Colonel had purchased and shipped to Saigon before we left the States, I would read about places that filled the globe. I'd copy the illustrations that were within the bindings of these helpful books, filling the pages of my notebooks with colored renditions.

Vietnam was one of the many countries we studied. I drew a map of Vietnam to reveal a country lying between the southwestern border of China and the Gulf of Siam. It looked like a man wearing a bamboo hat bent over from years of toil. Vietnam occupies the gateway both by land and by sea between China and the vast regions of Southeast Asia. It is twice the size of New England. The country is divided at the 17th parallel, with South Vietnam being almost the size of the state of Washington. Vietnam's current population of twenty-five million inhabitants makes it the largest in Southeast Asia after Indonesia. When my family was there, it was a country that was primarily agricultural, with rice making up three-fifths of its agricultural activity.

Rubber was another important product that grew in the "red soil" area that covered one hundred sixty thousand acres stretching from the northeast edge of the Mekong Delta northwest into Cambodia. The fertile soil was mainly in the delta of the Red River in the North and the Mekong River in the South. Most of the Vietnamese people were grouped in these plains. I noted that twenty percent of the population was Catholic and eighty percent was Buddhist. I included this report in the notebook with reports on the other countries we had studied so far.

My notebooks were beautiful as far as I was concerned, complete with drawings of peasants bent over rice paddies in Vietnam, *gauchos* in Argentina, Spanish dancers in Spain, and farmers in Mexico. I'd draw the countries large and cut their shapes out from separate pieces of paper so that they were taped and folded up on the appropriate page. It was with this artful work that I gained the attention I sought from the Redhead. I'd eagerly turn to the first page when the workbooks would be returned after grading and bask in the light of the "A+ Good Work" written in red pencil across the page heading.

Since then, I've always associated the color of red with her. She worked it like a painter would a canvas. Even the glow of her cigarette matched whatever she had on. Moving to the front of her desk, she would perch there and beguile us with tales of places around the world that she had visited. It was like she knew about the entire world. I would say we were completely enamored of the Redhead. She was a mystery to each and every one of us and remained such for the entire school year. Without being fully aware of it at the time, I think I unconsciously memorized everything about her.

I owe Lucy a debt of gratitude for bothering with a squirming eleven-year-old in her efforts to make me understand history beyond the Redhead's attempts. I refer to these times as Lucy's history lessons. In American schools and maybe in other places, history is learned by remembering things that happened on various dates, things considered to be in the past, historical events—the same way we learned when the Colonel reviewed the long list of dates in Vietnamese history when we were first flying over. This was what the history tests were like in sixth grade. I was great at memorizing dates, but what relevance they had to my life or anything else was a mystery. I would memorize what I had to for that week's test, but it would be out of my head by the next week. I didn't understand the importance or the connection of history to life until Lucy started to give me her lessons about Vietnam.

For Lucy, history was not about the past. History was the present, not to be altered but to be understood, asserting its traditional place in life and nature. Her stories didn't rest entirely on dates of events. They were more about the relationship of culture to history, and in Vietnam culture was everything. Lucy's history lessons weren't about clippings out of the newspaper.

I think the Redhead was trying as best she could to get us involved in things that were going on around us. She wanted to take us out of our comfort zones and away from our self-imposed mantra "Everything is okay; everything is normal." We brought in newspaper clippings of current events and discussed them in class. Somehow, it still didn't register with me in terms of my own life. *Life* magazine was portraying America's involvement in South Vietnam as a success. This seemed at odds with what was going on around me, what the Colonel was pointing out and what Lucy was saying. My American *Stars & Stripes* newspaper clippings showed images of dead bodies and soldiers, President Diệm with his cabinet, and captured accused Viet Cong prisoners. The subheadings were congratulatory about the struggle being won by the South Vietnamese Army. Lucy didn't dwell on these things, scoffing at the images I showed her. She talked about the cultural changes that had taken place over time instead and what was happening in the moment in Vietnam.

Lucy started bringing me a Vietnamese paper that the Nhus were putting out. The ridiculousness of the printed information usually made her laugh. In it, Nhu would profess his theory of personalism, which had everyone confused. It had something to do with "everything in the human being that is internal, whereby each human being is an eye witness of its own self." Nhu was known for going on and on for hours at a time pontificating about this philosophy to visiting American dignitaries, ambassadors, and anyone else who wanted to discuss the current situation in South Vietnam. Some were known to have fallen asleep in the middle of these long-winded monologues. No one had a clue as to what he was talking about. Nhu used the paper as a pulpit for his beliefs. Lucy never spoke of any of these things to either Mom or the Colonel. In retrospect, I could understand why.

In a child's limited way, I concluded that there were many conflicting things going on in South Vietnam, rooted in the internal political struggle within the Diệm regime and the rebellion that was occurring with the people throughout the country against foreign rule. No one in the United States understood that these were two very different things happening in Vietnam. Everything was blamed on Communist activity. It was great fodder for propaganda for the American people. Both the Diệm regime and the United States politicians used it as a way to get support for further involvement in this small country.

"No one understands what they are talking about. They have no connection to the Vietnamese people. I speak about President Diệm and the Nhus," Lucy said one day, continuing in her attempts to have me see the world as she did. "Our ancestors are everything. They are not the past but live on within us in the present. This is the lesson passed on from family to family. The definition of 'family' is changing in Vietnam, and you must understand the significance of this change. The French did the most to change it, but President Diệm and the Nhus are destroying it. Vietnam is involved in a struggle for nationalism, but also in a struggle for our culture. It is important if you are to understand Vietnam now and after you leave. Vietnam will change if it is not right for the people," she continued.

She always had my mind spinning. Vietnamese culture certainly wasn't anything that resembled my American upbringing. America is heralded as the land of opportunity, a place where an individual can get ahead with hard work. It is a place that certainly doesn't have the type of center found in Vietnam, where a child follows in his or her father's footsteps and ancestors provide the road map. In America, I was expected to leave home to create a life for myself independent of my family. I wondered how our American values were expected to be realized in Vietnam or even why we were attempting this type of alteration. Democracy would seem like an abstract concept to most Vietnamese.

"You think about these things when you are in your school. It is the only way to understand Vietnam," Lucy said that day as she gathered her things to leave. She had to get to class, and I wanted to get to the Cerc.

Later that week, the Redhead assigned a project in social studies class: we were to write about some part of the history of Vietnam. It was our choice as to what we wanted to cover. I remembered that the Colonel had mentioned the Trung Sisters in his history lessons when we had flown over from the States. The story is about two sisters of a warlord back in the sixteenth century recognized as national figures of independence for Vietnam in its struggle to free itself from China. I thought they'd be great to write about. For some reason the Colonel turned the project over to his Vietnamese secretary, and she typed the entire chapter out of an Army manual that told the story of the Trung Sisters. The report even came back from the secretary with an illustrated cover showing a map of Vietnam colored with red and black Magic Marker. It had holes in it, and the pages were assembled. I wondered why the Redhead gave me an A. It was obviously a rip-off from the book. I hadn't done the work. I hadn't even read the story in the book. I showed this graded report to Lucy.

"The Trung Sisters are part of our national heritage," Lucy said proudly, and with that proceeded to explain something not so clear in this perfectly presented report. "For the first time, Vietnam had independence of China. It lasted for two years. Then Vietnam was part of Indochina made up of Laos, Cambodia, and Annan. Vietnam became a country later. We were most vicious fighters and China gave up trying to control us."

"You see this picture of Madame Nhu," she said, showing a picture of Madame Nhu with a field of young girls in uniforms behind her in the local paper. "She thinks she is like the Trung Sister. See for yourself in this picture. She understands nothing." Lucy sighed in disgust. "She has never been one of the people. She is haughty and looks down on people not of her social class. Trung Sisters fought for independence from China for all the people." She paused to look at the picture and read the copy typed underneath. Everything around us was quiet. We were huddled together on the bamboo sofa in the living room with the fans on full speed above us. It was so darn hot.

It was exciting to hear that two girls had been the liberators and that it didn't always have to be boys doing things. I scooted over closer to Lucy and moved some pillows behind me. The drone of the traffic outside our wall was building now that the normal siesta hour was over. I was being lulled to sleep not only by her soft voice but by the time of day. Everything was quiet in the house except for the rasping sound of insects against the shuttered screens.

"The Colonel says we are helping the Vietnamese to fight the Communists here. Is that not what we are doing?"

"Communists never have won in Southeast Asia before in entire history. Neither non-Communist Vietnamese leader nor Communist leader believe in intellectual freedom—everything here founded on culture, not ideology. Our religion is a blend of Confucianism, Taoism, and Buddhism. I am a Catholic, but same thing—each has its own character, like a human being. Diệm says he is the chosen one of heaven. He believes he is the leader to defend Vietnamese morality and culture. Hồ Chí Minh says the same thing, but Diệm doesn't care about the people, only his family. Nothing is being done to help the people," she said ruefully. "Because of this, country will change for what is best for people."

"I'm confused. Aren't Americans here to help South Vietnam have independence? Aren't we fighting Communism?" I said, exasperated, not understanding her response.

"If this is the right thing for the people, then it will be. That is what it means that everything will be decided by the 'will of heaven.' Diệm and brother Nhu are not being right for the people now. They put their relatives in all positions; they take too much tax, destroy the village way of running itself; persecute the Buddhist monks and the intellectuals, religions not Catholic like their own. If a Catholic says something against them, then he too will be persecuted. This is not someone in harmony with universe and the people. Something will happen to say 'will of heaven' has changed; the 'Mandate of Heaven' is not with Diệm, and whole country will turn overnight. Why are you here? If you could understand our culture and history, maybe you would decide not to be here." Her voice was kind but had a slight bit of irritation in it.

My understanding of Vietnam was becoming even more confused with each of Lucy's lessons. That was combined with the ongoing exasperation that the Colonel was feeling about trying to do his job in making the South Vietnamese Army self-sufficient. As we gathered around the dinner table that night, I decided not to say anything about what Lucy and I had been talking about.

CHAPTER 24:

LONG LIFE FOR ONE HUNDRED YEARS— TET (FEBRUARY 9, 1961)

Vietnamese holidays were amazing. I liked them all. Tết Nguyên Đán, is the holiday that celebrates the Lunar New Year and was my favorite. This was as close to Christmas as it was going to get for the Vietnamese, as far as I could make out. It was a holiday greeted with as much excitement as any in the States. Tết starts on the first day of the first lunar month and is the first season of the New Year. It is a time of great celebration in Saigon and throughout Vietnam, complete with fireworks and dancing street dragons. Above all, it is the fete of the family and considered an opportunity for the household genies to meet. Those genies are the ones who help during the year: the Craft Creator, the Land Genie, and the Kitchen God. As the legend goes, each year on December 23rd of the lunar calendar, the Kitchen God takes a ride on a carp to the Heavenly Palace to make a report on the affairs of the household on earth and then returns on December 30th to welcome the new spring. It is also a time to welcome deceased ancestors back for a family reunion with their descendants. It is a sacred and secular custom. No matter what the circumstances, family members, both dead and alive, find ways to come back to meet their loved ones on this holiday.

Every imaginable scent was in the air for the Tết celebration of 1961. Incense had been lit. Red banners hung everywhere. The robust smells of traditional dishes blanketed the city. Everything and everywhere was Tết. The city was bustling with energy and goodwill. The servants would sit outside their small rooms and hold us transfixed with stories. Thi Ba let us try morsels of her tasty treats. She was preparing the traditional Vietnamese dishes of Tết to take to her family village. Of course, her daughter, Lucy, would be going with her. Mom helped with expenses for the supplies she needed on the condition she'd let us children sample some of the food. Her only requirement was that it be cooked. Mom was always up for trying something different and exposing us to new experiences.

Bánh dầy was tightly packed sticky rice with a meat or bean filling wrapped in banana leaves. The leaves would be folded up and tied. We were always amazed that Thi Ba didn't use tinfoil to wrap food in. We watched in wonder. Sometimes she'd let us do the wrapping, but I have the suspicion she rewrapped things once we were gone. All of the food preparation was time-consuming, taking days. Everything was a riot of tastes and smells. *Hạt dưa* was roasted watermelon seeds. She'd keep a bowl of these out and within easy reach for us.

That smelly fish sauce, *nước mắm,* was used in everything. It didn't taste like it smelled, and by the time the dish was served, the odor had been minimized. Thi Ba was careful to wash what she gave us with sterilized water. I liked it when we ate Vietnamese food. It is lighter than Chinese cooking. To me, it seemed like that was what we should be eating instead of the rich French food we always got. Thi Ba had worked for several French families before us and assumed this was what foreigners wanted to eat. My mother was too busy socially to do anything except train her on proper American hors d'oeuvres for the parties she threw at the house.

I busily cut branches of forsythia that grew on bushes in the garden, arranging them in a vase to create my own traditional Tết tree. We were told this was like our Christmas tree and were instructed on what we were to do. The branches of the forsythia bush were heavy with yellow (*mai*) flowers. To me, these cut branches looked more like a floral arrangement than a proper tree. I asked Lucy to get us the little red money envelopes that children tradition- ally hung on the tree. These were meant to be filled with money for children. Pati, Bob, and I had great hopes when we covered the branches with every red envelope we could get our hands on. It was like decorating a Christmas tree in a way.

There was much happiness in the streets during the days leading up to the actual day of Tết. As children, we found this exuberant energy exciting. Activity started weeks in advance. The streets were crowded with people trying to get their purchases made before the stores closed. Good- natured laughter filled the air. Saigon was vibrant and alive with goodwill.

Thi Ba packed up her succulent creations in carrying cases along with all the other things she had purchased for the day. She would leave early in the morning with Lucy on the day before Tết, as would Thi Tu. I never knew where Thi Tu went, and she never said. They called out, "*Chúc mừng năm mới*" ("Happy New Year") and "*Cung chúc tân xuân*" ("Gracious wishes of the new spring") to each other and to Pati, Bob, and me, who were sitting moping on the front porch, saddened that everyone would be elsewhere celebrating. We waved and yelled back a greeting Lucy had us practice for weeks: "*Sống lâu trăm tuổi*" ("Long life of one hundred years"), a traditional greeting of children to their elders. They laughed and waved back, showing wistful smiles. The gate swung shut. Left to our own devices for the rest of that day, we were somewhat let down by everyone's departure.

I had gathered an arsenal of things to do, all meant to bring good luck to me and those I loved. I was going to celebrate Tết with or without them. It was important to give people lucky presents on Tết, I had been told. A peach branch was good for expelling evil, and a rooster for wishing for good manners. That explained the reason Colonel *Sam* had given me a red rooster after I'd embarrassed his son by challenging him to a climbing game and winning. New rice was a gift for wishing to be well fed and red things symbolized happiness—like watermelon. Sprinkling lime powder around the house was good for expelling evil. I'd gotten a supply of it when I'd found it at the market. Mom kept asking why there was this weird white dust all around the house. She didn't realize I was convinced we had a spirit in the second house we had moved into. I was hoping to send it back to its family for Tết.

Days before the official day of Tết, Colonel *Sâm* and his family invited our family to the Chinese section of Saigon, Cholon, for dinner. *Sâm* wanted the Hanna family to be part of the festivities. He knew the Chinese would be completely preoccupied with their ancestors, relatives, and other family during the official days of Tết. The *Sâms* had five children, so with us four kids and the two sets of parents, we numbered thirteen. Tom was on holiday break from school in Baguio, so he was part of this celebration. We were to meet the *Sâm* family at the restaurant. As we lumbered along in the family car, glued to the windows, we could see festive decorations everywhere. The restaurant was set back at an angle from the road, with white stucco walls and open doorways with shutters. The crackle and boom of fireworks could be heard throughout the city.

A man with cardamom-laden breath greeted us at the doorway and directed us upstairs. The scent of magnolia blossoms enveloped the restaurant. We passed a succession of long white corridors before reaching the outside stairway that led to the second-floor dining room. This room was open and airy, with columns that boasted carved dragons painted red and gold. The dragon heads rested on the floor, with the scaled bodies wrapping around the columns reaching to the top. Gold lanterns with red fringe hung above the outside porches were swinging softly in the light breeze. Inside, the flickering of lit candles inside red lanterns created patterns on the wall. A huge table had been made up for our large group, and it didn't appear that anyone else would be seated in this upstairs room. Voices and footsteps could be heard from the guests dining on the first floor. As we arranged ourselves around the table, the owner came to greet Colonel and Mrs. *Sâm*. They were being treated with great respect. Our family was introduced and graciously welcomed by the owner.

It was to be an eight-course dinner, something we children had never had. The first dish was a beautiful thick soup, which we were told was shark fin soup. The spoon to be used was unusual and was more like an oval holder that we had to tilt to let its contents flow into our mouths. I shot a friendly sideways glance to the eldest of *Sâm's* daughters, who seemed to be enjoying the dish.

We were given chopsticks that were delicately designed: black with Chinese writing along the sides. Although we had been practicing at home with chopsticks, it was still a struggle. Bob and Pati had hidden rubber bands in their pockets and now proceeded to tie them around the bottoms of the sticks to make it easier. It was something Lucy had taught them. They seemed to be having no problem. The dish we tried out chopsticks on looked like French toast. It was fried, and sugar had been sprinkled on top. It tasted great. I leaned over to the other one of *Sâm's* daughters, who was on my right, and asked her what it was. "Red dog brain," she replied between mouthfuls. That was it for me! The last dish was finally brought out. It was a nest, an actual bird's nest, that sat in a pool of sweet milk. "The bird's nest in our soup has an interesting story behind it," *Sâm* said. "It is a delicacy in Chinese cuisine and has been used in Chinese cooking for over four hundred years. A few species of swifts, cave swifts, a small bird, are renowned for building these solidified saliva nests and are highly sought after." After hearing the story, I was glad I hadn't tried the nest, the house that spit built no less.

All in all, it was a happy evening. Outside the doorway that led to a small balcony, massive ramparts of crumbling chateaus were visible. Fading lights revealed shady streets off a quiet square. Fugitive aromas from the dishes being served on the first floor drifted upward and filled the air. Further out beyond the veranda, it was possible to spot a section of the Saigon River. Small boats with their inky reflections moved along it under a rising moon. The sounds of the street and the tinkering of the hundreds of wind chimes seemed to be everywhere. It all lay just beyond us. As I looked around the table, gazing at the faces of young and old, the smiling children, the attentive serving staff, the eagerly engaged adults, everything seemed to be at one with the universe. I silently wished all "*sống lâu trăm tuổi*" ("Long life of one hundred years").

A Moment in History

"The Tet holiday, which lasts several days, is considered the time to come home to be with the family and to honor ancestors. Some of the attacks made on American facilities were concentrated around the holiday of Tet: the Kinh Do Theater bombing on February 16, 1964 (two days after the start of the holiday); the Pershing Sports Field bombing on February 9, 1964; the Tet Offensive on January 28, 1968. These were symbolic actions not only to let the population know that Americans were not invincible, but also to make a point about what the goal of the Vietnamese rebels was: to come home. Americans during this period didn't understand a thing about this country's culture and its history. It was a symbolic gesture lost to most; the rebels were trying to find their way back home to their families and ancestral burial grounds."

—*Frances FitzGerald,* Fire on the Lake: The Vietnamese and Americans in Vietnam, *1972*

CHAPTER 25:

STAY-AT-HOME ORDERS

An overcast night hid his silent approach to the villa. Pausing, he pulled himself together before entering, taking a deep breath. It was early enough in the evening that the family was still in the living room working on various projects. The Colonel sat in his usual spot reading the latest edition of *Stars and Stripes*, the ice in his nightly Kentucky bourbon slowly melting next to him. Soft music played in the background. Colonel *Sâm* called softly from the doorway and entered the living room with his head bent. He was not in uniform. He had come to see the Colonel to discuss the newest trial he was about to endure. We kids were told to go to our rooms, but I lingered on the stairway, hidden behind the spindles, lying low on my usual perch. I didn't want to miss anything anymore.

"January 1, 1962, President Diệm signed my stay home orders without salary. I am no longer part of ARVN," Colonel *Sâm* said in a voice that was past defeat, past sorrow, simply resolved to accept things as they now were. He was breathing slowly, evenly as he spoke.

He was in a state of distressed confusion, though he had tried to hide it while the family was around. The air was still stifling hot. Beads of sweat had formed on his brow. He wasted no time. Mom quietly got up from her chair.

"I have been completely removed and am no longer in the military," *Sâm* said as the Colonel signaled him to be seated. He looked as though he hadn't slept in days. He seemed distraught and agitated; his hand shook as he pulled out a cigarette and attempted to light it. Unlit, it went back in his pocket. He willingly accepted the cold drink Mom offered him. He drank half of it before speaking again. She excused herself, knowing the two men wanted to talk in private. Finding me on the steps, she herded me into the bedroom. I glanced down at the top of the stairs, intent upon freezing the image of Colonel *Sâm* in my mind. I was suddenly afraid that I would have nothing left of him except what my memory could fill in. I climbed into bed and quietly waited. When I could hear no movement in Mom's room and only Pati's deep breathing, I slid back to my lookout on the staircase.

I could see that this announcement of Colonel *Sâm's* removal from the military came as a complete shock to the Colonel. He sat with a stunned look on his face. The two men had continued to work together over the previous year without any issues, even though *Sâm* was no longer Chief of Ordnance in ARVN. Now, to have him entirely removed must have been unthinkable to the Colonel. He was always telling us how *Sâm* was one of the few Vietnamese officers who listened to the MAAG consultants and took their advice. He described Colonel *Sâm* as hardworking, willing to do the tasks that were needed to improve ARVN's position. His background in Ordinance operations was excellent, and the Colonel relied on *Sâm's* expertise. More important, he trusted the man. This was a big deal for the Colonel. The officer who had replaced Colonel *Sâm* was a thorn in the Colonel's side, a man who did more to undermine the work than to move any project forward. As far as the Colonel was concerned, the man had no qualifications at all.

"The Nhus are advising President Diệm. This is very bad for the Vietnamese people. Mr. Nhu and Madame Nhu have Diệm's confidence, and he is not seeing what is going on," *Sâm* lamented, shifting forward in his seat to be able to speak quietly. "The Nhus are taking the power, and it is not good for Vietnam. It is the Nhus who are against me."

The Colonel was a born problem solver; nothing vexed him more than not being able to solve something. Colonel *Sâm's* situation was now a very big problem, as far as he was concerned. *Sâm* was in both Mr. and Mrs. Nhu's sights, and they were determined that he would not have access to anyone or anything when they got through with him.

"Mr. Nhu has organized spies in all restaurants, shops, and places visited by Americans. Those men working in it needed to report to Tuyen. Several Vietnamese officers' names got by them into their black records because they were together with Americans in those places. They know I am pro-American," *Sâm* said. He stood up and began to pace. "It is what I said in the papers I gave you. Mr. Nhu has a two-year plan. Three months ago, Mrs. Nhu has been sick at Huế. Our family doctor examined her and she said, 'Please help me. I need to live only two years.' A month ago, she said her sentiments secretly to top Catholic Mother that 'we do not leave; we stay here. President was stupid and incapable to challenge Americans. Now President Diệm is disenchanted. He trusted Mr. Nhu more than ever, and you going to see that, in two years, Nhu win and Americans down.'" It was a low moment for Colonel *Sâm*, and simply stating these things appeared to take him lower. "I am fearful of what else will happen to me and my family."

I watched as the two officers sat silent. Dusk had fallen early, swallowing the sunset. A blue night sky had already appeared as the earlier clouds moved across the broad expanse. Today was a sad day. Disappointment and frustration showed on both of their care-burdened faces as they sat silently staring at each other. I could see that the bond that existed between them would be there no matter what changes happened in the world around them.

"I have to be careful now when I come to see you. It isn't safe for me. I am sorry for all that is happening. I am sorry for Vietnam. I will come again," he said.

"Let me see what I can do. Don't give up hope. I will try," the Colonel said as the small, forlorn figure turned to go.

Colonel *Sâm* walked with a stiff upright gait toward the doorway. Stopping suddenly, he turned to give the Colonel an official salute. A fatigue that resembled death seemed to cover him. He moved slowly down the driveway. I could hear him pull the bolt lock on the gate.

Change was coming to South Vietnam, and I knew there would be little that could be done to stop any of it. Somber, deliberately, I slinked back up the stairs, just missing being discovered.

A Moment in History

"After the Geneva Accord in 1954, active Communist cadres in the south instructed their followers to disband and wait for the national elections. They hoped for the reunification of their country, a return to peace and a normal life free of foreign rule. In 1955, Ngô Đình Diệm repudiated the Geneva proposals and favored national elections and began his reign of terror against members of the resistance. His efforts were focused on destroying the remaining Viet Minh and reducing the villages to subservience. The Diệm repression only advanced the date of a new armed struggle. The National Liberation Front (NLF) was founded in 1960. Resistance members whose goals had been to defeat the French were now convinced they could not live in physical safety under the Diệm regime. The NLF proceeded with a ten-part program: peace, national independence, democratic freedoms, improvement in people's living conditions, and peaceful national reunification. They were trying to conquer the south by politics and culture, not by force."

—*Frances FitzGerald,* Fire in the Lake: The Vietnames and Ameircans in Vietnam, *1972*

PART III

"The further back you can look, the further forward you can see."

—Winston Churchill

CHAPTER 26:

BRINKS BOMB

Mom had calling cards with her name on them printed when we first arrived in South Vietnam. She did this as soon as she found out that calling cards were the fashionable thing for foreigners in Saigon to have, especially officers' wives. "Mrs. Ruby Nell Hanna," just that and no more, was printed in an unassuming typeface on simple white card stock. There wasn't an address or a phone number. That wasn't necessary. There were a limited number of foreigners in Saigon, and they all knew each other. The calling card was simply to be used when one stopped by to visit someone. It was probably good that it was so simple, because she didn't have to have the cards reprinted when we moved from Đoàn Thị Điểm to our second house on Phan Thanh Giàn. The card is usually presented by the maid to the lady of the house. This colonial tradition had been revived and was now flaunted by the ladies as the socially acceptable way to behave in Southeast Asia. French colonial ways were still alive and well, even though the French supposedly were on the outs in Vietnam after leaving in 1954, as per the Geneva Accord. The military and diplomatic service wives were having a ball!

It wasn't America, this country halfway around the world. Our mother loved it! After all, she had spent most of her early life trying to get off the farm in Kentucky. She had wanted a different kind of life. She found it as the wife of a military officer. The further away from anything she had grown up with, the better she liked it. She was the perceived rich American who had previously lived in the large villa on Đoàn Thị Điểm, one of the best streets in the city, just a few doors down from the American ambassador's villa. She had a house complete with servants. Now, with our having moved to Phan Thanh Giàn to a more modern-style villa in 1961, the ruse continued.

Mom was a member, along with our entire family, at the Saigon Country Club and the Cercle Sportif. She threw some of the best parties of the day at our house, where she confirmed her reputation as a brilliant and thoughtful hostess. As I mentioned, she was also beautiful; she had been a beauty pageant contestant in high school. All of this went a long way in assisting her in charming everyone she met. To top it off, she was smart and, like most Southern women, could manipulate the hell out of anyone without appearing to have done a thing.

She took her responsibility as an officer's wife seriously. She loved her expanded role in Saigon; she was no longer just a mother with us kids to be managed. As the wife of a military officer, she was as much under scrutiny by the service as she would be had she signed up and been given a uniform. An officer's wife is a critical part of a husband's advancement in the service. Mom was one of the best there at the time.

We children were treated as though we too were part of the service and instructed accordingly. We had always been treated this way, but in Saigon we were told we were now the representatives of our country. We were told that everything we did would reflect on our father. There was no room for error, just obedience at all times. In the States, we had to line up for inspection before going out. We reported our activities just as if we were regular military personnel reporting to the duty officer. In Saigon, however, our parents were not around most of the time, immersed in their exotic life. We kids considered things rather lax. No bouncing of the quarter on the bed by the Colonel to see if we had pulled the sheets tightly enough and had made hospital corners. The servants were doing these chores now. Happily, we were left to our own devices, although supposedly under their watch.

If we were afraid, we didn't show it. That wouldn't be acceptable. As the children of a military officer, we were told to grin and bear it, whatever it was. And that we did. As far as our parents knew, we were living relatively normal lives: school, homework, movies on the weekends, friends in for sleepovers, Girl Scouts, baseball, all stuff we'd have been doing in the States. But that wasn't the life we were living at all. We were completely ignorant of each other, presenting a selected fiction to our parents. We were good representatives of our country, however, every one of us kids. We thought so, anyway!

When first assigned the post in South Vietnam, the Colonel had the choice of taking his family with him or not. To leave us behind would give him a shorter assignment, one that would last only fourteen months. To take the family meant we would be there for a full two years. He didn't actually have a choice, though, because there was no possible way Mom was going to miss this adventure.

Most of the officers in Saigon at the time had not brought their families with them, so Mom proceeded to adopt each and every one of them. She made our house a second home for anyone who needed one. Many of these men found temporary comfort with Vietnamese girls that Mom would not permit at her parties. She was cordial when she did meet them at the various events held on the rooftop garden of the Brinks BOQ, however. This was the officer billet for those who didn't come to Saigon with their families. It was a place where Americans gathered for drinks and dinner. The rooftop gardens put one above the hustle and bustle of downtown Saigon.

These "Pearls of the Orient" who accompanied so many of the Americans were usually made up like beautiful dolls. They sported heavy eye makeup, very red lipstick, and beautiful silken áo dàis. They floated through the room, their strong perfumes wafting—heavy and musky, full of mystery and intrigue. In all honesty, I think Mom liked these women and was very kind to them in these social gatherings.

There was a big party coming up at the Brinks BOQ. Mom had a beautiful blue silk áo dài made for herself. White satin pants had been sewn to go with it. An áo dài is a high-collared dress of sorts. It is slit along the right and left sides running all the way up to the waist, so it is necessary to wear loose, flowing pants under it. Long sleeves contoured to the arms end in the middle of the hand. She had found a pair of high heels that had a beaded dragon design on the straps and were lacquered red and orange. For the party, Mom had asked the servants to help her with a fake hair piece that could be wound into a bun at the back of her head. Vietnamese women traditionally wore their hair twisted into neat buns. Mom had washed her hair with a dark hair rinse earlier that day to match it.

She stayed in her dressing room for hours. She had closed the doors to the bedroom that afternoon and told us kids we weren't allowed in. She said she had a surprise for us. Positioned on the winding stairway, we waited, killing time with card games: Rummy, Go Fish, and Old Maid. The door to the bedroom finally opened and a tall woman with brownish skin stepped out. The stranger appeared to be Vietnamese with her áo dài and high makeup. Her giggle gave her away. Our mother had a signature giggle that could not be mistaken. We were dumbfounded. She had transformed herself into one of the "Pearls of the Orient." Pati, Bob, and I scrambled down the stairway in front of her to where the Colonel was waiting. When she made her grand entrance, you could see the twinkle in his eyes. He was secretly pleased at the ruse they would be pulling off tonight at the party. He liked this playful side of his wife's character. They would tell us kids later in detail about the party. It became one of our favorite stories.

The couple arrived at the Brinks roof garden party fashionably late to guarantee that most of their friends would already be there. With the Colonel gently holding on to Mom's arm, they walked in as the party was in full swing. The shrillness of the gaiety was deafening. Roars of laughter filled the air. Colored bulbs crossed and recrossed the rooftop, lending it a festive air. Music blared from the speakers hidden by potted palms. Everyone was holding a chilled drink, enjoying the moment.

Getting made up had taken longer than our mother had expected. Eyebrows were raised as they entered. Men grouped and whispered among themselves and generally avoided the Colonel. They were displeased with him. Our mother was someone they liked. They hadn't thought it possible that he would not be with Ruby Nell. They knew he adored her, so what was this about? Eventually an officer, one of their closest friends, approached Mom and asked her to dance. The Colonel stood off to the side chatting with some other officers. She nodded an acceptance shyly, gracefully joining the officer on the dance floor.

The officer was examining her closely as they danced to a slow song. Mom played coy, keeping up the charade with her head bent low. It proved to be too much for her, however. This was a good friend, and she couldn't help but giggle. She had been in character for nearly an hour, and it was killing her to stay so quiet. She liked to talk. The minute she giggled she heard, "Ruby Nell? Is that you?"

"Yes," she said.

"I can't believe it. You have everyone mad at your husband," he said.

"Yes," she said smiling. "But wasn't it fun?"

It seems that at this same party, a young lieutenant approached the Colonel. He asked to speak to him in private. "Sir, we have a situation downstairs that needs your attention immediately," the lieutenant said in barely a whisper.

The Colonel quietly left with the officer without saying a word to anyone. Everyone was still gathered around Mom, congratulating her on the success of her ruse. Even the attending "Pearls of the Orient" appreciated the charade, smiling and giggling, drawing close to her.

Meanwhile, the two men moved quickly downstairs to the bottom-floor parking lot of the Brinks. A military jeep was parked unattended in the center of the lot. It looked innocuous enough. However, on closer examination, a bomb was found lodged underneath the vehicle. It was booby-trapped to go off when the ignition key was turned. Quietly and efficiently, assistance was brought in from the Colonel's Ordnance team. They removed the detonator mechanism of the bomb and arranged for the vehicle to be quietly towed away.

The Colonel returned just as stealthily as he had left and ordered a bourbon straight up. His usual drink was a gin and tonic at these affairs. He leaned on the railing of the roof garden and peered down at the street. A jeep was being towed away without any attention being paid to it. The moon was full that night, and a festive air surrounded him. It was an evening of fixed and falling stars. On top of this seemingly carefree roof, he could almost disconnect from everything else that was going on around him. He breathed a sigh as he turned to watch Mom. She was a marvel, giving equal attention to everyone. Each person felt she was completely attuned to whatever he or she was saying. He stood silently watching her as he sipped his drink. After they arrived back home that night, he told her about the jeep incident. The next day after telling us the story, he made a point of reminding us kids we were not to *ever* go anywhere alone!

A Moment in History

December 25, 1964, *The New York Times*,

"Terrorists Bomb Saigon Quarters of Officers; 2 Americans Reported Killed – 52 Others and 13 Vietnamese Wounded; 8-Floor Billet Ruined; Blast Believed Part of Plan of Viet-Cong to Sap Morale and Cause Withdrawal."

This explosion was done in the same manner as I described earlier with a vehicle parked underneath the building in the parking lot, but it was carried out in a much more elaborate fashion. The purpose of this bold act was to show that an American institution in the core of the heavily guarded capital was vulnerable and that Americans could not be relied upon for protection.

CHAPTER 27:

VICHY GIRLS

He seemed so young, Chou, the Colonel's driver. He had clean, sharp features on a baby face, clear skin, and greased-back black hair. It was shiny like glistening coal. One day, Chou came by the house on his day off with his family. He was dressed in his Sunday best. There were five of them, on one bike no less. His wife was petite and delicate, almost childlike. She was also in her best áo dài, with white satin pants, sitting on the back of the bike's rack sidesaddle. Chou stood holding the bicycle upright with all of them astride. He was beaming with pride, especially since all the children were boys. A baby, no more than six months old, sat on his mother's lap on the back. Another child was sitting sideways on the crossbar, and the last one was on the handlebars. It was a miracle of balance and maximum surface usage.

Us kids stood in the driveway in awe of the arrangement until the Colonel stepped forward to welcome them all into the house. As usual, the day was hot, and lemonade was served to everyone. Chou was grinning from ear to ear at the respect being shown him in front of his family. The children were shy and clustered around Chou's tiny wife like chicks around the mother hen. We couldn't entice them away, so Pati, Bob, and I sat on the porch steps quietly waiting for something to happen. Nothing did. Pleasantries were exchanged between the grown-ups. We children simply stared at each other.

The heat of the day was continuing to mount and served as a clear signal for Chou to load his family back on their bicycle and leave. We watched as this amazing feat of balance was accomplished once again. Chou turned the bike around, balancing it with one hand as he waved. He departed with the entire family in tow. Peddling his way down the street, he merged with the traffic, not seeming to think anything was unusual about the whole affair.

Chou normally drove a U.S. Army jeep. He was authorized to use it only for military purposes, not personal ones. Chou's jeep was his pride and joy. After seeing how he had to move around with his family, it was no wonder he adored the jeep and being the Colonel's driver. To be assigned the responsibility of chauffeuring the Colonel was a high honor. He lorded it over his friends.

Chou sometimes picked Pati, Bob, and me up from school when the Colonel wasn't using him. One day, his jeep was parked in front of the school. He stood leaning against it with cigarette in hand. Dropping it, he stamped it out as he saw the three of us. We spotted him and headed for the jeep.

"I take you home today," he said, helping us climb in. Pati and Bob were in the back. I hopped into the front seat next to him. He swung himself into the driver's seat with ease and comfort.

Pushing the clutch in and shifting into gear, he slowly pulled out of the school driveway. Instead of the usual right turn toward home, however, Chou took a sharp left. We were gradually gaining speed as he traveled north along the Biên Hòa Highway. On the smooth asphalt of the road, the jeep glided easily along.

"Where are we going? This isn't the way home, Chou," I said.

"Yes, yes, just a minute. Have to stop to pick something up," he said as we whirled down the road.

"Chou!" I yelled at the top of my lungs, the rushing wind making it hard to hear each other. "Where are we going? You tell me right now!" The Colonel's warnings hadn't gone unheeded by me. I wanted to be sure I knew what was going on. Besides, I had the responsibility of looking out for the younger kids.

"Have to go to military camp. No problem." His jaw was set as he said it. I decided to settle back and make the best of it. After all, the Colonel trusted Chou. Pati and Bob sat in the back seat, completely windblown in the open-air jeep. They didn't seem to mind this departure from our regular routine and were now laughing as we flew down the highway. The moving air from the speeding jeep felt good even when it was just hot air. It was a beautiful cloudless day. Normally, we'd be dumping our school bags, changing for the Cerc, spending the rest of the afternoon soaking in the swimming pool until it was cool enough to attempt going home. My thoughts were on the pound cake and Coca-Cola that I was missing due to this little side trip. I felt a stab of hunger, then remembered I had some of my French bread left in my school bag. I pulled it out. Tearing it into pieces, I offered some to Pati and Bob. The bread was a bit stale, but it served its purpose. My stomach ceased its complaining grumble.

Before long, the jeep turned onto a dirt side road with a barbed wire entrance and metal buildings. We had arrived at our destination. The ARVN sign was overhead. A uniformed Vietnamese guard waved us through as Chou smiled and yelled something in unintelligible Vietnamese. We squealed through the gate with a mountain of dust following us. I dreaded stopping now, knowing that we'd be covered in a blanket of this red dirt. As Chou put on the breaks, that cloud of dust rose behind, drifting over and covering us. We quickly took the bottoms of our shirts and held them over our faces. The coughing fit that followed seemed to leave Chou puzzled but not disturbed. He swung out of the open side of the jeep and gathered up some things to take with him.

The ARVN compound was just at the outskirts of the city on the way to the Tân Sơn Nhứt airport. I'd seen the entrance several times when we'd gone that way but never had entered it. Two little blond girls dressed in school dresses with a small brown-haired boy sitting in a military jeep in front of one of the Quonset huts had to look out of place to anyone paying attention.

"I be right back," Chou said before we had taken the cloth away from our faces. He sprinted off, taking a quick right at the end of the building.

"What do you think he is doing?" Pati said from the back after recovering from her coughing fit.

"Who knows? Maybe he had to go to the bathroom," I said, setting us all off laughing. Luckily, he'd parked in the shade. We dug in our school bags, determined to get our homework done so that we could go to the Cerc right after we got home. I remembered I'd hidden some bubble gum in my bag several days before and began digging in the bag for it. Pati and I split one tattered piece. I gave a full one to Bob, as he seemed completely restless. We all practiced blowing bubbles for what seemed like forever. Pati and I finally spit out the poor, tired, tasteless gum. Bob kept his. Finishing our homework, we started looking around to see what else was going on that could distract us.

The sun had shifted and was now directly on us, leaving us sinking into a cloud of listlessness. My skin was already nearly black from the months of exposure at the pool, as black as I'd ever get at any rate. I didn't seem to burn anymore from the sun, but Pati was different. She was fair, and her skin easily burned. Bob had olive skin and just kept getting darker and darker.

"You stay here. I'll see if I can find him," I said, sliding off the front seat and landing on the ground. I'd been eyeing the Vietnamese enlisted men who were now passing by us staring. I don't think we were supposed to be there. Ever! As I moved in the direction we'd last seen Chou, I heard whooping and cheering. A sudden cry of pleasure rose above it all. I didn't feel comfortable about wandering away from the jeep, but what else was there to do? I shot a glance back to be sure the kids weren't following me as I slowly turned the corner of the building. In front of me was a wide-open field surrounded by high wire fencing.

Young Vietnamese girls in uniforms were directly in front of me. They were like the ones we had seen at the birthday parade for President Diệm. I'd also seen them in newspaper pictures with Madame Nhu. They were practicing drills on an obstacle course that had been set up. They were busy practicing their routines, so no one noticed me. They were dressed in gray outfits: shirts with neckties, slacks, and wide-rimmed cloth hats with drawstrings around their chins. I watched for a while, trying to remain invisible. The brightly colored dress I had on was not an ideal formula for obscurity. I had been told earlier that Madame Nhu was behind a Vichy-style youth organization. I didn't know what that meant at the time. However, watching the young women as they did their military drills was exhilarating for me. Seeing females in this male-dominated role was an eye-opener.

I was just about to slink back to the jeep when the sound of Chou's high-pitched laugh could be heard above a loud cheer from a crowd. Keeping close to the metal huts, I continued moving in the direction of the voices. The buildings were closed, so there was no way to tell what was inside. A temporary metal roof had been attached to one of them, forming an overhang to cover equipment. This was where the shouts seemed to be coming from.

There he was! Chou, squatting and throwing dice, surrounded by a handful of Vietnamese soldiers! In the center of the group, shaking a fistful of piasters, Chou was yelling, a wild and crazy look on his face. He was winning, it seemed. Just then he lost the roll of the dice and stood up swearing. He spun around, catching sight of me. Visibly surprised, he threw down some cash and leaped out of the circle. He began taking queer jerky strides in my direction, smiling nervously. I quickly ducked behind the building, heading back at full speed toward the jeep. He was still grinning when he reached the jeep, but I didn't like the look in his eye.

Pati was now sitting in the front seat looking totally intimidated by the surroundings. Bob had settled across the back seat, sound asleep. As I jumped into the back of the jeep, I nearly crushed Bob. Chou swung behind the driver's wheel. Turning his head around, he looked straight at me. I was one move ahead of him though.

"It will cost you, Chou, if you don't want me to tell the Colonel," I said before he could say anything. I delighted in making him so alarmed. Chou's entire being shifted from the angered aggressor to the subservient driver.

"You no tell your father," he shot back. His voice now sounded desperate as opposed to how mad he was when he had gotten into the jeep.

"Depends," I said, barely above a whisper. I was working on presenting a calm persona.

"On what it depends?" I thought he was going to cry.

"Whether Pati, Bob, and I get to stop for sugar cane sticks on the way home," I said.

"No problem, no problem." With that, he turned the engine over, did a 180-degree turn and shot the jeep through the sentry post's open gate onto the highway. He now headed in the direction of home. We pulled over to make the blackmail purchase of three succulent sugar cane sticks from a sidewalk vendor. We gnawed on these sweet fibrous stalks as we sped down the highway. Chou, now seeming to be in a hurry to get us home, didn't want one for himself. We finally reached the villa and turned into the driveway. Chou jumped out to open the gate. The Colonel was home, and we could see him moving at a fast pace toward us from the direction of the house.

"Where have you been?" he blustered, visibly upset about something. We all froze. This was not going to be any kind of silent inquisition.

"I asked Chou to take us to a store in Cholon," I said quickly, glancing toward a sheepish-looking Chou.

"Whatever the hell for? Didn't you know we were worried? I was just getting ready to have the military police after you, Chou! What were you thinking? This vehicle is not for my children's pleasure to be driven around town. I never want this ever to happen again! You bring them directly home no matter what they try to talk you into," he said, calming down. A wave of relief seemed to be passing over him as he spoke.

Chou kept his eyes on the ground, waiting for the storm to blow over. He shot me a grateful glance as the Colonel walked back toward the house. I wasn't sure what had worried the Colonel so much. I was to find out later that a missionary family had been kidnapped upcountry that day, children and all. This signaled a change, and he wasn't one to miss subtleties. Up until now, foreign children had not been bothered in any way by anyone.

It was good I hadn't said where we had gone. Being in the ARVN base might not have been such a good idea, considering the strained relations with the Americans now in evidence. The foreign community would now respond with tighter controls on their families. The Colonel laid down the law and didn't sugarcoat it in case we hadn't clearly gotten it the first time. "Absolutely no independent trips out unescorted! Understand?"

No matter. Chou was mine. I didn't take advantage of it. Not yet, anyway. He now regarded me as a trusted friend. I viewed this as something good to have in my back pocket if I ever needed it. I was always saving up favors and taking advantage of opportunities. If I wasn't blackmailing someone, I was squealing on that person, it seemed. The time would come when Chou would rue the day he ever owed me anything. I was living one day at a time, and that was fine with me.

Chou was the Colonel's jeep driver. His own personal
form of transportation for his entire family was a bike.

The ARVN military post was located just outside
Saigon. Like on most military and government facilities,
a large placard featuring the image of President Diem
was prominently displayed.

CHAPTER 28:

CITY OF
RUMORS AND SPIES

The older American boys had no boundaries, it seemed, even with the safety warnings from their families. They would roar down to the docks along the Saigon River in their semiformed gangs. One or two of them seated on each motorcycle, clinging, they would laugh and talk as they sped along. Their wheels spun and engines sputtered. Sometimes they would hit puddles of water left from a recent downpour, and a refreshing spray would cover them. The Vietnamese who hung around the docks were like ancient inhabitants of the city peering from the dark openings of the nearby buildings. They watched the boys pass. Patched and faded walls bordered the slow-flowing river that meandered past the docks. The intensity of the river smell caused the boys to wrinkle up their noses as they passed through. They would speed up as they reached the end of the docks and headed out onto the main highway.

The boys were oblivious, unaware of this dock world they had innocently entered. The fact was that when the country was divided in 1954, the group that controlled the Saigon–Cholon area were the *Bình Xuyên*, a band of river pirates who ran a vice racketeering operation. They controlled the opium and prostitution businesses and were licensed to control the national police by none other than Emperor Bảo Đại. Their headquarters were around the docks. Many were still there now, but not in the kind of numbers as when they had ruled this section of the city. Now, they formed a group along with a religious group, the *Cao Dai*, acting as spies for Nhu.

There was a complex history between the *Bình Xuyên* and the two religous sects, the *Cao Dai*, and the *Hòa Hảo*. The most pressing problem facing Ngô Đình Diệm when he was called to office from France by Emperor Bảo Đại in June 1954 was the existence of these groups who held sway over vast quasiautonomous territories. Charged with the task of unifying southern Vietnam, Diệm realized he had to break the power of the sects, especially the *Bình Xuyên*, whose interests conflicted with his. He had two alternatives: he could either eliminate these groups or integrate them into the body politic. In either case, he needed a strong and loyal army.

Madame Nhu was to boast later that she was the one who spurred Diệm to call on the army in 1955 and virtually eliminate the threat these groups posed to his position. Ironically, it was her husband, Diệm's brother, who later in the '60s utilized members of these various groups to be part of the intricate spy rings he created, as he and Diệm no longer trusted their own army and were leery of the Americans. These rings were a complex network of spies who reported the whereabouts of every American and any Vietnamese in contact with them. They reported to Ngô Đình Nhu.

"Those guys over there always seem to be following us. Have you noticed that?" Tom said one day between puffs on his cigarette. My older brother was somebody who paid attention to subtleties too. He was home from the Brent School in the Philippines. He had changed from the quiet boy he had been. He now had an adult-like appearance. Fantastically, he now had hair on both his arms and legs, was taller, and didn't look like himself. This had his younger siblings staring in wonder. His previously round, full cherub face was now slim, with visible cheekbones. I had to admit, he was bordering on being good-looking.

With a cigarette pack rolled up in the sleeve of his short-sleeved shirt, James Dean style, he spent most of his time hanging out with his old gang. Many of these kids had also been sent away to school and were reunited when they got back to Saigon. Not supervised, they were wild. Tossing his cigarette butt on the ground, Tom was making an exaggerated effort at stamping it out as he gazed up the alleyway they had just come from. His foot moved back and forth as he looked in the direction of two figures lingering at the corner. They were dressed plainly, like most of the young Vietnamese men of the time, with short-sleeved white shirts, black pants, and black dress shoes. They too were casually smoking cigarettes.

"Are you getting paranoid?" his friend Terry asked with a short laugh.

"No. Let's just see if they end up where we are next time," Tom said. He knew to pay attention, since the Colonel had made a point about staying alert and not taking unnecessary risks. Tom had been removed from the goings-on in Saigon while away at school. There had been sporadic acts of terror throughout the country that he had not been aware of. An atmosphere of unrest ran beneath the surface of life in Saigon. He was on curfew these days, so he knew something was up.

Motorbikes revved up with the engines gassed. The entire gang blazed out of the side street, hurling past the two men who were stationed at the corner. There were six American kids in the pack, and they had the entire day to do nothing but go from one place to the next. Smoking ciggies, listening to music, playing pool, and drinking 33 Premium Export *ba muoi ba* were the activities of the day. It was a life of complete freedom, something they would never have again when they returned to the States. This time in their life was unique. Tom would later refer to it as the best time of his life.

Eventually, the crew made it to the Cerc to ogle the French girls clad in skimpy bikinis, play chess, and wait for the day to end. In the club library, Tom found the chessboard with all its pieces lying in a jumble. He and his friend Terry sat and concentrated on the game in front of them. No longer concerned with the men who were tailing them or where those men might be, they settled into a long game. Everyone was on curfew, so they had to pack it all in by sundown. The rest of the afternoon passed peacefully. It was easy to get a quick lunch served as they attempted to slaughter each other at several games of chess. They finished their last game and gathered their friends. It was time to move on.

No sooner had they exited the Cerc onto Rue Chasseloup-Laubat than the same two Vietnamese men appeared again. They had been waiting out front near where the boys had parked their bikes. It seemed that they were to be permanent appendages to the pack of American boys. Tom swung a glance back over his shoulder, having caught sight of them in the rearview mirror. He'd have to remember to tell the Colonel about this. Maybe not, though. He might not be able to go out anymore if he did.

The pack headed back toward the Chinese section of Cholon again, screaming past the buildings along the waterfront where they had been earlier. Behind them, men stepped out from doorways or looked up from the nets they were untangling to watch these pretentious American youths, always strutting with bravado. Why not? They felt entitled. Weren't their fathers there to save the country? The Vietnamese men that followed the boys would always be there, maybe not the same men, but there always seemed to be somebody tracking the whereabouts of each kid and every other American now. It was exactly as Colonel *Sâm* had said it would be.

One day, Tom asked me if I thought anyone was following me. He made a point of saying I should stay alert because he was pretty sure he was. That was when he told me what was happening to him and his friends.

When Tom was sent to the Philippines, it was a rude awakening for him to suddenly no longer be part of the family. At age fourteen, as I mentioned, he had been shipped off to school in another country far away from us with little warning. When he returned to Saigon for Christmas break, he was no longer the naive kid who had been our brother. He seemed like a stranger, someone with his guard up at all times. He didn't bother with any of us younger kids now. His world revolved around his friends, his motorbike, and his freedom, away from everyone. He had become an expert at masking the scar tissue of old emotions and now remained aloof from us all.

"You're stupid!" Tom yelled as he harassed Thi Tu one day in the back courtyard near the servants' quarters. She stood with her head bent and tears forming in her eyes. For whatever reason, Tom enjoyed humiliating the servants. He did this type of thing frequently. I stood nearby, embarrassed, watching Thi Tu's sad downward glances as she struggled to maintain her dignity.

"Leave her alone, you ass!" I screamed, finally deciding to come between him and my beloved Thi Tu. I couldn't stand the arrogance that Tom and his friends now showed the Vietnamese people. I didn't understand it then, and only later realized that it was simply a reflection of the American attitude toward these people—an attitude of superiority. It was no different than the prejudice that permeated America's South, it seemed to me. Vietnam was viewed as an uneducated poor country, and nowhere in their imaginations could Americans believe that they wouldn't reign supreme in this relationship. How could they not realize the breadth and depth of this two-thousand-year-old country? The behavior my brother and his friends displayed at the time baffled me. America's puritan culture was at odds with this culture they had no concept or understanding of. It was a culture that was centuries old, compared to the relative infancy of America. Just as bizarrely as Tom's verbal assault had started, it ended. He stomped away, slamming the door to the house as he entered.

"Your brother is very mean," Thi Tu said as she walked to her room and closed the door. I stood in the courtyard feeling crushed by it all. I was sure we weren't doing a very good job representing our country if this was how we acted toward someone like Thi Tu. She had never been anything but nice to each and every one of us. Behind me, I heard the gunning of the motorbike engine. Tom peeled out onto the roadway on his bike with the tires squealing. I don't think he thought twice about his behavior. There was no reason for him to do this, really. He was no different than any of his friends. It was accepted. Perhaps persecution of the servants was Tom's way of not feeling at the bottom of the heap, a way to feel better after the put-downs "the old man" would give him. Maybe he could feel superior by being able to pass on the abuse. Honestly, it just made me irate. I didn't understand a thing.

A group of older boys who'd been at the ACS had established the precedent for this type of arrogant behavior that the younger boys embraced, Tom included. They were called the CLODS and had pretty much been around since the late '50s. I have no idea where the acronym came from or what it meant. They prided themselves on their irreverent attitudes and behaviors. They seemed to either disgust people or were copied. Whichever view you took, they were a creative bunch! By 1961, the founding members were gone, some of them most likely deported for unacceptable behavior.

One stellar afternoon at "the underground theater," I'd sold all my goods at the market and went back to the theater. Waiting for a break in the circle traffic to cross and catch the bus, I watched the horses and drivers pass by me. These carts plodded by, with both driver and horse looking half dead. The moving wagonloads were inhumane. The stacks sometimes measured at least ten feet high. I was struck by how hard everyone worked in this country. "Zenning," I got across the circle just as the younger kids were boarding the bus. Tom wasn't with us.

We arrived home that day to find the Colonel yelling at Tom for some unknown reason. He seemed to always be finding fault with Tom. It had become a regular occurrence. Tom would just stand and take it, showing no emotion. Tom's life wasn't easy with the Colonel. The Colonel seemed to have it out for him. It was like Tom couldn't ever do anything right. He had a knack for embarrassing Tom when other people were around, as if he needed to put him down, thinking it would give him a backbone. Maybe he wanted Tom to stand up to him. My brother never did, though. His only defense was to just act unfazed, disinterested. This infuriated "the old man" even more. He couldn't get a handle on his son no matter what he did. "The old man" couldn't manipulate or control him. They both knew it. It was sad to watch the two of them go at it, because I think they missed out on the relationship they should have had, and maybe even wanted. It was a relationship all of us wanted to have with our father, one of support and love. As soon as the Colonel left the room, Tom bolted for the bathroom.

"Hey, I can't ever please the old man, so I've given up trying," Tom said, wiping the vomit from his mouth after he'd come back to the room. Caught smoking a cigarette, Tom had been forced by the Colonel to smoke a cigar, the entire thing in one sitting. It was punishment, not only for smoking, but also for having been caught pilfering cigarettes from the downstairs cigarette holder. This was the Colonel's idea of how you cure a smoker; never mind that he smoked a pipe. Tom accomplished the task and didn't make a dive for the toilet until he was sure "the old man" wouldn't see. How he held out like that, I'll never know, but he managed it. I guess anger and resentment can help you master a lot of things. Tom would tell me years later that he felt that being sent away to the Philippines, far from "the old man," probably saved him in some way.

"I could give you a whole list of reasons for why he is such a bastard, but it would take up most of my life. I'd rather just avoid him and live my own life separately," Tom said after I asked him if he was okay. He'd had enough. He left through the villa gates shortly afterward and flagged down a nearby cab. I didn't see him for the rest of the day. Tom flew back to school the next week.

A MOMENT IN HISTORY

Ngô Đình Nhu created not one but ten secret intelligence agencies, all competing to bring news of traitors, spies, and foreign plots. Since he could not control everything, he made sure no cooperation could occur between any of the agencies. Since the agencies viewed the Americans in the same light, they assigned individuals to track their whereabouts. Probably not so important were the children, but they were keen on knowing which Vietnamese associated with Americans. Those Vietnamese would be passed over for promotions and, in many cases, dismissed from their duties without any warning. The Diệm regime was not pro-American.

—From the Archives of Colonel George T. Hanna (Colonel Le Van Sâm's Notes)

CHAPTER 29:

PALACE BOMBING (1962)

On February 27, 1962, two dissident Republic of Vietnam Air Force pilots, Nguyễn Văn Cử and Phạm Phú Quốc, bombed the Independence Palace, the official residence of President Diệm and his family, with the aim of assassinating them.

The sun was just coming up as we waited for our ride to school. Our transport was a big green Suburban with a private driver who took us back and forth every day. When we reached the American Community School, he suddenly turned the vehicle around without stopping, as someone signaled to him to keep moving. The man yelled something in Vietnamese to him as we passed. Squealing out of the driveway, we headed back toward town. We were the only American family who lived out on Phan Thanh Giàn, so we were the only ones ever riding in the van. The air conditioner was on high, blasting cold air. It was like sitting in a refrigerator. We moved quickly down the boulevard, as fast as traffic would allow. Pati, Bob, and I were surprised by the driver's sense of urgency and confused by the change in our morning schedule. The ACS was outside the central part of the city. As we got closer, the traffic began to build.

"What's wrong?" I asked the driver, having kept quiet until my curiosity got the better of me. This was not our usual route. Not going to school was good news, but now I was wondering why.

"When you get home, you ask. There is problem in the city. We take this way around it now," he said. His face showed no emotion, and he kept his eyes on the road. He was a middle-aged Vietnamese man, short and stout. He swerved this way and that to avoid the mass of bikes and taxis in his way. The vinyl seats in the back had Pati and Bob sliding from one side to the other. Vietnamese along the way were shouting at him as he barely missed hitting them. Everyone seemed to be in an anxious state.

Nothing else was said to us, but I continued bugging the driver with questions. I figured he'd eventually say something just to shut me up. Swarms of people outside our windows were visible as we now moved at a snail's pace along the roadway. Planes were flying over us. Finally reaching our house, we quickly jumped out. Tearing through the gate, running up the outside steps to the roof garden, we reached the railing, searching the sky. From the top floor, two flights up, we could see everything across the rooftops.

The sky had a low level of cloud covering. Against this overcast background, planes could be seen circling low and hovering over where we knew the Independence Palace was located. They appeared as small as birds. A plume of smoke was rising in the distance. We found out later that one American-made WWII-era fighting plane had flown down the main boulevard and released a bomb. The pilot had been trailed by another aircraft that released another bomb, hitting the opposite end of the palace. As we stood there, the first plane was now returning for another run.

His bomb had not exploded. The sound of this next explosion was like the muffled bang of a toy gun, and our villa vibrated slightly. In the distance, smoke rose skyward.

Frozen in place, leaning on the railing, we gripped the metal as we watched. We didn't talk. There was nothing to be said. I was lost in my own thoughts and worried. I didn't know where Mom was. The kindergarten where she taught was in the Norodom Compound next to the palace. I didn't know where the Colonel was either.

That morning, as we watched from the top of the roof garden at Phan Thanh Giàn, we stood like good soldiers and waited. We would learn later that Mom had run into traffic and hadn't made it to the kindergarten. Her small Renault taxi got stuck in the long line of vehicles that had no choice but to turn off their motors and watch the circling of the planes and the dropping of the bombs. At a standstill, she waited in the breathless sweltering heat. Loyalist aircrafts were in pursuit above; tanks and jeeps armed with .50-caliber machine guns patrolled the smoke-filled streets below. She would eventually move past the congestion and head home.

It would be hours before we knew anything. Pati, Bob, and I stayed on the roof all that morning. Our eyes were focused on where we thought our parents might be and the gate below in case they showed up. We didn't talk about the *what if?* idea. We just waited. My mind was racing, however. I was going to have to orchestrate the next move for Pati, Bob, and me if anything happened to our parents. I'd call the Bingham family and have them help me. We could go live with our grandparents in Texas. I'd have to find a way to get in touch with Tom. He was back at school in Baguio. *I'm sure the Army could get us all on a transport back to the States.* I had money saved; I'd be able to take care of us all. *What would I do with the bodies? Stop thinking that*, I told myself. What eleven-year-old kid comes up with a detailed next-step plan in the middle of a bombing?

We found out later from the Colonel that one of the bombs that had hit the Independence Palace had crashed through the roof but not exploded. It had settled quietly on the first floor just above where President Diệm, Ngô Đình Nhu, Madame Nhu, and their children were breakfasting. It had just lain there in wait. President Diệm and his family were rushed out through an underground tunnel to safety. Only Madame Nhu sustained minor injuries. The Colonel and his team were brought in to examine the unexploded bomb and coordinate its removal.

The Colonel arrived at the palace with a demolition crew in several jeeps. The place was crawling with palace guards. They entered, climbing over the long metal object. They determined what would be necessary for the removal of the bomb. After they took out the fuse, it was tossed into the back of a nearby jeep to be driven off later. The bomb would be loaded into a separate vehicle. Cleanup was almost complete when the Colonel took time to look around him. He concluded that the damage incurred was manageable, that things could soon be put right, though reconstruction of the building would take time. Most of the palace was still somewhat intact. Work would need to be done to repair the bomb's entry trail. In the meantime, President Diệm and his family would move to nearby Gai Long Palace. The Colonel turned and walked outside, swinging himself into the front seat of one of the waiting jeeps. It was the same vehicle that they'd thrown the detached fuse into.

As the jeep drove away, the Colonel heard the fuse ignite behind him.

"Wouldn't you know, that thing was still live," the Colonel said when he told his story later that night. He seemed amused by the surprise of it. "Scared the piss out of me," he added. It had been only a matter of time—that bomb might have taken everyone out.

The *ACS Bamboo Beacon*, our school newsletter, released an extra edition that week. It was always handwritten and run off on a mimeograph machine. This time the headline read: "Extra! The Palace Is Bombed."

A Moment in History

"The 1962 South Vietnamese Independence Palace bombing in Saigon was an aerial attack on February 27, 1962, by two dissident Vietnam Air Force pilots, Second Lieutenant Nguyễn Văn Cử and First Lieutenant Phạm Phú Quốc. The pilots targeted the Independence Palace, the official residence of the president of South Vietnam, with the aim of assassinating President Ngô Đình Diệm and his immediate family, who acted as his political advisors. The pilots later said they attempted the assassination in response to Diệm's autocratic rule, in which he focused more on remaining in power than on confronting the Viet Cong. Cử and Quốc hoped that the airstrike would expose Diệm's vulnerability and trigger a general uprising, but an uprising failed to materialize."

—*Stanley Karnow,* Vietnam: A History, *Penguin Books, 1997*

Independence Palace was the residence of President Diệm
and his brother's family, the Nhus. A second coup in 1962
was orchestrated by officers from Diem's Air Force. They
bombed the palace hopeful it would signal a rebellion
from the populace against Diệm's corrupt regime.

CHAPTER 30:

THE MARS BOX

A s Thi Tu turned the doorway key from the outside one evening, we kids scurried up the winding staircase. The servants had started locking us inside the house whenever we were to be alone. Mom and the Colonel were going to another party somewhere. It was becoming a regular thing, our being locked inside. After the palace bombing, we were under close guard and restricted in our movements. The doors and windows of the villa had ornate iron grillwork on them, classically decorative but impermeable as far as anyone's getting in or out. In retrospect, it probably wasn't a good idea to lock children in like this. But then again, they were weighing the odds of death by fire against the danger of an intruder. A cavernous house, our Phan Thanh Giàn villa was a bit spooky at night. Our footsteps and voices echoed on the marble floors, which amplified all sounds. We took refuge in our parents' bedroom that night. Closing the bedroom doors and locking the only one that had a lock, we turned all the lights on. Another door, which locked from the inside, opened to a small hanging balcony. It too had a prison-like metal covering, but we could open it from inside. That night, we stood outside on the balcony, leaning over the railing. It was still early evening. The life below us ebbed and flowed.

The colorful nightlife so prominent in other parts of the city was absent in our neighborhood. Although the vendor stalls across the street had their big metal grilles pulled down and locked, a stream of humanity continued to mill about at all hours. Flickering street lamps created moving shadows along the street and in the garden below us. Children and adults gathered around the constantly flowing water faucet in front of our outside wall. This went on all night, the bathing and collecting of water in large tin containers. Screams from the street children pierced the air as they sprayed and splashed in the water. The free-flowing water offered coolness for everyone. Sirens from the emergency vehicles passing on their way to the Saigon hospital blared to force the moving river of bodies and vehicles out of their way. Everything here had its own pace. Very little could or would change that.

As complete darkness fell, Pati, Bob, and I returned to the sanctuary of our parents' bedroom. Propped up on the large double bed, we played games, hoping we'd get tired enough to fall asleep. Tom was away, so there was no big brother to rely on in case something happened, but we weren't afraid.

"Did you know that Dad hid something in his closet?" Pati said, triumphant that she had something to tell that she thought no one else knew about. "I saw him put it there. It's a candy box!"

The Colonel had recently returned from a trip to the Philippines and attempted to hide a box on the top shelf of his closet. His mistake had been to put whatever he was trying to hide in a cardboard Mars candy box. How could a child let something like that go unexamined? This was like waving a red flag in front of a bull. With great pomp and ceremony, standing on a nearby chair, I pulled the Mars box down and handed it to Pati. A maroon fez rested on top of the box. This was given to Bob. He immediately put it on his head and began doing some type of contorted dance.

The Mars box itself was like any box with candy that one could get at the PX. Setting it on the bed, we formed a circle around it, sitting with our legs crossed. Our faces reflected pure confusion when we finally opened it. Inside it was one Kotex pad, three little rubber cartoonish toy pigs, a metal windup toy, two woven grass things you put your finger in, and rope puzzles. The puzzles were braided pieces of jute with red ribbons tied at the ends. This made no sense at all. We were completely puzzled. The Colonel's actions were baffling at times, but this took us to a completely different level of wonder.

"Maybe these are his toys," Bob said somewhat half-heartedly, looking quite official in the fez that rested just above his eyes. He was smiling. Cute. He looked as irresponsible as a flower.

"I don't think so. This isn't like the Colonel. He doesn't play. Must have been something he had to do in the Philippines. I mean, that's where he got this stuff," I said, trying to sound authoritative.

"Do you think he'd let me have the pigs?" Pati said with a slight smile. She clearly felt he shouldn't have them if he wasn't going to be playing with them. "Think we can ask him about it?" she ventured.

"No, I don't think that would be a good idea," I said, wondering what type of punishment would be associated with this act of mutiny.

We could come up with no satisfactory explanation. Just then the door to the balcony suddenly slammed open. Pati and Bob screamed. I froze. All our heads jerked toward the balcony. Staring into the black night beyond the doorway, silent, we waited for what might come next. Nothing happened.

"Who's there?" I finally yelled.

Outside, it was a night of pure and complete darkness. The wind had kicked up, and a freak rainstorm was now showering the balcony. The rainstorm came in like a freight train, pelting the glass. Lightning flashed. I jumped up to close and lock the door. The booming thunder sent all three of us headlong under the covers. Eventually, listening to the soothing sound of falling rain, we fell fast asleep. When our parents returned, they found the Mars box and its contents spread across the bed on top of us. Putting everything back in the box, they returned it to the top shelf of the closet. They never said anything to us about it. We didn't voice any of our questions either.

I couldn't wait for Tom to come home, so I could corner him about what we'd found in the Mars box. Tom seemed to already know all about it when I finally could talk to him. He said the Colonel was being indoctrinated into his 32nd Degree from the Masons. He told me that "the old man" was moving up the ranks in what he thought was a secret organization. This was part of an initiation. Tom thought he had to wear them in a parade or something. Strange. He mentioned something about the Shriners and a parade in Manila. I couldn't get it out of my mind. The Colonel's life was already a mystery to me without this new information. But you had to be humored by the thought of this strict military officer walking down the streets of Manila with these weird-ass things hung around his neck, especially the Kotex pad.

"You didn't bother the other box, did you?" The concern on his face now had me wondering what was in the other box on the top shelf. It was an unimpressive cardboard box. I hadn't given it a thought.

"No. Something good in that?" I said.

"Don't touch it, and make sure none of the other kids ever get into it. Do you hear me? I'm not kidding, Sandy! It's a box of grenades."

"What the heck is he doing with a box of grenades in the closet? That's crazy! And why didn't he tell me about it? What if Pati and Bob got into it?"

"Well, he told me they were there, and he also told me what to do if something happens," he said.

"You're just trying to scare me, aren't you?" I said, knowing he loved to do that whenever possible.

"Now listen, and I'm serious. This is what he told me. If there is trouble and anyone comes into the house for us, I'm to put you kids in the back of the closet and pull the top mattress off the bed. I'm supposed to pack it on top of all of you. Then I'm to get my M1 rifle and take up position, hiding myself as best I can under the mattress too."

"What M1? You have a gun?" I said, shocked at this new revelation.

"Yes…and you better not touch that either, unless you have to. It's on top of the armoire in my room. If I'm not here and the old man isn't around, you are going to have to do everything I just told you. Damn, Sandy! You should have tried to learn how to shoot that gun when we were in Texas. I'll show you how to do it, but you stay away from that box! Understand?"

Now, I had gone through Tom's closet a million times, snooping, and it had never occurred to me to look on top of it. He didn't say any more, but I knew that he wasn't playing around this time. I took his orders like they had come directly from the Colonel. No way was I getting near that other box, though. No way.

Sometimes, there are things to be afraid of that you don't know about. Other times, there are just things that go bump in the night. There would be such a night, what I'd call a bump in the night, but it wouldn't be an imagined sound or a thunderous rainstorm. This was to happen a few weeks later, after the Mars box incident.

Standing on top of the roof garden of our villa always gave me an exhilarating sensation of height and space. I felt free when I climbed up there to scan the world that surrounded me. It was a great place for thinking or simply daydreaming. I could gaze down on the bustling street, Phan Thanh Giàn, to watch a virtual beehive of activity. During the daytime, men on bicycles with no less than thirty ducks tied by their feet off the backs of their bikes whizzed by. Women moved to and fro with tin buckets filled with water on the ends of sticks. Young female students in bright white áo dais, wearing bamboo hats, zipped through traffic on fat-wheeled motorized bikes. Children were everywhere. The older children were dressed in school uniforms consisting of blue shorts, white short-sleeved shirts, scarves, and little blue hats with drawstrings. They carried leather satchels as they made their way to and from school. Food vendors scooped noodles into small bowls for their customers. Other vendors handed out big chunks of sugar cane to pass-ersby, collecting the piasters handed to them. Cyclos and motorcyclos buzzed up and down the street. Cicadas filled the air with a drone that wavered from intense to even more intense. The air was pungent with smells. Faces were filled with reverberating expressions. My roof garden looked out on this marvelous vibrant world.

As I stood on the rooftop one day, I heard the small cries of kittens coming from under the terra-cotta roof tiles. Carefully lifting them, I slid through into the attic space. I discovered Momma Cat's four-week-old kittens with their small, weak voices inside. I had wondered where she'd been hiding them this time. Crawling out and putting the tiles back carefully, I vowed to keep her secret.

We had been having electrical problems, and some Vietnamese electricians came to the house to do some repairs a few days later. I was in my sanctuary on the rooftop at the time. They told Thi Tu that they needed to get into the attic. Mom and the Colonel weren't home, and the servants weren't about to let them enter the house. So, climbing the outside steps, they made their way to the roof garden. Thi Tu told me what they wanted to do, so I excitedly showed them a way into the attic, proudly removing the roof tiles one at a time.

That weekend, I went on an overnight to a friend's house—my first friend, Janis, near Don Thi Diệm. Awakened early the next morning by her parents, I was told I needed to go home immediately. I gathered my things quickly. Chou was outside waiting for me. The streets were already packed with vendors and shoppers as we sped along. What appeared to be pure chaos with cars, people, and bikes filling the roadways was more like a well-orchestrated dance. Everyone moved and everyone shifted. Very rarely did I see any type of accident. In the middle of the circles were traffic police in white uniforms with white gloves and hats. They directed traffic. We American kids had come to refer to them as "the white mice." When Chou pulled in sharply to the driveway, I jumped out. The whole family, as well as the servants, was gathered in the second-floor hallway.

"Good, everybody is here," the Colonel said as I joined the group. "There was a break-in last night. Robbers got into the house through the roof, coming through the trapdoor here," he announced, pointing. "The tiles from the roof were removed. They slid down the electrical conduit." My sleepy eyes now sprung wide open.

There were footprints all along the wall, and the electrical conduit had been pulled away from the wall. The ceiling in the hallway was at least fourteen feet high. Somehow, the robbers had known that the other door to my parents' room had a wicked squeak. The entry through the children's room made no noise. This was the way they had taken.

"I can't imagine how they knew all this," he said. Raising my hand, I now spilled the beans on how they even had known how to get into the attic.

The Colonel kept his .45 automatic with a clip of bullets in the top drawer of his dresser. He usually pulled his wallet out of his pocket before going to bed and set it on top of the dresser at night. Whoever the intruders had been, they had intended on getting the revolver. I think the money must have been an afterthought. The wallet had been left empty.

Everyone was safe and no one had been harmed, but I think this was just pure luck. My brother's room was next door to my parents' room. He was home after having completed a full year of school in the Philippines and had awakened to the sound of the robbers coming or going.

Either way, it was good he hadn't bothered to check it out. He'd just turned over and dismissed the noise, going back to sleep. Mom had also woken up, but it was when the robbers were leaving. She thought it was just Tom making the noises. She too hadn't gotten out of bed to inspect.

It no longer felt safe at home, even though the tiles were cemented back in place and the trapdoor was nailed shut. This event of the outside world's entering our home had a strange effect on me. I now looked at people differently. We didn't let any Vietnamese workmen back on the property for the rest of our stay. One question that plagued us all was how they knew exactly where the gun had been located and how to get to it noiselessly.

CHAPTER 31

MONEY LAUNDERING

No one saw me do it. At least, I don't think anyone did. The servants never bothered to tell on us kids anymore. They'd given up trying to have any influence on us, especially on me. I had long ago stopped listening to their caring chatter as they scolded me about my wily ways in their indifferent English and French. Quickly, I rifled through my mother's purse. I had only a few minutes before she'd be back. It sat on the glass top of the dining room table, almost begging to be disturbed. Mom had gone back upstairs to get something, a forgotten address or perhaps a tube of lipstick to be ferreted away in the side pocket of her beige bamboo leather-strapped handbag. It was a last-minute thought that had her stop midstride in the dining room, turning 180 degrees on her heels to quickly mount the stairs again.

What had she planned for today's outing? I wondered. She usually made a list of the places where she was going, shopping with the addresses written down, especially when she had the Colonel's driver, Chou, at her disposal for the whole day. Mom's comings and goings now were a mystery to me. She had a life all her own. It felt like we weren't a part of it anymore. The luxury of servants at her disposal had given her a freedom from her four children that had not been possible prior to these Saigon days. Then again, I guess I could say my life would be a mystery to her, if she even had an inkling of what I was up to. In her innocent ignorance, she assured me she always knew where I was. After all, I was only a child. What could I possibly be up to? Years later she would find out, and it would leave her speechless.

Inside her purse was a piece of paper folded perfectly and tucked neatly into one of the side pockets. A list of addresses was written in a gentle flowing script on a piece of Mom's personal stationery. It stated her intended stops for the day. I knew most of them, having accompanied her before when she'd had the time to take me along. Today appeared to be a full day of activity, and she intended to be on her own, unencumbered by children. She had made that perfectly clear to us at breakfast. I silently read the list.

CAMTAU 17, Passage De L'Eden, Saigon

This is where you could get beautiful jewelry, good silver pieces at reasonable prices. Mom loved beautiful things. I was sure she made this little shop a monthly stop. I knew this from the collection that was growing in her jewelry box, a beautiful rosewood thing that she had purchased in Hong Kong on one of her trips there. Those trips were usually made with the Colonel, without any of us kids. Her passport was covered with stamps from the various out-of-country trips she'd taken.

QUANG-CHAU, 37, Nguyen-van-Thinh, Saigon

This was a tailor of civil and military uniforms used by everyone there. The uniforms would be starched so they stood on their own, just the way the Army liked them. She also used this place to have our clothes tailored when she wanted to supplement the Sears mail-order ones—tight-fitting things that didn't spare any fabric as far as room was concerned. These clothes were like having a second skin, they were so perfectly formed to one's frame. She would insist we wear these until either the buttons no longer met when we tried to fasten them, or we'd worn them out, whichever came first.

ETS THAI-THACH Import and Export, 58/70 Rue Tu-Do, Saigon

This place had all the finest and choicest grocery items from all parts of the world, to suit all tastes available, "at most reasonable cost," it claimed. Some things were not available in the military PX and commissary, so this was a required stop for most military personnel and foreigners.

The BOOKSHOP, 33, Passage Eden, Saigon (in the Arcade)

Here, there were American magazines, bestsellers, pocket books, children's books, and textbooks. Not everything was printed in English, but there was a decent selection. It was a great place to pick up a few good books to fill the hours. This was also a hangout for ex-pats and aspiring young poets. The older kids hung out there, mimicking the Beat generation in style, writing poetry, and reading Jack Kerouac. We didn't have a television, so books were something Mom would always have on hand to be sure we had something with which to occupy our time. If we said we were bored, she'd hand us books. It got so I read anything I was given, including books about basketball, something I am amazed at now, because I can't stand any sports. I think she picked them because they were at least written in English and said to be age-appropriate.

The Record Center, 28, Passage Eden, Saigon (in the Arcade)

This store boasted Saigon's best collection of American recording artists, air-conditioned comfort, private listening booths, and Saigon's lowest prices. Mom liked to find things for Tom here, as well as music that could be played at the house for parties. The Colonel had bought a do-it-yourself record player kit and a beautiful rosewood cabinet on one trip to Hong Kong. Tom and his friends considered this store a second home, making routine stops during the week to see what was in the stacks. They'd listen to what was supposed to be the latest release. Many of these records would arrive in Saigon well behind what anyone in the States was listening to. It didn't matter. It was a lifeline, making them feel as if they weren't completely cut off from the world they had come from.

Pan Am, 31, Tu-Do, Saigon

"Jets to Take You Around the World" was Pan Am's slogan. Now this was a far stretch for Mom to think about. Our family was always traveling standby on military transports whenever we went anywhere. Those trips came complete with brown ration boxes of unidentified food items. The Army dictated that military families fly military aircraft. There wasn't any questioning that. I was certain that flying Pan Am was something well beyond our dreams. But here it was, written in Mom's fine cursive script, as if it were just a normal item to list for the day's activities. Very curious.

As I sat there with the thin piece of paper in my hand, I had a sudden foreboding of something I'd tried not to think about during our entire stay in Saigon. It hit me like a thunderclap. How long had we been in Vietnam? I had to think. Had it been two years yet? I didn't want to think about our leaving anytime soon. I liked my life of independence and intrigue. I liked the money! I liked everything about Saigon. It had felt like we would be in Vietnam forever. I started rummaging through my mind. The thought that our stay might end soon gave me a cold feeling, like ice on the back of my neck. This singular item on the list, out of all of them, had me hugging my hands in my armpits, a nervous habit I had.

I refolded the paper neatly and put it back in the purse the way I had found it. As an afterthought, I pulled a piaster note that was peeking out of the opposite side pocket of the purse. To me, Vietnamese money was simply a thing of beauty. I didn't want to keep it, just admire it, holding it up to the light. I never tired of looking at piaster notes, and besides, it had a calming effect on me as I attempted to get my racing thoughts under control. There was a sort of magic in these notes. An invisible world lurked within. If you held a piaster up to the light, the image of a tiger in a clump of bamboo, or the face of some personage of importance would appear like magic. Hidden, it could be seen only when the note was held up where light could pass through it. This sorcerer's trick fascinated me.

Across the tile floor, the sound of clattering heels could be heard again as Mom made her way to the top of the staircase. Stuffing the money back in the purse pocket, I dove onto a nearby seat. With one leg hung over the arm of the bamboo sofa and the other one on the floor, I struggled to appear natural. I quickly moved a few pillows to carelessly support my head. It was all I had time for as she whirled by me at a fast pace toward the front door. She grabbed the purse as she passed. She was wearing a fitted sleeveless sundress that complemented the color of her purse. A waft of her perfume passed over me as I heard the jingle of her bracelets. She didn't seem to notice me at first, but then again mothers have eyes in the back of their head, don't they? Somehow registering my presence, she moved over to brush a kiss across my forehead.

"Be good and don't bother the servants," she said in her calm, melodious voice, and was out the door before I could reply. As if I ever bothered the servants! That was Tom's thing, not mine. Chou had been patiently waiting for her and was relieved to see her finally appear. The sound of the jeep wheels squealing out of the driveway could be heard as Chou gunned the engine. I imagine he was trying to impress her. She was clutching the side strap tightly as they made the left turn out of the driveway and onto the street. I doubt she was impressed, but this mode of transportation let her get everything done without having to hail a taxi or cyclo to go from one place to the other. Today's list would take her through the whole of Saigon and back for almost the entire day.

I started up the stairway two steps at a time and rushed out to the balcony of Tom's room just in time to see the servant closing the driveway gate. The scraping of the metal lock sliding into its holder could be heard. Thi Tu turned away from the gate and slowly moved back down the driveway, disappearing from view. She didn't look up. When Tom was away, I would take over his room. From there I could lean over the balcony without anyone's noticing me and not be bothered by anyone. I didn't think Tom would mind. Heck, he didn't even know about it. He was home now though, so I had to be careful. I'd heard him leave early that morning, so for now, I was safe. Turning away from the railing, I re-entered the room and sunk down on the bed's fresh linen to stare at the high ceiling and think. A small green lizard was resting in the crack between the ceiling and the wall, frozen. The sound of children playing in the waterworks beyond our stucco wall drifted skyward, filling the room. Their laughter was high-pitched and full of glee. The sound of a horse-drawn carriage slowly passing by created a steady beat, like a single drumstick on a stone surface. I was glad to be alone to have time to pull my thoughts together. Before I knew it, I was whispering curses under my breath. Darn parents don't tell you anything! I needed to talk to Tom! Were we being transferred soon? Where was he, anyway?

The thought of Pan Am was stuck in my head. Not knowing what was going on was irritating me. The three-day trip in the propeller-driven military plane we had come over in was something all of us dreaded a repeat of for the return flight back to the States. Pan Am would be like going from rags to riches. Mom had to be dreaming, but then again, she had always been a bit psychic. She had a way of knowing about things that was always surprising. Like the time the Colonel had said, "You'll never guess what happened to me today." Her response as she stirred the pasta sauce was, "You walked into the women's bathroom and made yourself comfortable reading your newspaper." From that point on, the Colonel took whatever she said as gospel.

Vietnam had been a marvelous escape from our former lives, and the thought of its ending soon was unacceptable, as far as I was concerned. We had brilliantly adapted to this life, I thought. I, for one, wasn't planning on going quietly.

I lay under the breeze from the whirling overhead fan. My thoughts were disturbing. It had to be a sign that things were going to change soon. No telling when us kids would be told anything. Our parents had an unsettling way of waiting until the very last minute to disclose any world-shattering plans that involved us. It was like waiting as patiently as a dog for a signal. Maybe this was it.

Okay. I needed to come up with a plan now for how I was going to cash out all my ill-gotten loot. I didn't want to return to the United States with perfectly worthless piasters on my hands. How was I going to exchange all my piasters before we moved? It had to be done before we left, that was for sure. I had several thousand dollars by now from the baby powder and Hershey bar business. Vietnamese money wouldn't be usable in other parts of the world, including in the United States. Heck, most people wouldn't even know where Vietnam was or how much the money was worth. I had worked too hard to not get its full value at this stage of the game. I propped the pillow up and crossed my legs. I had to come up with a drop-dead, no-holds-barred plan.

As I mentally reviewed my options, a single mosquito droned nearby. Its death was immediate. I didn't have time for its troublesome ways. The two years in Saigon had made me an expert at swiftly crushing them in my bare hands. As I lay there, I concluded that my beautiful piasters were simply going to have to be exchanged for a more viable currency, one that would be of value in the United States. That wasn't going to be easy, as American greenbacks weren't that plentiful. Tom had told me the Colonel could be court-martialed if piasters were brought back into the States and exchanged by any one of us. The exchange in Saigon had to be for greenbacks, something less interesting than piasters but something that would have value. That would solve the problem. This was probably my only alternative. I was sure we'd be on a military base at some point when we got back to the States so if I could make the exchange of the smaller amounts now into ten and twenty-dollar bills, I could consolidate them into one-hundred-dollar bills in the States. The Colonel's grumbling dissatisfaction with what was going on in Vietnam had me concerned with how long we'd stay in the Army, though. I didn't realize then that he had committed to stay four years in the Army in exchange for the MBA program he'd attended at the University of Chicago before we were assigned to Vietnam. He would still have two years left that had to be served.

No need for the Colonel to find out anything at this stage. He'd been in the dark about my activities for two years. Now at the ripe old age of twelve, I should be able to handle things myself. The best places to make exchanges would be at the airport, the PX, and the commissary. Tom had taught me that. If I did it over time, no one would be the wiser. I was going to have to rely on Chou for the airport run. We were sent to the movies enough that my wait for the bus near the PX could be put to good use. I'd still have to make extra trips. Might as well get started! The degree of freedom I'd had up to this point probably bordered on being dangerous, but I had never considered it a problem. I didn't take any of the recent rules about not going out unaccompanied as etched in stone, especially in a situation like this.

Mom would be out of the house for the entire day, so it seemed like a good day to start preparing for a move. Tiptoeing down the stairs, I slipped out of the house without being seen. Creeping like a mouse, my pockets bulging with piasters, I slipped through the gate. It was late morning. The heat of the day remained tolerable. It was the weekend. Pati and Bob were out back with Thi Tu. I left a note on the table—"going to the stamp store, back in a few hours"—completely ignoring the Colonel's orders to not go anywhere unaccompanied. I waved down a cyclo and headed downtown.

"*Allez tout droit*," I called out as the vehicle leaped forward. "*Doucement!*" I wasn't in that big of a hurry yet. The driver looked down at me with his hands on his hips and laughed.

Light clouds filled the sky, and there was a thrilling rush of wind from the whirling cyclo as we sped by the many streets along the way. The tall eucalyptus trees shaded the boulevards, and the sounds of the city filled the air. Pulling up to the front of the PX, I paid the driver and rushed up the steps. I wanted to get this over with as fast as I could before anyone noticed I was missing. The cashiers seemed miffed at my wanting American greenbacks. I was out of there in less than ten minutes, waving down yet another cyclo for my ride back to Phan Thanh Giàn. Returning home, I found the note still on the table and felt a wave of relief. Pati, Bob, and Thi Tu were still busy in the courtyard. Mom wasn't back yet, and who knew where the Colonel or Tom was? No one was the wiser. I deposited the efforts of my first money-exchanging foray into my trusty cigar box. I had been storing the money box in a place no one ever entered, my little science lab.

The Colonel had set up a makeshift lab for me in the old washtub room that wasn't being used in the servants' quarters. I had told him I wanted to be a horse vet so he'd think I was more than just a useless girl. I wanted him to know I had ambition. He'd picked up a microscope and a chemistry set for me on one of his R&R trips to Hong Kong to really make it official. This was his way of showing support for the idea. There were several large rat holes in the room, which always had me peering over my shoulder in case a rat showed up when I was there. Surely, we'd both have been surprised. Anyway, I told the younger kids that the rats were big enough to eat small children, and they never came near. They had seen a few of the gigantic rats that the cat and dog had killed, working together. They believed every word I said. These fat, ugly, glistening creatures were enormous, and that is no lie! We'd often see them scurrying as they feasted on the garbage along the roadway when we'd pass by at night.

The servants never bothered with the lab room, and I had the only key. Lucy was the only one who ever checked up on me. She was always curious about what I was up to. As far as she was concerned, I was under her tutelage. As I closed the lab doors, turning the key to lock them, I spotted Lucy outside.

She sat in the corner of the courtyard reading in the early-afternoon light. Stroking her hair with calm gestures, she was dressed to go out. Her hairstyle was that of the modern youth, short and curly. Her student attire was the traditional white áo dài with black pants. Her bamboo hat rested on the ground next to her. She was lost in the pages of the story she was reading, not noticing anything else around her. Lucy, daughter of our cook, Thi Ba, an example of the modern youth of Vietnam, was a person straddling the split between the world of her ancestors and the modern changing world she was a part of in Saigon. That world consisted of the traditional Vietnam and one that had been created by the Western influence of the French and now the Americans. I moved quietly toward her, hoping to surprise her, but she caught sight of me before I'd made my surprise leap. "*Faites attention!*" I yelled.

"You should know by now you can't surprise me, little sister," she said. She was only twenty, but always referred to me in this manner.

"What are you reading?" I asked, sliding up next to her to look at the book, which was written in the now popular *nhug ghi* writing. It was nothing I could make head or tails out of, unfortunately, but at least it had recognizable letters, as opposed to the Chinese symbols originally used centuries before. My all-knowing sixth-grade teacher had told us that this form of writing eliminated the illiteracy of the peasants and was really what had made it possible for the Vietnamese to be able to communicate with each other, eventually gaining freedom for them from China.

"Oh, it is a great novel written a long time ago, maybe in the '30s, by To Nguyen Tuong Tam, that I would translate to you as *Breaking the Ties*," she mused. "It is something that many of us read now, because it is similar to our plight."

"What do you mean by 'plight'?" I knew what the definition of the word was but wasn't sure what she was referring to.

"We modern young Vietnamese have a difficult position in our society now. We are the products of the old and the new without any definition of how we should be in the present. It is the perfect example of yin and yang tugging at each other," she said. "My mother has asked your mother to take me with you when you leave for America," she said matter-of-factly. "My mother agrees with me that I go, as she knows that I no longer have the will or the mind to be able to follow the traditions of old. I want to live differently without the weight of yesterday and tomorrow on my shoulders. Besides, I come from a level of society that would only leave me in what I would consider a deplorable level. I do not want to be a servant or a concubine. I would have to be subservient to a husband. It is not how my education has formed me now. I have been educated in the Western tradition of the individual, but our country is still steeped in the ways of Confucius," she rambled on.

Now, this was getting into territory I didn't know anything about, but I was willing to learn. Hesitantly, I threw out the next question.

"Okay, let me hear about Confucius," I said with a gulp. I knew Lucy would be very detailed and that I might as well settle in for the long haul. I kept an eye out for when everyone was going to the Cerc to swim, however. I had no intention of missing an afternoon cooling off in the pool.

"No, better I tell you a love story instead," she said with a laugh.

"Ugh, love story. I'd rather hear about some old wrinkled guy named Confucius," I said. I'd seen pictures of him before.

"This book I am reading is about a young educated woman who has her marriage arranged by her family to match their level in society. In Vietnam, the families related to the Mandarin marry into families of the same class, and so on down the line. They don't marry for love like in the French and American stories. The female must be subservient to the husband and to the husband's family. She is taken from her family and expected to be a part of the new family, to be agreeable and serve them. For me, she is no better than a slave or a prostitute!" Lucy said.

Now this was a different side of Lucy than I'd seen before. She was always polite and quiet, always so nice to me and respectful to her mother. But here was a woman who was obviously angry about something. I had a fairly good idea she saw herself in this story.

"Lucy, is there going to be an arranged marriage for you?" I said timidly.

"In proper Vietnamese culture, this would be how it is done. But as you can see, I am the daughter of a servant, so my prospects are not good for moving above my class structure in terms of this type of society," she lamented. "That is why I want to go to America. There I can be just Lucy, without any obligation to my culture."

"What did they say?" I was now excited by the idea of having Lucy in our family. "Did they say yes?"

"They said they would think about it." She seemed sad, as though this lack of commitment now was more than she could deal with, tiresome and difficult. She went back to reading her book.

"Okay, let's talk about Confucius. Is he like Jesus? I can tell you some really weird stories about some of the religions I've seen in the States," I said with an all-knowing smirk. I was hoping I'd be able to talk to her about the drowning part they did during revival meetings in Kentucky. Instead, I was given a lecture.

"Confucianism is a belief in a proper social order. It is a dictate on how a society is to be ordered, structured, and properly run," she said in a low, modulated voice. "Our country has had this belief as its foundation for centuries. Foreigners seem to have no understanding of this way of behaving. What is happening now is the questioning of that order. It is a difficult time here in Vietnam. We will talk more about this later," she said as she looked at her watch.

Taking her hat up and placing it on her head, she got ready to leave. She had to go to school, even though it was Saturday. Her bike was set near the gate. She placed her brown satchel filled with books and papers on the back carrier of the bike. It was one of those bikes that was very popular with the young women. It had a motor attached to the front fender with a shift to put the motor into its proper gear. No peddling; it simply glided along. She turned back to look at me as she passed through the gate, smiling and waving. The sound of her bike engine could be heard droning and hissing down the street.

Our ride to the Cerc had just arrived. It was early afternoon and Mom still had not returned from her outing. Just as I'd expected. I knew her errands would keep her out all day. The honk of the horn from the front driveway was the signal to get moving. I ran into the house through the back door and out the front screen door, grabbing my swim things. I jumped into the van along with Pati and Bob. For some reason, the Colonel had arranged for this van pickup. He didn't seem to want us taking a taxi or cyclo today. I'm sure my unaccompanied trip that morning to the PX would have made him furious. We were scheduled to pick up the Bingham kids. I was looking forward to seeing them.

As we traveled down Phan Thanh Giàn, we were surrounded by a mass of young men and women on their motorized bikes. They looked identical. Woman in white áo dais with black pants wore bamboo hats. Men in white button-down shirts with collars and black dress pants carried satchels on the backs of their bikes. They moved as one entity in the same direction. That morning, I had learned from Lucy that they were not all content. They were not a mass of people all the same, but individual Vietnamese people caught between the old and the new.

I felt sad for Lucy and wondered why my parents were hesitating about taking her with us. I mentally apologized for their lack of commitment to her. She had seemed so hopeful. If they hadn't said yes immediately, her chances seemed slim at best.

After we arrived at the Cerc and I took that first cool plunge into the crystal-blue water, all my concerns were washed from my mind. It was heaven to sit by the side of the pool in this completely isolated exotic world the French had created. My friend Janis and I had things to catch up on. I told her about my suspicions of our moving soon. Later, going to the bar area, I slowly ate my single piece of pound cake and sipped a Coca-Cola with its single ice cube. Heaven. Aromas rose from the club's kitchen as the cooks prepared evening dinners for the members and their guests. The smell of fish, cardamom seed, cumin, and garlic whirled through the bar's enclosure.

Another day in Saigon would be ending soon, fading into the violet darkness. I shut my eyes and let the warmth of the sun dry my wet swimsuit and add another layer of brown to my already dark skin. A wind was kicking up and blew across the water, catching the exchanges of small talk all around me, sending snippets into my dreams. I awoke to the touch of small, warm, soft fingers on my face. Pati and Bob broke into laughter when I finally opened my eyes.

A Moment in History

"What allowed Vietnam to finally create a separate state from China was the introduction of a written alphabet known as quoc ngu that wasn't dependent on the symbolic writing of the Chinese. This new script made it possible to communicate across the country and to unify the people. "Quoc ngu was developed by a Portuguese Jesuit missionary in the seventeenth century. It was neglected until the nineteenth century, when it was taken up by the French colonial government as a means of breaking the grip of Chinese culture and fostering Western ways of thinking. Its simplicity and the ease of its use—it was much simpler than Chinese characters—resulted in its gradual spread, especially when it was seized on by the Vietnamese reformers in the twentieth century as a means of breaking free from Chinese tradition and spreading mass literacy. It was eventually chosen as the official Vietnamese written language only in the twentieth century. "

—*Christopher Nguyen,* Origins of the Vietnamese Writing System: Quoc Ngu, *April 2, 2015*

CHAPTER 32:

FIVE WAYS OUT

L ike the spark of a single match, small flashes of distur-
bances were happening everywhere around us now.
All of them indirect, like the sound of a shot that wasn't
clear, resembling more the rustle of leaves on a still night.
In 1962, the breeze was steadily picking up. A storm
was brewing.

I had been listening to the Colonel's growing disillu-
sionment with Vietnam and the interference of Washington
politicians in military operations here in Vietnam. Their
seeming dismissal of the information the MAAG advisors
were providing about the situation in Vietnam was at the
core of his disappointment. His frustration with all of them
had him in a constant state of irritation. The lack of cooperation from Vietnamese officers was no longer subtle; now it
was obvious. The promotion of inappropriate individuals to
various military offices was almost comical. The Colonel's
mood was alarming when he was home. Curt and somber,
he seemed to be in a world that was separate from all of
us. The Colonel began to mutter one phrase an alarming
number of times during the day: "Damn politicians!" We

stayed quiet and steered clear whenever possible. His mood had all of us kids tiptoeing around him.

Tom was back from school now on summer break. His report card hadn't been up to the Colonel's expectations, perfect fodder for a storm with "the old man." Tom knew to keep as far out of reach and sight as he could get, after having had a full-frontal attack by the Colonel on the subject when he arrived home. This included an in-the-face interrogation with the finger-thumping-on-the-chest move. The Colonel seemed to focus on Tom the most of all us kids. It was as though he saw Tom as a reflection of himself, and Tom had to be better than him. The weight of that responsibility was more than Tom could tolerate. It wasn't a pleasant thing to see. When the Colonel decided to focus on any of us nega- tively, Mom stayed out of the conflict. Her strategy was to discuss it with him the next day when he was calm. It was the Southern way. This was how she handled him, never having a direct argument. She was clever.

We'd been in Saigon almost two years now, though I wasn't sure of the departure date. The Colonel hadn't pulled the globe out to announce a transfer yet. It had been packed and put in storage before we had left the States. All of us were buried in our separate worlds. Our parents had their lives. We children had our own. One thing was being made crystal clear now to all of us kids: no going anywhere alone! The routine of the movie theater stayed the same. I didn't heed their warnings as far as the black-market was concerned, however. The servants would accompany us to the PX and wait until we boarded the bus. They were also supposed to be there to bring us home when the bus returned. What we did in between, however, was unaffected. I was back at the black market without any issues. My customers continued to buy my goods, leaving me with stacks of pias-ters to fill my pockets. My disheveled smoking Vietnamese lookout still showed up to hide between the stalls. My little vendor and I continued to barter to our hearts' content for the treasures he sold. As Tom was home now, I could count on him for support; sometimes he went to the market with me and then swung by to pick me up. He was back to his old ways and wasn't about to miss his pool games and *ba muoi ba*. Tom was spending his share of the money on *ba muoi ba*, black market cigarettes, and pool hall bets.

The new curfew was to prove a major problem for Tom, however. He had bought a motorbike earlier that year, but being away at school, he hadn't had much chance to use it. He wasn't the extra passenger on the back seat of his friend's bike anymore, but the one driving. It was killing him not to be able to go out at night. He'd gotten an Itom motorbike, Italian made, and it was probably his first real love. It was red and white. Allowances were made for him in the daytime, as long as he didn't go anywhere alone. For us three younger kids, the only reprieve we got was when we'd be dropped off for the movie bus. The driver became our chaperone.

Tom didn't ride the bus with us, so the little kids and I continued buying items from the PX prior to boarding the bus. I'd do a little money exchange once Pati and Bob had left the building and were out of sight. They were more than willing participants in the business now. I paid them off in candy and whatever else they wanted. Their dental issues were incredible when we got back to the States. Mom seemed baffled by how that could have happened. We all played dumb regarding any questions.

Roaring up on his bike in front of the black-market sometimes at the close of business to get his cut, Tom dropped me back by the gates of the storefront of "the underground theater." I hated motorcycles, so sitting on the back seat and clinging to him had my nerves frayed. That didn't happen often. He still viewed me as an unreliable partner and encountered me as little as possible. I'd gotten a watch so I could keep to a tight schedule and not miss the kids or the bus home. No need to be caught at this stage of the game.

These days, Lucy was becoming more and more restless. Sometimes, she would be the person assigned to accompany us to the PX and pick us up. Were my parents going to take her with us or not when we left? I began to share her anxiety about the situation.

"Lucy says her mom asked you to take her with us. Can we? We love her! She'd be great to have with us. Can we? Please," I said, trying my utmost to be such a pain in the ass that Mom would give in to my begging. It didn't work, of course.

Although open to the idea when it had been proposed, Mom and the Colonel were too distracted now to commit to anything. Maybe the Colonel wasn't sure he could get approval. I never knew if he tried or not. I want to believe he did. Lucy seemed so disappointed at their lack of commitment, as was her mother. They were worried about what was going to happen to them after we left. They knew things were changing in 1962. It was obvious that Vietnam would not have a quick resolution to its problems.

Ongoing protests were taking place around town, and the papers were full of the issues that now troubled the country. Students were protesting the government's harassment and the persecution of their teachers. Buddhist monks had become actively involved and were being imprisoned. Lucy sided with these protests, but she was also worried about the fact that her family worked for Americans. People were being targeted by Nhu's spies in every part of the city for these associations. Still living in a French colonial fantasy, Mom didn't let herself get pulled into the mood of alarm.

"You'll stay with the house of course," Mom said to the servants. "You don't need to worry. There will be another family moving in." She would throw these remarks out as she scurried out of the house to yet another bridge game with the embassy wives.

That wasn't what worried Thi Ba, Thi Tu, or Lucy. There was more going on beneath the surface than any of us realized at the time. We had inklings. If I'd been older or clearer about what Lucy was saying to me in my many "lessons" with her, I might have had a better understanding of how fragile the world we were living in was. It was already a tentatively bolstered-up world, an artificial structure that had no real base.

Colonel *Sâm* had made visits to the house at various times over the previous year, even after he had been relieved of his rank and duties in the South Vietnamese Army. He and his family hadn't been harmed so far. After *Sâm* was let go from ARVN, the Colonel had gotten him a job with an American construction company subcontracted to build airfields throughout South Vietnam. *Sâm* was grateful. Nothing had changed the friendship or loyalty that the two felt for each other. It was probably the only time I ever saw the Colonel allow someone other than family into his emotional life. He always kept people politely at a distance. He held Colonel *Sâm* in high regard. This wasn't something he easily granted anyone. They seemed to be united by a curious sort of bond. Mom had previously always been responsible for developing the friendships and creating the social planet that whirled around them.

One day, late in the afternoon, Colonel *Sâm* arrived, driving a small two-door Renault. Tom had been told to go down to the gate and quickly let him in when he arrived. He was to shut the gate behind *Sâm* immediately when he was inside the yard. *Sâm* drove in and parked the car where it couldn't be seen from the roadway. He seemed in a hurry. He jumped out of the car and moved toward the villa at a fast pace. Small and graceful, he crossed the room to where we kids were spread out on the sofa and floor. He was a beautiful man with distinct features and a comforting smile. Glad to see *Sâm* again, the Colonel motioned for him to sit down. *Sâm* always greeted everyone first before sitting and proceeded to do so.

"Sorry to interrupt. I wanted to see you before you and your family leave," he said to the Colonel once he had finished with the pleasantries of the day to our mother and acknowledgement of us children. He was such a kind person.

I sat straight up and focused my attention on the two men. Leave? *How is it he knows stuff I don't?* I thought. *He probably even knows the date too.* I was fuming, and my mind was ricocheting. *Why can't these parents of ours ever let us know what is happening? I have a lot to do before we leave town! What about the animals? What will happen to them? And how can we leave Thi Ba, Thi Tu, and Lucy?* I fell into a sulking mood distracted by my thoughts, barely hearing any of the conversation between Sam and the Colonel. I had to get busy!

Pati noticed the cloud brewing over my head, something that was to be checked on in case it was to affect her and Bob. It was one of the survival techniques she had developed for herself.

"Something wrong?" she ventured, showing a keen and mobile face. Her tone was low and puzzled.

"Shut up. I'm listening," I snapped back with a testy growl as my attention returned to the two men nearby. I strained to overhear their conversation.

Sâm eyed me, hearing my comment. Turning, he said to the Colonel, "Maybe we speak in private?" His sunken eyes had a look of pain and chagrin, highlighting his premature wrinkles. He motioned the Colonel outside. *Sâm* lit a cigarette. Bolting from a reclined position, I rushed toward the stairway and mounted the steps two at a time. Reaching the upstairs balcony, I quietly moved into position overhead to continue listening.

"I am to go upcountry to work on another airfield. I was worried that you might be leaving before I got back," he said slowly and thoughtfully. "There are many problems now. As you know, Nhu has everyone watched, and it is dangerous for me to be seen with you. I could not let you leave without saying goodbye from myself and my family. My wife, Ngai, and my children send their kind regards and affection. You have been a good friend to us," *Sâm* said. He said this but couldn't look the Colonel directly in the eye; it was too hard for him.

"*Sâm*, do you want me to get you and your family out?" the Colonel said. "I can arrange it for the whole family, but I need to know soon."

"No worries. I have five ways out for my family and myself." He began to talk about a few of them. Their voices lowered for some time, so I didn't catch any of it. I would never know what the five ways out were. I turned and bounded back down the stairs in time to see the Colonel and *Sâm* reenter the living room.

They stood together in the entryway of the house. With parting farewells to Mom and the rest of the family, *Sâm* turned to go, extending a hand to the Colonel. He stopped suddenly. Instead, he embraced him. His eyes were glistening. He quickly turned and walked down the driveway. Rushing out to open the gate, Tom quickly closed it behind him. *Sâm* was gone just as suddenly as he had appeared. The sound of his car engine could be heard for a short time afterward. There was a disappointed and forlorn look on the Colonel's face that remained there for the rest of the afternoon. He was convinced that he would never get to see his dear friend again.

My mind was racing. I was annoyed. He was hiding something from me. I was in a fever. I was stuck in the house and wasn't allowed out alone anymore. My only hope was Chou. Later that week, he appeared at the school to take us swimming at the Cerc. He stood in the driveway waiting for us with an air of involuntary boredom, patiently smoking. With all the signs pointing toward the possibility that everything was soon coming to an end for us, I had hatched a plan and was well ahead of schedule. I'd taken to carrying the larger Vietnamese piaster notes with me at all times. Pati and I climbed into the jeep. Bob had stayed home this day. Whispering my directions in Chou's ear, he bolted back with a baffled look. I simply said, "Drive on."

"No! Colonel going to kill me!" Chou cried in distress at my proposal.

"Either you take us to the airport or I tell about when you took us that time we went to ARVN headquarters!" I wasn't backing down, not now, not when my entire financial future was at stake.

"You bad girl! Colonel know how bad you are? Your monkey named Mou Hou Lui, but you Mou Hou Lui! You no good girl!" He eyed me, no longer seeing the little girl he thought had saved him. I was going to get him in trouble, and he was worried. I gave him my best "do what I say" sneer, the one that worked so well with the younger kids. He put the jeep in gear.

Giving me a look of complete irritation, he said, "You going to make big trouble for Chou!" Pati and I clutched the sides of the jeep for dear life as he wheeled out of the school entry circle. Bob was sick with some intestinal thing from eating who knows what and wasn't with us. I guess Chou figured if we were going to be able to cover for this side trip, he was going to have to make time. Faster and faster we drove, weaving in and out between the bikes and horse-drawn carts. Small banging cars and masses of people on bikes and scooters surrounded us. A multitude of smells mixed with the trail of dust we were churning up. We pulled our shirts up over our noses.

The day was like every other day, a perfect blue sky with the sun at its peak. To my surprise, we made it to the Tân Sơn Nhứt airport in half the time it usually took. Windswept, with my short hair standing straight up and a layer of dust covering my face, I slid out of the jeep and headed for the terminal doors. I caught a glimpse of my reflection in the glass as I passed by. A skinny, stringy-looking kid in Vietnamese tailored clothes, appearing more like a boy than a girl, with dark brown skin, stared back at me. I had to laugh. I was no longer that chalky, innocent-looking ten-year-old with permed blond hair in new Sears clothes who had gotten off the plane two years earlier. Shrugging it off, I pushed the door back.

Chou and Pati waited. Chou had a cigarette lit before I'd even made it past the front of the jeep. Pati, wondering what adventure we were now on, was willing to patiently wait it out. *This could be fun* was always the thought she'd have to keep herself from getting frightened. It was midday and the sun high in the sky. Luckily, Chou had parked under a covering that gave some shade. His lit cigarette smoldered in the corner of his mouth. They waited.

Now, there were several parts to my carefully laid-out money-exchange plan. Not all of it had been completely worked out, but it was a changing masterpiece as far as I was concerned. I had hundreds and hundreds of dollars' worth of piasters by this point. I don't think Tom had a cent left from his share, but I'd successfully hidden my money over the two-year period. I wasn't going to find myself duped out of it by not getting the money exchanged now. I had already changed the smaller bills at the PX, and now it was time for cashing out the larger notes.

In the airport, I counted out my piasters and asked for the exchange to be in American greenbacks. The exchange rate at the time was seventy piasters to the dollar. On the black market, it was around ninety piasters to the dollar, Tom's choice of money exchange when he used green-backs. The man behind the counter didn't even bother to look up, let alone acknowledge that a child was making the trade. He could not have cared less. I came out of the airport exit with a smile stretched across my face from ear to ear. Things were going to be just fine. I'd figure out the next part of what to do with the money once I knew where we were headed. For now, this was good enough.

Our two-year stay in Vietnam had changed me. My approach to the world was completely different now than when we'd arrived in Saigon. I had become wary of the world around me, always keeping track of everything and everyone. Sizing up any situation quickly, I made my moves accordingly. I was vigilant in my watch over the younger kids. Memorizing every detail of where we went and how we got there, just in case something happened, I would be able to take charge and find our way home. I even paid attention to how Chou drove the jeep with its stick shift in case I had to jump into the driver's seat during an emergency and drive us all somewhere. I kept money in my pocket at all times. On constant alert, I was no longer a distracted, self-absorbed American kid. Saigon had changed me, and I didn't know yet if it was for the better or not.

Chou dropped us at the Cerc and quickly left to pick up the Colonel. He was glad to be done with me. The trail of smoke from his cigarettes lingered. We stayed for a little while, swimming, and caught a cyclo home with Thi Tu a few hours later. As Pati and I pushed the screen door open, the room's coolness could be felt. A sweating pitcher of lemonade waited for us on the dining room table. The room was always filled with the essence of lemons; the same smell that had greeted us on our very first day met us every day. Some things were constant, without change; this was one of them.

Pati and I trudged upstairs, leaving a trail of towels and wet clothes as we made our way skyward to check on Bob. He'd spent an entire day in bed. He looked like a pampered kitten sitting up with a pile of pillows behind him. He'd been told that if he was sick, he had to stay in the bed all day. Lots of games, comics, and empty plates surrounded him. He loved it when he got to stay home and had this kind of attention, though I suspect he didn't want to have to stay in bed the entire day.

It was rather amusing to see Bob lounging so comfortably. I was sure he wasn't sick at all. Good for him, though. He had gotten what he wanted: love and attention, female warmth from whoever would give it to him. Being the youngest child in this family wasn't easy, I was sure, though I'd never stopped to consider his situation specifically. I sat down opposite him, leaning forward and staring into his eyes.

"You weren't really sick, were you?" I said, putting my warm hand on his brow.

"I'm not telling you. You'll tell!" he said coldly, pushing my hand away and giving me a look of defiance. Pati just laughed, glad to see someone take me on. In the end, we were all laughing and jumping on the bed. Luckily, no one saw us. How much easier it is to settle things in childhood. When we became adults, it was so much harder to dismiss the things that life dropped at our feet.

A MOMENT IN HISTORY

"President Diệm had been holding his own. The economy had not been booming, but it had not been contracting either. Now the American Institute's 'broad social program' was imposed to raise living standards in South Vietnam. The seventy-one percent tax on luxury goods and the tax on foreign exchange—an indirect tariff on all imports—sent prices up in the cities, which meant a decline in purchasing power related to country goods. The military situation began to erode almost immediately.

As the economy contracted in the spring of 1962, Diệm pleaded for relief from the 'buy American' rule. It also led him to increase his authoritarian attempts to regain control, seeing no other solution and by now wary of the advice of his American counselors. But the accumulated social tension of an economy in sharp contraction grew to be an explosive force and could not be contained in authoritarian hands."

—*Jude Wanniski,* The Way the World Works, *1978*

CHAPTER 33:

KEEP CALM AND CARRY ON

A s I mentioned, when we lived in the first house on Đoàn Thị Điểm in 1960, we were just down the street from the American ambassador, Elbridge Durbrow. He had made his career in the Foreign Service and left Saigon on May 5, 1961. The entire family met him once, though I couldn't tell you when or where. In 1962, his replacement was Frederick E. Nolting Jr., also from the Foreign Service office. Nolting was a firm supporter of President Diệm. He was to leave office on August 15, 1963, to be replaced by Henry Cabot Lodge, a political appointee and not a supporter of the Diệm regime.

After a random bombing and a few other strange incidents around Saigon in May of 1962, Ambassador Nolting issued a letter to the American community. It was meant to calm everyone. Unfortunately, it displayed an obvious ignorance of the shift away from support for American involvement that was going on all around him.

The Colonel read it to us that evening when we were all together spread out on the floor. He thought it best to remind us to be on alert and thought Nolting's communiqué would serve that purpose.

TO ALL AMERICAN CITIZENS IN SAIGON
May 20, 1962

During the past few days, unknown assailants (presumably Viet Cong Terrorists) have made two grenade attacks within the city of Saigon. These attacks have caused injuries to ten Vietnamese, including two children, two Germans and three Americans. Despite the nationalities of those injured, there is some reason to believe that the attacks were directed primarily against Americans. It is my conviction, however, as well as that of my staff, that the American citizens living in this area should not become unduly alarmed by these incidents.

The attacks serve to remind us that similar attacks have occurred from time to time in the past and that they may quite possible [sic] occur in the future. Certainly, they indicate that the assailants have both an intention and limited ability to attempt to create panic and disorder. The very fact that they have had little success so far is a tribute to the efficiency and devotion to duty of the Vietnamese police and security authorities.

Considering the entire matter in perspective, both the incidents which have already occurred and the possibility that more may occur during the imme-diate future, I urge all American citizens to retain their customary composure [and] to continue to carry out their duties and at the same time to conduct themselves with prudence, taking such precautions as common sense suggest under the circumstances, bearing in mind previous notices on this general subject.

Frederick E. Nolting, Jr.
Ambassador[5]

"He's kidding, right? Can he be serious in writing this?" Mom said when her husband had finished reading the letter, annoyed that he might be hiding something from her.

She shook her head in disbelief. He offered no response, and so we would, in fact, go on about our business as was recommended in the letter. We would continue to conduct ourselves with "prudence" and "customary composure"

The calm of this country had changed. Change sometimes is not a thing that comes suddenly. It can be slow, like the tide. Once living outside time, Vietnam had been a country bound by a cherished order. A new fear now gripped it, and the terror orchestrated by the Diệm government, as well as by the rebel forces, could not be dispelled. The stability of Saigon had been undermined forever. The politicians, military, and agencies from countries trying to gain control didn't seem to be aware of it. For that matter, was the reigning regime even aware of that fact?

The official transfer orders finally came through for us. The Hanna family would be leaving Vietnam in June 1962. Although told we were being transferred to a military base stateside, we kids weren't sure where we would be going. At first, we heard it would be Pennsylvania, then it was to be Virginia. We would be returning to the United States, and for the moment that was enough to know. As usual, our parents didn't say anything to us about exactly when in June we'd be leaving. That wouldn't happen until a week or so before the actual date of departure.

"You can only take a couple of things with you, so start thinking about what that is going to be," Mom said. "Set them aside and put your names on them, so I know which ones you have picked."

Our toys, the ones we were to leave behind, would be given to the Vietnamese children who surrounded our compound, those playing in the nearby waterworks and street. I kept a tight watch on my cigar box's hiding place and chose two things on which I wouldn't compromise: one was the microscope I'd gotten from Hong Kong, and the other was the carved mahogany horse head bookends we'd picked up from the Philippines when we were there to visit Tom at his school. Pati and I had both gotten porcelain dolls from Hong Kong. She chose these and smuggled mine in with hers, I found out later. She was a much nicer person than I was. Bob chose something and later wondered why he had picked it.

Tom was hoping desperately to get his motorbike approved for a return to the States. He'd been a biker raging through the streets of Saigon on it. Free. It represented something to him that he wasn't about to let go of. "The old man" dragged out approving Tom's request until the last possible moment. Tom, in turn, tried to appear not to care one way or the other, trying to demonstrate to the Colonel that he didn't have complete power over him. Tom was miserable but kept a level head throughout the psychological manipulation imposed on him by the Colonel. It was always confusing to me watching this moronic dance between the two of them. The Colonel finally agreed. Tom had long ago given up trying to please him. Getting the okay to bring the bike back to the States meant a lot to the boy. The Colonel knew it.

My total act of rebellion had to do with Mou Hou Lui, my monkey. I threw tantrums, stomped around angrily, and swore. This resulted in my having a soap taste in my mouth for days. Ivory was Mom's bar of choice. I tried everything I could think of, even being sweet and hoping to appeal to the kinder side of either of my parents. They had long since given up taking sides with us. In the end, all the animals would have to be found homes. This was my darkest hour.

They were my friends, all my animals—my family, as far as I was concerned. I was miserable. Pati and Bob wailed with me on the injustice of being a kid with no rights. The servants simply viewed our carrying on with humor. They knew there would be no winning this one. From their point of view, the will of heaven would prevail and we would have no influence on any of it. We were finally given the exact date of our transfer by Mom.

The days dragged on. The usual goodbyes were said. Not ones like, "I'll see you in the States" or, "Catch you later." We knew we most likely would never see any of our friends again. Funny how leaving never seemed to cause any of us issues. There was never an expectation of seeing anyone we knew again anyway. It would be unusual if we did. BRATs are used to it. To make a big deal about this would have been much ado about nothing. It was the same for all of us kids in Saigon.

Things were speeding up now. What had once seemed a slow progression of the seasons now was a life cramped into a short time frame. The Army had our house packed up, and even that beast of a car was taken away to be shipped. The Colonel had hoped to sell it in Saigon, but he hadn't had any luck. We waited for the day we'd be departing. Pati and I were housed at a friend's house. Bob and Tom stayed together somewhere else. Pati was a good sport and just followed my lead whenever required. We'd been read the riot act about being on our best behavior or there would be consequences. We saw neither of our parents during this time.

"Do you think they forgot about us?" Pati said one day when we were all at the Cerc together. A look of sheer alarm flashed across Bob's face. Our host families made the Cerc a regularly coordinated activity each day, so we kids could see each other.

"No, they are just busy," I said, though the thought had occurred to me. I wasn't worried yet. I knew I could find my way around Saigon by myself if I had to go looking for them. Each night, we'd sit outside on the veranda of our borrowed lodgings, Pati and I, watching the lengthening pale violet rays of the afternoon slowly fade. We'd linger near the garden, listening to the sounds of crickets with their busy night songs filling the air. The family we were staying with had agreed to take my monkey, Mou Hou, so Pati and I would take her out of the cage on these evenings. She was as displaced as we were.

"What do you think Tom and Bob are doing?" Pati said quietly.

"Probably the same thing as us. Just waiting to be picked up." I could tell it was important to her that I wasn't worried about anything. It allowed her to feel safe. I kept any concerns I might have had to myself. It was a lonely time, but I kept calm and carried on. The evening would end with our crawling into our bed to wait for whatever the new day would hold. Where our parents were staying, we had no idea. We never asked. We were good soldiers. We took it all on the chin, in true military fashion. We were settling into our unpredictable future, a process that is part and parcel of every move for a BRAT.

CHAPTER 34:

UNTIL WE MEET AGAIN

On February 8, 1965, military dependents were evacuated from Saigon at the Tân Sơn Nhứt airport. My family and I had been deployed three years earlier, in 1962, without the type of curt sendoff so many of the remaining kids got at that time. Most of those kids during that evacuation were simply told by their parents that they would or would not return home after school, that they might be leaving Vietnam instead. They were told to pack things they might like to take with them in case they had to leave. One girl was told that she and her family were going to the beach. She brought her pail and shovel along with her swimsuit. It was orchestrated so that it would not be obvious that an evacuation would be taking place. Our exit in 1962 was more traditional: orders received, belongings packed and shipped in advance, all of us kids spread out around town sleeping with friends until the assigned departure date. We'd be riding in the same plane we had come over on, a four-engine prop. At least, that was the way it was supposed to happen.

Prior to our leaving the house on Phan Thanh Giàn, I'd spent days trying to figure out where all my animals would go. The turkeys found a home with an American civilian family working with one of the government-contracted construction companies. They lived over in the "Little America" subdivision near the airport. These people weren't on two-year limits. They took my red rooster too. I made them swear they would not eat any of them. Fluffy, that ridiculous poodle-shepherd mix, would be left with the house we were leaving and taken care of by the servants until the new residents moved in. I hated leaving our best dog, Inky, our first pet. His old love, our maid Anna from the first house on Đoàn Thị Điểm, came to get him. She took him with her to a new house she was to be at in Cholon. We'd gotten him as a puppy at the first house. He was a loyal family member.

The stork had died earlier that summer, killed by a bunch of bananas that had broken off during a storm. He had lain lifeless under its weight. We had a massive funeral, a mix of Eastern and Western ideas. I read a verse from the Bible over him, lit incense, and had the two younger kids attempting a Buddhist chant in the background. It was quite colorful. Our sense of all things religious had become a confused mess. Momma Cat was given a new home across town. To our amazement, she somehow made her way back to our house by the next day. It was decided, after such a valiant effort on her part, to let her stay with the house. The servants promised to take care of her too. My monkey, Mou Hou, was the hardest one for me to leave. Luckily, until we were to catch our flight I was staying at that friend's house who was taking her. Mou Hou was upset by the move. I found out later, after we left, that she had chewed through the wire that same day and gone over their wall, never to be seen again.

On the day that we were to leave, Mom arrived to collect us. She had called the houses her children were staying at to tell them to keep us there until she arrived. She found us ready and waiting outside in the soft air under a cloudless sky. We stood at attention near the gate with our packed bags next to us, waiting. She arrived in one of the big black government sedans that were so much a part of the American presence in Saigon. It was a beautiful day with a light wind. We made our way to the airport, navigating through the throngs of humanity already swarming the highway. Mom said that our father was completing some final work at the office and would join us at the airport. Tom and Bob were already in the car when Pati and I climbed inside. We were happy to see everyone, relieved that our mother remembered to come for all of us. The sweetness of their voices as they greeted Pati and I signaled that they were just as relieved as I was to be together again.

Pulling bags out of the vehicle, climbing over each other, we lumbered into the terminal, burdened down with our possessions. We had arrived at the airport with hours to spare, only to find out there was no flight available for the family that day. An engine had dropped off the plane en route from Thailand. It was not going to be making any flights that day and would return to Bangkok for repairs instead. After hearing that announcement, I was more than happy to not get on that plane. We weren't looking forward to what we knew would be a long and tedious flight back to the United States. We knew that multiple stops over many days awaited us.

The Colonel had the transfer orders in hand when he finally arrived at Tân Sơn Nhứt airport, only to find that the flight had been cancelled. Completely irritated, even though it was something that could not be helped, he ordered us to return to the houses where we had been staying. He dashed back through the airport doors. Luckily, Chou was still there waiting. Orders would have to be changed now. The Colonel took off in the jeep with tires squealing. He'd need new paperwork to leave on the next available flight, whatever day that might be.

Mom hailed a cab. Our government sedan had already departed. Leaving our baggage at the airport, she stuffed us kids into the small blue-and-yellow Renault taxi, retracing her route to the airport and dropping Pati, Bob, Tom, and me off at our assigned houses. Mom left for who knows where. Pati and I settled in for what we thought would be the rest of the day in the spacious garden with Mou Hou. While the Colonel was trying to work things out in some kind of official military way, Mom had beat it over to Lieutenant General McGarr's house and was in negotiations there. In retrospect, I think our mother was a complete mystery. She was probably one of the best manipulators ever born. Those Southern ways of hers were totally disarming. I came to this conclusion after studying her for years after this singular event occurred. I don't know what she had on the general, if anything, or if it was the general's wife who finally got to exercise some power over the general. Maybe she was just able to charm him like she did everyone else. All I know is that only a few hours later, we were picked up again and taken to the airport. Instead of a military transport, what awaited us—and had been waiting for some hours—was a beautiful Pan Am 707. We kids were dumbfounded. The state department kids had talked about their luxury trips over to Vietnam on these jets. We military kids had been more than jealous.

The small taxi Mom had picked us up in looked like a clown car as the five of us climbed out, one right after the other. We slid into the terminal and headed for the ticket desk. Six neatly-dressed stewardesses who had planned on riding standby back to Hong Kong stood near the check-in desk. They had been given orders to disembark, but they waited near the gate hoping that a change might occur. Fat chance! We were the ones who would be replacing them, taking their seats! Seeing our motley crew arrive, their eyes took us in and registered a clear understanding of how things stood. Their chances of getting out of Saigon now were slim to none. We let out a cheer right then and there in the terminal at the sight of that beautiful blue-and-white jet waiting for us. No multiple days of travel with fights and squabbles or those dreaded brown ration boxes. We were going to ride home in luxury. Had Mom known this was going to happen?

The Colonel wasn't with us, however. He told us later on the plane what happened. At headquarters, while he was trying to arrange a new departure date, he'd finally gotten word of the miraculous change of events. Handed a new, expedited set of orders, no doubt issued by the general, he tore out of the office. Chou was waiting in front for him.

He jumped into the jeep, shouting, "Get the hell out of here! Tân Sơn Nhứt airport, Chou!" They sped toward the airport, only to be stopped by a line of Vietnamese uniformed guards just outside the terminal area. There was a problem.

As the rest of the family anxiously waited at the terminal exit door leading to the jet, the Colonel wasn't that far away. He and Chou were sitting on the opposite side of the airport tarmac, as a regiment of police and palace guards were keeping traffic from crossing. They were told that President Diệm was landing in a private plane. He was returning to Saigon from a trip upcountry.

"Just drive through!" the Colonel shouted at Chou.

"No. You leave and me stay. I no do because no good for me or you. When you gone, I still here," he said emphatically, perhaps the first time he'd ever disobeyed an order from the Colonel.

As they waited for what seemed like forever, President Diệm's cavalcade of vehicles finally passed. Diệm sat in the back of his chauffeured car in his signature white suit and dark sunglasses, looking through the closed window. There had been rumors of another coup brewing, and everyone was on high alert. There was no getting past the guards, no matter who you were.

When Diệm's procession of vehicles finally passed by the two men, the guards opened the roadblock. Chou gunned the jeep, shooting past everyone, hitting the brakes only when directly in front of the terminal building. Chou and the Colonel leaped out of the jeep at the same time. Grabbing the gear, Chou ran into the terminal, neck and neck with the Colonel. The Pan Am passengers had been sitting on the plane now for three hours, waiting for who knew what. They weren't a happy lot. Mom hadn't boarded yet, and we kids refused to make a move without her. She wasn't going out the terminal door until her husband arrived. Luckily, the pilots were under orders not to leave until the entire Hanna family was onboard. That order had come from above.

"Colonel! Until we meet again!" Chou shouted, throwing his travel bag to him. A broad smile stretched across his face. The Colonel slid through the entry gate with his bag in hand. Chou waited with his hand held high in the form of a wave, then slowly moved it down to his brow to form a full salute when the Colonel looked back at him.

The Colonel spun around and froze in place, returning the salute. Both men had smiles on their faces and sadness in their eyes at this final parting. Pulling a cigarette out from the pack in his upper shirt pocket, Chou turned and walked slowly back toward the jeep. He pushed the airport door open into the glaring light of the now sweltering afternoon. We kids could see him pulling himself into the jeep. As I thought about Chou, I imagined him now heading back to Saigon at full speed with the wind blowing in his ears, singing at the top of his lungs. That would be just like him, free, heading back to that timeless city—one that now showed a heartbreaking indifference to the departure of the Hanna family.

Spotting the Colonel running through the terminal, I started to walk lightly, effortlessly out the terminal door toward the plane. People on the plane were happy to see us, but were no doubt wondering who this motley crew of Army BRATs and their parents was who had caused such a delay. I thought the Colonel cut a very official-looking figure in his starched military uniform. We collapsed into our seats. It had already been a long day for us all. As the plane doors shut and the stewardess announced the services for the flight to Hong Kong, we settled back in our seats. I looked around at the decadence of this flight in comparison to the one we had come over on. Thanks to an act of God, we were not returning on it. I would most definitely choose this one. I felt like pampered royalty.

Mom had told me long ago that I had taken my first flight on a civilian airline when I was four weeks old. She had pulled out a certificate from the Sky Cradle Club to prove it. Yes, I'd been indoctrinated as a full-fledged member of the American Airlines Flagship Sky Cradle Club on the June 26, 1950. The plane was flying from Boston to New York. The stewardess, captain, and first officer had signed the certificate of membership. I wondered if Pam Am would give us a certificate of some sort for this trip too.

The stewardesses, beautiful women in smart blue dresses and sensible heels, with blue pillbox hats, came by with Pan Am pins for us kids along with coloring books. I slipped the pin into my cigar box that I clutched by my side. It made me think about the other pin I had there. It was from the visit I had made with the Colonel to the nuclear submarine, the *Nautilus*, earlier that year. Both pins were now nestled in the cigar box with my hard-earned money. I kept it all close to my chest. A big blue rubber band kept the box shut, keeping the contents inaccessible to anyone who might get curious when I dozed off. My thoughts were now focused on what lay ahead of me. and when I would get the chance to change my greenbacks into larger bills. I wouldn't be able to relax until this last step was complete.

I had a window seat. As I stared out at the billowy clouds above us and the surrounding landscape, a sudden wave of sadness covered me. My mind filled with thoughts of Saigon. I realized that everything would now become part of my past. The smell of the city was still entrenched in my nostrils. Its colors and sounds filled my brain. It would be a long time before these completely faded. I knew I would regret their loss when it happened, but I had always known that time would come. It was always that way.

The stewardesses we'd bounced off the flight were standing along the gate, no longer looking hopeful and probably muttering under their breath. I know I would be. The plane taxied down the runway. Metal buildings filled with workers inside and outside lined the tarmac around the main terminal. Huge flame trees bordered the roadway beyond the terminal. The plane sped forward as its engines revved up to a high-pitched whine. The nose lifted effortlessly skyward. Below us spread the buildings and streets of Saigon, the outlying rice fields, the Saigon River. The landscape resembled pieces of a puzzle as we flew over the villages and rice paddies. Forests and roadways created patterns discernable only from high up through our windows. Eventually, it all disappeared. We had entered a huge bank of bilious gray and white clouds.

The image reflected in the window pane was of a boy-like child with dark circles under her eyes. It was me. A furrow was etched in my brow. The reflection before me seemed to be the face of an older person. Across the aisle, dressed fashionably and sporting an air of self-control, sat our mother. The Colonel sat next to her, looking tired, with eyes closed. Tom, slim and good-looking, was stretched out in his signature dragon shirt. It suited his current projected air of superiority. He wasn't going to be taking crap from anyone now. Pati had the same short hair and tight-fitting, boyish Vietnamese tailored clothing as me. She didn't look as much like a boy as I did. She was just too cute. I was sorry she wasn't in one of the dresses I knew she liked. Bob had dark circles under his eyes too, and all his hair had been shaved off. He looked like life had been hell. We kids had lived a life separate from our parents. We had reached a place during these two years where we now treated each other with a reserved affection, behaving more like friends than sibling rivals. I closed my eyes and attempted sleep, drifting off into a world unto itself as the noises blurred around me. When I awoke, I quietly climbed over Pati and walked down the aisle to where the Colonel was seated. He gazed up at me with a questioning look.

"What is it, Sandy?" he asked in a low, puzzled tone.

"Did it make any difference? Our being in Vietnam, did we help? Will everyone be all right? Will Colonel Sâm, Lucy, Thi Ba, and Thi Tu be okay? What's going to happen now?" I asked in a hushed tone, a voice squeaky and nervous—a schoolgirl's voice.

He considered how to answer me. After pausing, he decided to offer a simple response. "It will be what it is going to be. We will be okay." It wasn't the answer I was looking for, but looking back, I don't know if he knew. For now, his concern was in just getting all of us out of Vietnam safe.

We had finally been told at the airport that we would be temporarily staying at the Fort Lewis Army Base near Seattle, Washington, until our car arrived. The delay at this military base would not be long. We stayed in Hong Kong and Tokyo for an extended rest and relaxation period before arriving in Seattle. This marvelous schedule had been worked out by Lt. General McGarr, though I'm sure Mom gave her input. I guess he selected what was available on Pan Am that day. That was fine with me. I wasn't ready to return to the States yet anyway. I needed time to adjust.

What a pleasure the return trip was compared to the one that had brought us to this part of the world. Night and day! The hotel rooms in Tokyo and Hong Kong were opulent and extravagant. There were glass chandeliers everywhere. You could drink the water directly out of the tap and brush your teeth with it without any fear of getting sick! Food could be ordered and delivered to the room at any hour of the day or night. I loved the English four o'clock tea schedule in Hong Kong. I would order it daily, with as many sweets as I could find on the menu.

"I take my afternoon tea with lots of milk and sugar, thank you," I said as they wheeled in a full cart with the tea service and towering plates of desserts. The attendant would pour my first cup of tea, looking so smart in the hotel uniform with its shiny buttons. Very proper. I'd sign for the delivery. Our parents were usually out shopping, so I stuffed my face until I couldn't eat another bite. Mom wondered why I never seemed to have any appetite when it was time for dinner. Pati and Bob joined me without complaint.

Eventually, we made it back to the United States and to the base, where, as I mentioned, we were to wait for our car to be delivered. It had been shipped weeks before on a freighter, but there was some sort of delay. A two-week stay in the guest quarters on this military base in Seattle was anticipated. That was the plan. The Colonel wanted us to be able to see the 1962 World's Fair and didn't mind the layover. I had a big problem, though. Although our parents had indicated that we were to be stationed at another military base in Virginia, Fort Monroe, I wasn't sure I could trust this information. The Colonel had gotten final orders when we were in Japan, but I wasn't taking any chances. I decided I had some work to do!

The day we were to go to the World's Fair, I feigned illness. I begged to be allowed to stay in bed while the rest of the family went to the fair. I put the thermometer under hot water before showing Mom, and it made a convincing argument for my being sick. I willingly took the aspirin she prescribed for a fever. She gave me a number to call if I got worse. They didn't want to cancel the day's outing. As soon as I was sure they were gone, I hightailed it out of the guest quarters to make the rounds of the Army post. First the PX, then the commissary and any other place that looked good for money exchange, including the base bank. These were all good targets for consolidating my smaller into larger bills. No one would take notice if I did this at several places. By the end of the day, I had changed all of it into larger bills. My new money wasn't as pretty as my Vietnamese piasters. At least I had money that was usable anywhere we went in the United States and easier to handle. I barely made it back to our quarters in time. Luckily for me, my exertions had resulted in a sweaty kid nestled under the covers when my family opened the door. They had shortened their stay at the fair because of me.

Mom shook her head as she felt my forehead. "How are you feeling?" she said with true motherly concern. She tucked the blankets closer.

I thought I'd die with heat but moaned my gratitude instead. "*Je me sans beaucoup mieux.*"

"Okay, now I know you're not well. You are talking in French to me, Sandy." She seemed even more concerned as she left to find something else to give me for whatever she thought ailed me. Pati and Bob stood near her, waiting.

"How was it?" I managed to say in a forced scratchy voice after she left, complete with all the drama a kid can muster when playing sick. The French was just another stroke of genius on my part as far as I was concerned.

"It was great! You have to get well so you can come tomorrow," Pati said, proceeding to jump on the bed. Bob moved over close to me and looked into my eyes.

"You aren't really sick, are you?" He had a smirking grin on his face like he understood everything these days. With that we all broke into uncontrollable laughter, the kind when you double up, nearly joining your knees to your nose. We couldn't stop. We needed this emotional release. It would be something that no adult would understand.

As I lay under the pile of covers, my trusty cigar box next to my side, I had to laugh. Life's possibilities were swirling in my mind now. I was thinking about the future: the horse I would buy, the Olympic trials I would compete in, the ribbons and trophies I would win. My plan started to grow to mythical heights. In a single moment, I had moved on. Saigon had been left behind, it seemed. Like all good military kids, I was on to the next chapter of my life, seemingly with no regrets. No looking back. I had money and felt I now had control of my life. Everything would be okay. I was sure of it.

We would drive back across the United States the same way we had come two years earlier. Disney World wasn't added to this return trip, however. We would arrive in Texas at our grandparents' house on Tom's birthday. We were always arriving somewhere on Tom's birthday. It was July 17, 1962.

Returning to the United States, we were all feeling somewhat displaced and distant from each other. We stayed on an Army post near Seattle to visit the 1962 World's Fair.

CHAPTER 35:

IN THE TIME OF MADNESS

So, we got out. Out before the world went crazy in South-east Asia. We left Vietnam, a country ready to explode, and entered the United States at a time when the threat of the entire world's being reduced to a nuclear wasteland was at its height. The exchange didn't seem fair. The tension we experienced while in the Far East was now magnified exponentially. We had been assigned a post in Fort Monroe, Virginia, in 1962. This was the headquarters of the United States Continental Army Command. Most of the officers there had also returned from overseas assignments. In fact, it was a place filled with high-ranking officers. The Colonel referred to it as having "a lot of chiefs and very few Indians."

We had crossed the country packed in the Ford Fairlane station wagon with all our baggage, from Seattle down to Texas, over to Kentucky, then to Virginia. Our furniture and other possessions had been sent directly from Saigon to Fort Monroe. Mom quickly set up house and put us all on schedules. It wasn't long, however, before we found ourselves smack dab in the Cold War with Cuba and Russia. For thirteen days in October 1962, the world was on the brink of a nuclear war. Confrontations between the United States and the Soviet Union over ballistic missiles in Cuba had brought about the crisis. Most Americans were not aware at that time that the missiles along the shores of Cuba were pointed at all the major cities in the United States and were fully loaded with nuclear capability. The Joint Chiefs of Staff were behaving as though this wasn't a possibility and probably would have died believing this. Fort Monroe was on high alert, on lockdown. What did we kids do? Simply settled into what seemed like just another time of unpredictable insanity. That is what all good military kids do, and we did it without asking any questions.

A simmering world meltdown was what was at stake. I had thought that by returning to the United States, we'd all be back on safe shores. We saw very little of the Colonel during those explosive days. With his Ordnance Corps expertise, he was shipped down to Homestead, Florida, to coordinate equipment and supplies for a potential invasion. For me, it seemed that the end of the world was coming, and nuclear bombs would be showering the earth from everywhere. I felt helpless. There wasn't a thing I could do.

Then, just as crazily as it had started, the crisis miraculously ended. President John F. Kennedy had initiated secret communications with Nikita Khrushchev of the Soviet Union. Kennedy had realized he couldn't count on the advice of the Joint Chiefs after the failed CIA-led Bay of Pigs invasion of Cuba in 1961. Neither Kennedy nor Khrushchev wanted to be the instigator of a nuclear war. Concessions were made on both sides for each of them to save face. The disarming and removal of Cuba's nuclear weapons began with the United States' reducing its missile inventory in Turkey. All of this was broadcast by the news stations, and I was watching closely.

Visible signs of sanity emerged, and I discovered to my utter amazement that I was going to live to see another day. With this sudden wave of relief, I found myself completely furious at the entire world for the kind of stupidity that would lead up to something like this. We were so close to the edge with these "war games." The arrogance of these men, thinking nuclear weapons would solve all their problems. Idiots! It was a time where insanity ruled, and every kind of possible craziness unfolded. It was a time of madness!

The Colonel's response to it all, once he returned from Florida, was simply to set Tom and me up in a liquor distribution business from the basement of our home. In true Colonel resourcefulness, after discovering there was no liquor sold on the post, he applied for a license to sell alcohol at Fort Monroe. The Cuban Missile Crisis had increased everyone's intake of alcohol significantly. Thus, began the start of the second business that Tom and I found ourselves partners in. "Damn if he isn't doing it to me again," Tom said as he ripped open a box of Johnny Walker bourbon. "You were too little to remember this, but the son of a bitch used to have me work all summer in that snack bar on the golf course at Fort Sill when we were in Oklahoma. I didn't get to play baseball or do anything else. He'd have me there from eight in the morning until dark. Stacking sodas and candy bars—you name it, he had me doing it. I was only eight years old, for God's sake. I did it for two years, and to top it off, he kept the damn money I had saved in the bank."

"Do you think other kids are doing this kind of stuff?" I said, moving the finished orders toward the doorway. I knew he had more information about the ways of the world than I did.

"No way! Everybody else is having a childhood. Just not us!" We were just about at the end of the day and were hopeful we'd have some free time that day. I decided to talk to him about a lingering fear I had. Now seemed as good a time as any.

"The world is crazy, Tom!" I said. "They were going to kill us for sure with those stupid bombs, and we weren't going to have a life! The whole world was going to be wiped out with their stupid bombs," I blurted out.

"I'm not going to worry about any of it. When it is over, it is over, and I intend to cause as much trouble as I can in the meantime. I always thought we wouldn't have a life anyway," he said in that nonchalant manner. I wondered if that was true or if he was just trying to look unfazed in front of me. Not long after this, the world began to fall apart around me.

On Sunday, November 3, 1963, the *Stars and Stripes* news service reported "Diem Toppled – Military Force Rules Saigon." The day before a military revolt topped the government, President Diệm and his brother Nhu were assassinated in the van transporting them from their hiding place in the Catholic Church in Cholon. They were shot and bayonetted by members of their own military. Even the Colonel didn't think they'd kill them. The leaders of the coup didn't want to risk them being able to regain power.

Later that month, it seemed like it was going to be just another day of classes. Our schools were off the Army post in the nearby civilian town. I was sitting in my seventh-grade English class in Hampton, Virginia, daydreaming and busily dissecting sentence structures. The squeaking sound of the intercom being turned on had all heads in the class lift and look toward the speaker hung high over the blackboard. The school principal thumped his finger against the microphone. Maybe school was going to be dismissed early. We sat silent. Hopeful. The principal's broken voice came over the loudspeaker. His words came in pieces, between strained silences. "President Kennedy was...shot... today...in Texas. We will...pause for a moment of silence." Silence. Black hole silence. Deafening stillness. Children began to cry. Some tried to catch the eye of another. Others simply kept their heads down low, wiping their tears on their sleeves. My reaction was one of sheer unadulterated anger. I let out a single dry, weary sob. It overwhelmed me to the point that I began to shake. A feeling of complete loss of hope for the world and for myself took hold.

I wept bitterly then, as I still do to this day for that moment. It was the day my country lost its innocence, as far as I was concerned. To me, it seemed that pure madness now reigned! The dice had been thrown, and the ball was in motion. There was no stopping it now. It had been only twenty days after President Diệm's assassination that President Kennedy was assassinated. They killed him in Texas, Vice President Johnson's home state, on November 2, 1963. Suspect events had preceded this killing—actions that might have been at the root in instigating such a tragedy. On October 11, 1963, President Kennedy had issued a security memo, NSAM 263, that not everyone agreed with. It is believed that Kennedy had been in the middle of changing his position on Vietnam. He had done something unprecedented. He had hired a historian on his staff in an effort to understand Vietnam and what we were doing there. He had issued an order for the removal of all American military from South Vietnam starting in 1963, scheduled to be completed in 1965. I wonder if he was using the same type of behind-the-scenes diplomacy with North Vietnam through Hồ Chí Minh that he had successfully used with Khrushchev in Russia. He must have realized the futility of the United States' involvement in Vietnam. I hope this was the case, but who knows? I'm sure neither Vice President Johnson nor the Joint Chiefs of Staff agreed with Kennedy's actions.

Lyndon Johnson, upon taking over the presidency after the assassination, revised Kennedy's orders only days after the funeral—November 26, 1963—with NSAM 273. This reversed the direction that Kennedy had intended with NSAM 263, though hadn't made public. Johnson had met with the war-hungry Joint Chiefs of Staff and joined forces with them. "We will escalate this thing in Vietnam," Johnson said. I wondered if this was America's own coup d'état orchestrated by American military and politicians. The American populace was too much in shock after the assassination to even notice, I think; too naive, too innocent to understand that such a thing could happen in their America. Too many people had too much at stake to let there ever be peace. These political dogs of war thought themselves invincible then, as they still do today. Madness!

Like dominoes set up and then pushed to fall one after the other, America's great leaders fell in the blink of an eye over the next few years. It would be a deep and mournful period for America—like rain that splashes on your face in the early summer, hard, sudden, lasting. These were leaders who had been looking for peace, for sanity in a world gone crazy. Eliminated. Shot down! Martin Luther King Jr., the great civil rights leader working for equality of the races, was assassinated on April 4, 1968. Robert Kennedy, a shining light of sanity, was assassinated as he began his presidential run on June 6, 1968. It seemed like it was never going to end. Madness!

Consistent with all good nightmares, the Colonel received orders to return to Vietnam without any dependents. If he went, we would be left behind. We were at the end of our two-year posting at Fort Monroe. It didn't take the Colonel long to make his decision. He had reached eligible retirement age after twenty-five years in the service and had finally gotten his "birds," promoted to the rank of full Colonel while in Virginia. He was still angry at the officer who had blocked him from getting them in Saigon because of the issue of the Toyota jeep purchase in 1960. His grilling before the congressional subcommittee over the matter hadn't escalated beyond that. He'd get his military pension now and take up civilian work. He had no intention of returning to Saigon. He had no illusions about the situation in Vietnam. Before we left Vietnam in 1962, it had been the consensus of all military advisors there that this was a civil conflict that the U.S. should not be involved in. The commander of MAAG, Lieutenant General McGarr, even sent a report to that effect before his time in Saigon was over, advising against escalation.

Our family departure from the military and Fort Monroe didn't go as we expected. Something happened that none of us could have predicted. About a month before the end of our Army career, my parents were entertaining some friends at the house, a couple. They'd been drinking freely, at least the Colonel had, prior to making the planned move to the Officer's Club for dinner. Perhaps he was celebrating early his upcoming release from the Army—who knows?

He was loaded. The Colonel never liked being in a group of equally-ranked men, being just one of many officers. And as I mentioned, Fort Monroe was the holding fort of so many officers returning from overseas assignments. After waiting forty-five minutes for his drink order, he finally lost it. I mean lost it! A full-scale Colonel verbal frontal attack was showered down upon the club's managing officer, a major. The major immediately put the Colonel on report right after asking him to leave. By early morning the next day, we kids were suddenly loaded with whatever clothes could be assembled quickly into the family car and driven by Mom to Horse Cave, Kentucky.

The Colonel was called before the four-star general, the Commandant of the Continental Command at Fort Monroe. "Well, George, I guess you did it again," he said. Fortunately, nothing terrible happened. We never did learn what past act the general was referring to with this statement. Tom asked him about it years later, but "the old man" wouldn't say. Anyway, the Colonel finally got his release papers, remaining ranked as a Colonel with a full Army pension.

We waited a month in Kentucky for the Colonel. He had to coordinate the packing and moving this time without the help of his wife. When he finally showed up in Kentucky, we were on the move again—the entire family. This time, we were going to a small farming town outside of Chicago: Naperville, Illinois. To put it simply, we would now be full-time civilians, and for the next few years, I was a fish out of water.

Civilian life proved to be an assignment more difficult for me than anything that had come before it. In 1964, I found civilians entirely frightening. There was no awareness of international events and political realities among my peers. Theirs was a standstill world. It was like walking out of a gigantic combustible bouncing ball into a place frozen in time. At fourteen years of age, I was scheduled to start high school in Naperville. Tom was shipped off again for his junior year of school, this time to Northwestern Military and Naval Academy in Lake Forest, Wisconsin. The younger kids would be on their own in middle school. The Colonel was now working for an American company, Corn Products International, just outside of Chicago. Mom was the glue that somehow held our disconnected group all together.

In Illinois, we moved into a gigantic split-level house with six bedrooms and a three-car garage. It was situated on two and a half acres on Wherli Road. The place was about two miles outside of town on what had once been farmland. Mom had made a ridiculously low offer to the bank for this foreclosure property. To our surprise, the bank accepted the offer. Our stored household goods from our nine military postings were delivered *en masse*. It resembled the coming together of the United Nations: possessions from England, Austria, Thailand, Germany, Hong Kong, Japan, the Philippines, and Vietnam arrived after years of storage.

Survival. I had been confident that our childhood had taught us kids everything we needed to know to handle any new situation. With each transfer, we had learned to reinvent ourselves. That's what military BRATs, our invisible transient tribe, do. However, this time around it was different. We weren't with our own kind. These were complete strangers to us, who had lives that were completely unfamiliar to us. We were now conscript in something we weren't prepared for: civilian life. Having returned from the foreign shores of Vietnam, we found ourselves in a world that threatened to atomize us in an instant. In this new world of the Colonel's retirement, we would find ourselves in more of a foreign land than any we had ever been in before.

We kids were registered for school and bussed back and forth. Our communication with each other was practically nonexistent. I can't say what was going on with any of the others. We were all so caught up in our own survival struggles, I guess. It was a strange and artificial world we found ourselves in. Civilian life was at odds with everything we had experienced so far. Adapting to these people was difficult. I was shy, was dressed strangely in my still-fitting Vietnamese tailored clothing, spoke another language, and had no way to connect to anything that made up these kids' lives. I didn't know television shows, and I had no understanding of small-town cliques. I was teased and bullied, as most people are who are not understood by the mindless masses. This new experience would leave me in despair and lonely, filled with melancholy.

My Saigon money remained tucked neatly in the same cigar box that had made the journey with me from Vietnam. My dreams remained in that box, untouched. Believing that the world was ending, I hadn't seen the point of pursuing anything, least of all my dream of getting a horse. I simply wanted to be invisible until this sentence in civilian purgatory was over. I now understood the civilian horror Tom had faced six years earlier in Hinsdale and agreed with him that living with civilians was hell!

The next two years passed uneventfully, apart from the constant cruel treatment by my classmates. There were no plans to move again; at least nothing was being said, though it was something I got down on my knees and prayed for nightly. I knew something had to change if I was going have any kind of life in this barren wasteland. It was the summer of 1966.

Commanding Lt. General McGarr with Vietnamese military officers. McGarr would recommend no escalation of American involvement in 1962.

CHAPTER 36:

MINISKIRTS AND HORSES

Fishnet stockings, white lipstick, and miniskirts were the fashion in the summer of 1966. Having made it to the grand old age of sixteen, I had watched these trends come into fashion with horror. I knew I was going to have do something with myself if I was ever going to meld with these Midwestern teens. I was entering my junior year of high school in Naperville, Illinois. Discarding the brown nondescript dresses I'd been wearing, I grew my hair out over the summer and employed Sun In, a hair bleaching product, to create dramatically streaked highlights. I styled my hair like Hollywood movie star Veronica Lake's. That involved flipping my blond locks over to one side, slightly covering my right eye. It was a look that was a far cry from the cropped hair I had insisted upon, or the boy-like look I'd adopted to avoid attention in Saigon. Like the chameleon that steps on a different-colored leaf, I changed to blend in. I wasn't that far off from what the "Pearls of the Orient" were attempting, I thought at the time. Tanning all summer left me with a golden and healthy look. Having gotten a job at the local drugstore, I could now afford to shop for fashionable clothes without having to explain where I'd gotten the money, and besides, that was the funds for my dream horse. I wasn't touching the money in my cigar box because I'd had no idea how I was going to explain how I'd gotten it. Thanks to the recent discovery of Twiggy, the model who was the rage at the time, flat-chested and skinny were popular. When I returned to school that autumn, no one recognized me. Even the tireless bullies did not know it was me. Summer lightning falsely promises rain. I deceptively played along with their thinking that I was a new kid that year. They looked only at appearances, not at the person. It was a shallow, empty world, but at least I wasn't tormented anymore.

The cadmium yellow school bus would drop me in front of the house after school. Pati and Bob were in middle school, catching their own bus at a different time. I rode the high school bus alone to and from school. With our older brother gone, we were no longer a cohesive unit watching out for each other. We would see him only on holidays and during the summer breaks. It was a lonely life out on Wherli Road. The house had two staircases, which made it possible to avoid human contact with everyone, if desired.

One day, entering the house and mounting the front stairs to the kitchen on the second floor, I discovered Mom sitting on the banquette seats at the breakfast table. She was waiting for me. In front of her was a large stack of money. Currency in all denominations was spread out in front of her on the kitchen table, beautiful American greenbacks. My coveted cigar box sat open next to them, empty. The big blue rubber band that had held it closed for so many years sat broken nearby, resembling a flattened worm. That box had been resting quietly now for several years in my closets, both in Fort Monroe and now in Naperville. Putting my schoolbooks down on the nearby counter, I slid into the seat opposite her. She seemed composed, but then again, Mom was very good at not showing you what she was thinking. I braced myself to see how this was going to go. The afternoon sunlight was streaming through the kitchen window. Mom seemed to be aglow in a rich golden light. As always, she looked beautiful.

"I wasn't snooping. I was cleaning your closet and happened to knock this cigar box over. Guess what I found. I think I deserve an explanation, young lady," she said, really calm. I was impressed.

So, the moment had come. She was finally asking. Remember, if they didn't ask, we didn't tell. Those were the rules we had grown up with, our little gang of four. But if they asked, it was up to any self-respecting BRAT to tell.

"Oh, don't worry. That was a long time ago, and besides, I earned it," I said, not worried yet.

Now I'm sure this comment led to a few leaps at the synapse that I wouldn't want to know about. I could see she was pacing herself. "Earned it? Exactly when and where was that?" she said, continuing to look at the self-styled trollop in front of her. Spots of red appeared on her cheeks.

"Like I said, it was years ago, when we lived in Saigon," I said, turning my attention to admire the stack of money in front of me. It was impressive. I'd been so distracted with my civilian survival nightmare, I hadn't taken the money out to look at it in a long time. All my plans were still on hold.

I wonder if the word "prostitute" ran through her brain. I know I looked like one in my miniskirt and fishnet stockings. None of this was connecting to anything she could figure out. "I knew where you kids were all the time. You never went anywhere I didn't know your whereabouts when we were in Vietnam. Tom was with you or the servants. Always!" She was starting to sputter. "Where was I?" she now demanded to know, looking me straight in the eye. The veneer was starting to crack, and I could see things were going to get ugly soon.

"Probably at the golf club, playing bridge, or in Hong Kong. I don't know. You just weren't around." *Can a person create steam that will come out of their ears?* I wondered.

"Okay." She closed her eyes. "Why don't we start this conversation again from the beginning? What were you doing?" She was trying to be calm now, but her tapping finger was giving her away.

"Tom and I had a business," I said, looking directly at her.

"Tom! Tom was in on this?" Mom flushed at this last statement, her entire face turning a bright shade of pink. What was she thinking? Tom was pimping for me?

I now decided to be more forceful in my explanation, as she looked like she was about to lose it. Words poured out of me in a torrent. "We were selling baby powder and Hershey bars on the black market in downtown Saigon."

She looked like she had been hit full force in the face. "When and how in the world did you get downtown to the black market?" The completely confused look on her face made me take pity on her.

"Well, it really was because you sent us to the movies so much, and after seeing *The World of Suzie Wong* about a billion times, I couldn't take it anymore. Tom was already selling stuff there and sneaking out of the theater so he could get money to buy beer and cigarettes. I just black-mailed him into letting me be part of it," I said, talking fast.

"He was thirteen; you were ten! What do you mean he needed beer money? What beer? You both had an allowance," she said, completely frustrated. "Where were the little ones while you two were off gallivanting?" The look of total exasperation on her face had me feeling more compassionate toward her, so I decided to let it rip.

"They called it *ba muoi ba*; 33 Export was the brand, to answer the question about the beer. All his friends were drinking. But to answer your other question about Pati and Bob, they stayed in the theater. I told them I'd sell them if they came out before the movie was over. I could have made a lot of money from them. They were cute. They believed me and were more than happy to stay inside. I also bribed them with candy, a surefire way of gaining loyalty!"

"Why in heaven's name did you need all this money?" She now was staring at the pile on the table, and her glance toward me revealed the look of someone who was having a problem figuring out who the person sitting in front of her was.

"I needed money to buy a horse. I want to go to the Olympics," I said. My answer was matter-of-fact. After all, I'd been working on this plan for some time now.

"But, Sandy, you don't even know how to ride," she said in sheer amazement.

"That is a very small detail!" The sticking point in my grand plan had always been that up until now. I had no idea how to ride a horse. Still, it had all made sense to me, though the look on Mom's face had me doubting my logic for just about a second.

Sitting back on the banquette, I was pleased at how well this mother-and-daughter talk had gone. I'm sure I had a self-satisfied smirk on my face. I waited. No telling where this would go from here, but at least everything was now out in the open. I couldn't take my eyes off the money. Mom didn't make a move. She was thinking, it seemed. After a short time of dead silence, she responded.

"Let's put the money in the bank for now. I think we should start by getting you riding lessons. Would be a good thing to know if you intend to go to the Olympics. Discussion about buying a horse will have to come later. I'll talk to your father about this. I think I will need to take this one slowly," she mused.

She'd gone full circle and was now on my side. I was beaming. As far as I was concerned, there wasn't a better mother on the planet. The sun was setting over the wide-open corn fields behind our house, giving everything a golden hue. It was as if the room were lit by an inner light that set everything and everyone in it aglow. The world was suddenly big and beautiful to me, as if the weight of the world I'd been carrying around for so long had suddenly been lifted. Sometimes, there are moments that come into our human existence, like a key in a lock, opening an entire new world before our very eyes. What a wonderful day it was to be alive. As the saying goes, "*La vie est belle!*"

The reworking of my reality at this point was like the rewinding of a clock to tick steadily, one second after the next with predictability. The world of life and death, intrigue and subterfuge, coups and assassinations, nuclear meltdowns, the Cold War, Saigon, and America shifted. In this singular moment of my life, none of it mattered anymore to me. A new reality entered my mind, and it slowly opened like the bud of a flower suddenly throwing back its petals to reveal its center. The possibility of a future now existed—a future to grow up in and perhaps even to regain a lost child-hood in. Yes. Anything was possible that day!

I found her, my horse, at an old, dilapidated auction house. She stood knee-deep in manure and was the last horse on the auction lot. Ribs showed through her dull, thickly furred hide. Her white-stocking legs were stained green from the manure she stood in and had stood in for some time. The Colonel and Mom had a friend, Mary McGregor, who'd told them we should look at this animal. The Colonel had been humored by Mom's story. I'd been taking riding lessons for some months by that time, and he'd suddenly decided that it was time for me to buy a horse. My dream horse was an Arabian thoroughbred I had been taking lessons on. It was for sale for two thousand dollars, and I had that amount. The animal I was now leading out of the airless, dark stall at the auction house was of no comparison. I couldn't believe the condition this horse was in. Spur marks had left scabs on her sides. Thin beyond belief, she stood almost lifeless. She had no will of her own. She was broken. Her winter coat was coming off in thick hunks. The auctioneer didn't hesitate to throw on a saddle and bridle. Mounting up, I rode her around the ring once. Twice. She would have run into the fence if I didn't turn her. Her mouth was damaged and hard from abuse. She barely registered the pulling of the reins, the pressure of the bit. And then, I'd had it. I was mad! The auctioneer patiently stood by the fence. The Colonel waited nearby in his Texas alligator boots and signature Stetson hat, tamping his pipe, watching. I stopped in front of them both and dismounted.

"I'm going to count out one hundred seventy-five dollars and leave it here on this post. If it is gone when I come back from putting this poor thing back in her stall, we have a deal. I'd take it, mister, because I don't think this animal is going to live that long. As part of that deal, you are going to throw in the saddle, the bridle, and deliver her," I said. I wasn't about to leave this poor creature there, but I wasn't going to pay more than she was worth at this moment. I took the saddle off and dumped it at his feet. I slid the bridle over her ears as I released her into her stall. She turned slightly and looked up at me. "Don't worry, girl," I whispered. "I'll be seeing you soon."

The Colonel seemed amused at my dealmaking. We drove home together without talking. I think he was wondering what we'd gotten ourselves into with this animal. I hadn't planned to buy her when I saw her, this big-boned, big-hooved strawberry roan mustang quarter horse with the "WE" brand seared on her haunches. But I had! Just like that, and without a second thought. She arrived two weeks later in an open truck with her head high and visible from all four sides. The saddle and bridle were delivered with her. She had been sick after the short outing she'd had with me. It took me six months to get her well.

Winnie became the friend I'd never had, the one that didn't get left behind no matter where I moved to over the following years. I named her that because whenever she saw me, she belted out a high-pitched whinny. She turned out to be a great horse, willing to jump higher than I had the courage to go. I couldn't stand the idea that she might get hurt. My dream of going to the Olympics was easily tossed to the side, no longer important. Over the following years, when life became too hectic for me to spend the time needed with her, I found kids whom I would teach to ride and trust her care to. Twenty-eight years after our first meeting, one rain-soaked night, she died in my arms at the age of thirty-six in Langhorne, Pennsylvania. Sitting on the barn floor, I cried like a baby for hours after the quiet had settled around me. Alone in that dark barn with her big beautiful head resting on my lap, I said goodbye to the only living being I had ever truly loved unconditionally in my life.

When I'd bought Winnie, I'd gotten the support I was looking for from the Colonel, the recognition and attention I so hungrily needed. He even built a barn for me to keep the animal in our backyard. His way of expressing love was through his actions, not necessarily his words. Words were difficult for him. Eventually, Tom would realize his support too. It would take longer for him, but it was perhaps an even greater step taken on the part of the Colonel. In 1971, Tom was one of the last of five men who were called up for the military draft in Chicago. The draft was a conscription program in the United States, employed by the federal government requiring military service. They were going to be discontinuing the draft in Chicago after this last recruitment call. America had entered the conflict in Vietnam and was waging an all-out war there. President Nixon, who had expanded the scope of the thing after Lyndon Johnson's presidential term, was now faced with civil unrest and antiwar movements. The Vietnam conflict was tearing the country apart. Nixon was trying to find a way out of this quagmire. The Colonel backed his oldest son up in helping him get a 4F designation, a ruling of being unfit for service. Whatever he said got Tom his deferment. Tom told me later that the Colonel had told him that if he couldn't get him out, he could get him stationed in Hawaii passing out ping-pong balls.

"I'm not about to have my oldest son killed in Vietnam. It is a pointless war. It is a war we should never have entered. We will not win it. The military and government know this; they just won't stop it. There has already been enough death on both sides," he said, explaining to his oldest son why he had supported him.

I have often wondered if it was because this struggle in Vietnam couldn't be won that the Colonel had chosen to step away from it all. He didn't do anything unless he could win, that was for sure. His time with General Patton in WWII had formed his character and reinforced a singular can-do attitude. Vietnam would prove to be something that wasn't understood from the very beginning by most. The Colonel would try to explain it to me years later, long after his retirement from civilian work. This happened many years after a cerebral hemorrhage nearly killed him, long after his retirement from civilian life, when he was living a simple life. When he finally spoke up, it was the moment that all the pieces of our life in Saigon fell into place for me.

I bought my horse, Winnie, from the auction house. She wasn't the thoroughbred I was considering, and I didn't go to the Olympics. Instead, for twenty-eight years, she was my best friend; the one I'd bought with my Saigon baby powder and Hershey bar money in 1965. She died in my arms in Langhorne, Pennsylvania, at the ripe old age of thirty-six. Picture taken with Laura, one of her child caregivers.

CHAPTER 37:

THE COLONEL'S COLLECTION

The Hanna family had been away from Vietnam for several decades. My siblings and I, now adults, were spread across the American continent like pebbles tossed to the wind, having landed randomly in every direction possible. Tom had gone from Alaska to Kansas, Pati from Kentucky to Michigan, and Bob from Illinois to Kentucky. I had recently moved from Massachusetts to New Jersey. Our mother and the Colonel had settled in the South, creating a comfortable life for themselves. They had built a Spanish-style white stucco house in Elizabethtown, Kentucky. It was meant to see them through the remaining days of their lives after they retired from the military and re-entered civilian life. It allowed them to tap into all the benefits of a retired military officer at nearby Fort Knox. The years had softened the old war horse, or perhaps it was the cerebral hemorrhage he'd survived in his late fifties. It had left him a changed man. Either way, he was no longer the same stoic warrior we kids had grown up with. Instead, he had become the dear man we had always known lurked somewhere under that tough exterior. As a military officer, he had demanded obedience at all times, even after he finally gave up on the Army. In those later days, he was just a gentle soul.

Over the years, I visited my parents on and off. Whenever I was there, the Colonel would descend into the basement and return with objects from his past life to either show me or give me. He called them his collection. I called them my dowry. This collection was made up of things he'd gathered over a lifetime and hidden from all of us. In the faded light that filtered through the basement windows, he would unearth things whose whereabouts were known only to him. He was in his late seventies, sweeter than you could ever believe. He was now too changed and too sweet for my brother Tom to have it out with him about anything from the past. He wouldn't have understood.

The Colonel was now a man who had a little garden, played golf, and argued with the television news programs. Out of hiding places from the basement time machine, he pulled relics from what seemed like lost civilizations. They were all attached to stories he'd tell whenever he could find someone to listen. I never could find where he kept his stash. It seemed unlimited—things that time had forgotten but he hadn't. On one occasion he climbed up the steps from the basement with a four-by-five-inch glass large-format camera negative. He held it up to the light with a twinkle in his eye, as a devilish grin spread across his face. "You know, the press corps asked old Georgie what he was going to do when he got to the Rhine. Do you know what he said?"

"No, Colonel," I said, knowing he was talking about General George Patton, his hero and boss during World

War II. He had been Patton's ordinance officer. The broad mission of any Odnance Corps is to supply Army combat units with weapons and ammunition, at times involving their procurement and maintenance. The Colonel was one of the best. Let us just say he was incredibly creative in his job! After the war's end, before returning stateside from Europe, he'd packed a trailer with items he had confiscated, bringing them back with him. This negative was one of those items.

"Old Georgie said, 'Gentlemen, I'm going to piss in it,'" he said in a spirit of pure mischief as he passed the negative my way.

The black-and-white reverse image showed the figure of a man standing relieving himself by a river. Yes, he was pissing. I handed the negative back to him. He was referring to General Patton as the pisser, of course.

The Colonel had been Patton's can-do man in WWII, and in his own words, referred to his time in Europe as the time his Texas horse-trading persona and talents had been put to good use. He'd been in the Armor Division at Fort Knox, Kentucky, and had gone to Texas A&M. The Colonel had also been a tank designer at Little Rock Arsenal and at the Aberdeen testing grounds. There is a plaque at Little Rock Arsenal on display honoring him for his work as a member of the design team. He worked on the designs of two armored tanks while stationed there, the M3 and the M4. The M4 was called the Sherman tank and would prove to be the American workhorse of the war. It was a diesel tank and is credited with defeating German General Erwin Rommel in WWII.

We played with the tank prototype models the Colonel had somehow gotten possession to bring home when we were small. Riding on top of them, we pushed them with our tiny legs. One of them had a big star on it, the signature marking of the Sherman tank. When General Patton was to receive a shipment of twenty-five hundred Sherman tanks, he demanded that someone who had worked on "the damn things" be delivered with them, because he was determined "to kill" whoever it was if they didn't work. My cousin Linda, when listening to the Colonel talk about it, said that the directive had actually been much more explicit. "He told us Patton said he'd cut the balls off the guy," she said. The Colonel, a reserve officer at the time, became part of Patton's 3rd Army Division. Patton had just transferred his procurement officer out, so the Colonel was moved into the slot, with the task of getting Patton nylons and chocolates as part of his responsibilities. Patton was pleased with the tank shipment I guess. The Colonel wasn't killed or castrated.

When the Allied invasion took place in Normandy, tanks couldn't get through the thick hedgerows that dominated that part of France. The Colonel, having been raised on a farm, suggested a series of spinning chains. This worked to get the tanks and troops through the thicket. The Colonel came up with other variations that could be done to the tanks, and many of them were employed by Patton. He was a hands-on problem solver, and Patton couldn't have been more pleased with him. History tells tales of Patton's army that are incredible, and the tales of the Colonel's time with the man were spellbinding.

Always the storyteller, his tales of his adventures had his listeners riveted to every word. He'd tell them again and again. His narrative very rarely described anything other than the comic side of life. Like his older brother, Homer, he would always start it out with a little chuckle.

He didn't tell me all the stories, however, the ones perhaps too horrible to relive. I was finally able to ask him about the images I'd come across when I was eight years old, the ones hanging on that clothesline in the basement in Illinois. He'd taken a lot of black-and-white photos during WWII as a semiprofessional photographer with a Leica camera, no doubt confiscated during the war. He had documented the world he found himself in like a hasty street photographer. He told me that one day, moving ahead of Patton to set up the base camp, he and his assistant came upon a concentration camp. His camera captured the horrors of the discovery. These images weren't printed until years later when we were in Illinois. I had never before asked the Colonel about what I'd seen, not when I was eight or even when I got older. He in turn had no reason to bring it up. Nothing had led to a conversation of this sort.

Now, with this visit to Kentucky, the Colonel added a new item to my dowry. I had already been given the table-cloth from Hitler's Eagle's Nest. He'd gotten to the holdout before everyone else as Patton's 3rd Army moved through the area. He had carefully folded it up and taken it with him. Now, sitting in front of him on the wooden kitchen table in Kentucky was a faded brown oversized file enve-lope, the kind used in government offices. It was tied shut with an equally faded pale pink ribbon. Looking up at me with his forehead furrowed, he carefully slid the envelope meekly over to me with trembling hands. He was thinking and remembering a time years earlier. There was an expres-sion of sadness on his face.

"Do you remember *Sâm*?" he said quietly.

"Yes. He was your counterpart in Saigon. Colonel *Sâm*, right?"

"Colonel Lê Văn *Sâm*," he corrected. "Yes. He was Chief of Ordnance for the South Vietnamese Army, ARVN, when we arrived there in 1960. I worked directly with him as a MAAG advisor. He gave this package to me one night when we were in Saigon. He showed up at the house late that evening. All of you kids were asleep. Something had happened between his wife, Ngai, and her cousin, a woman known in those days as Madame Nhu. You probably remember her as the infamous 'Dragon Lady,' I suppose. That was a name she more than earned! It was the one the press had a field day with later. There were certainly enough stories about her after we left," he said, getting up to pour another cup of coffee. The coffeepot ran from daybreak till lights-out. "Madame Nhu was the sister-in-law of the South Vietnamese President, Diệm."

"Ngai, Mrs. *Sâm*, had been vacationing with her children in Đà Lạt. You probably remember their kids. They came to the house several times, and we all had dinner with them once in Cholon. We never took any of you kids to Đà Lạt though. It was a resort town in the mountains north of Saigon. Anyway, Mrs. *Sâm* saw General Đôn entering Madame Nhu's boudoir. Madame Nhu saw her. What she saw set off a chain of events for Colonel *Sâm*," he said, taking a long breath. "Madame Nhu was someone who didn't like people knowing anything about her, especially about what Mrs. *Sâm* saw. *Sâm* was convinced there would be repercussions."

As he spoke, the story came back to me, the one I'd heard while sitting on the stairway spying on the Colonel and *Sâm*. His monologue rolled out. I sensed that a vulgar intrigue was about to be disclosed to me. I waited for him to get there, to get to the place where the full richness of life for the *Sâm* family became a broken happiness, a tragedy. There was no hurrying the Colonel though.

He finally unearthed all the facts. The relationship that existed between the two women was that they both were related to Emperor Bảo Đại; this is the strand of genetics that made them cousins. Bảo Đại, "the Keeper of Greatness," was the thirteenth and final emperor of the Nguyen Dynasty in Vietnam. Madame Nhu, at that time, was married to South Vietnamese President Diệm's brother, Ngô Đình Nhu. Ngai was married to Colonel *Sâm*; she was a career officer's wife. Although cousins, the women were not close.

"Ngai immediately packed up her family and returned to Saigon. When she told *Sâm* what she had seen, he became afraid. He was sure something horrible was going to happen to him and his family. Madame Nhu was a ruthless and unpredictable woman. Colonel *Sâm* sat down and wrote out an exposé on the members of President Diệm's regime, both military and political. He knew them all— where they came from, who they were beholden to. The intrigue reads like a script for a movie," he said, slowing down to sip the now-cold coffee. "He viewed this document as his insurance policy for the future. When he gave it to me, he made me promise not to do anything with it unless something happened to him."

Now deep in thought, he continued his monologue without pause. He had visibly traveled back decades in his mind. Like a lantern slowly flickering, memories were spurting out in bits and pieces. With his last statement, the Colonel began to pull the thin sheets of onion skin paper from the folder. These pages had the appearance of old-fashioned rice paper. They were yellowed from their many years of storage in the Kentucky basement. Time's imprint was stamped on them. Colonel *Sâm's* beautiful script now remained only as pale blue indentations. The faded yellow patina of the paper made the stack look fragile. He handled the sheets gently, almost as he would a small animal or child, carefully putting them in order. He looked through them slowly.

"Do you remember Vietnam?" the Colonel said, now looking up curiously at me. "Do you remember anything about it? You were only ten when we got there is why I ask."

Although I'd been only ten years old when we arrived in Vietnam in 1960, I remembered Saigon as though it was yesterday. Visions of the city filled my mind as he spoke, tugging at my memory. It had been some time since I had let myself go down that road. I remembered Colonel *Sâm* too. Something the Colonel didn't know then was that I had been there the nights that Colonel *Sâm* had come to the house and brought these papers to him, that I had been hiding on the circular stairway, peering through the spindles, listening. This was something I often did in those days. I was always trying to figure out what was going on around me and what the Colonel was doing. I considered myself quite a spy while in Saigon.

"Do you know what this is?" the Colonel asked. I shook my head slightly. He continued. "It's evidence in a way, an explanation and prediction of why American involvement in South Vietnam would fail. *Sâm* wrote it out to expose the fact that the ruling regime at that time was not pro-American. The history of that blasted country became a mess after World War II," he said, starting to become excited.

"Now this is where it gets tricky. The Geneva Accord agreement that was signed—Allies, French, North Vietnam

—created a two-year halt to the conflict between 1954 and 1956. Elections were scheduled to be held to let the Vietnamese people decide what they wanted after those two years: either the National Front for the Liberation of Vietnam, from the North, or the government of Emperor Bảo Đại in the South with Diệm as the Premier. Everyone had agreed to this plan!"

"Well that didn't happen, did it?" I knew my voice had a bit of sarcasm in it. Too many of my friends later in my life had been sucked into what became a full-scale war. So many of them lost, on both sides.

"Unfortunately, it didn't. Diệm had no intention of holding that election, because he knew he wouldn't win. He rigged his own election to make himself president of South Vietnam earlier than the one scheduled in 1956, one of his own, thus creating the Republic of South Vietnam. The United States went along with Diệm. It was a completely botched job, really. We Americans had no idea what kind of regime we were supporting or anything about the real history of the place. In other words, we didn't honor the Geneva Peace Accord that we as a country had arranged with our Allies. We are ultimately responsible for what history has revealed," he continued. Once he got started with a story, there was no telling what track he would go down and for how long. I sat back and waited for the rest of it.

"Colonel *Sâm* gave these documents to me at risk of his life one night and asked me to hold on to them. They provide a key to some of the reasons America's efforts in South Vietnam failed. Americans are still confused about the reasons for our involvement. I want you to do something with this exposé." With that said, he seemed to feel a momentary relief, like it was something that had been bothering him for some time, a headache-causing decision that was now off his to-do list.

I looked down at the packet and papers. The neat cursive writing covered the pages from top to bottom. The text ran on, page after page. I didn't read any of it at first, just scanned it. I noticed a handwritten letter wedged between the delicate sheets of paper. I pulled it out to read silently to myself.

Saigon, September 30, 1963
Dear Col. Hanna

I missed you almost two years. Mrs. Sam and all our children never and never forget about your family. We have six children; three boys and three girls. I had moved my family now to living in Cholon. Just a short distance from the church is what my wife likes.

My wife and I some time like so much to write to you, but we hesitate and at last we don't do that. As you know so much our situation and we beg you not forget it for us. Now let us show you some more trouble we have in our family. My brother-in-law Doctor Quyen at Hue was arrested by the government since months ago. As you know Dr. Quyen was Chief of Medicine at University and he also is chief of Hue hospital. Government accused him asking why he take care so much about students wounded and he protest also ill treatment to the monks and nuns and students wounded. At last he sent a letter to the President Diem that he doesn't want any more to work on his jobs. Almost a month and half we haven't seen him. We don't know where they confined him. What jail he is in. He spent almost 15 years take care of President Mother. Now Quyen got the same as I got before. I do not have so much time write to you I hope I'm going to meet you and your family in next letter. I am so fond with you that something I have told you before that now become true. I afraid too much the Mr. Nhu and Mrs. Nhu going to be used like advisor for Diem President. All Vietnam people now have trouble with them. We completely desperate.

A few weeks ago, I met Doctor Allardyce. She was friend of Col. Ulrich family. Now she try to help us also. Right now, Mrs. Sam talk to Dr. Allardyce and I'm writing to you.

Col. Hanna, don't forget us and Vietnam country. Please search the way that help us.

Let my wife and I send our compliments to Mrs. Hanna. I want to say hello to your sons and daughters.

Thank you and Mrs. Hanna.

Sincerely Yours
Sam & Ngai [6]

Another letter, this one typed, was buried in the pile. It was still in its original, stamped envelope.

October 1, 1963

Dear Colonel and Mrs. Hanna,

I have recently gotten in touch with the Le Van Sams and have been trying to give him some assistance by reporting to persons who can take some action. Perhaps we shall not exactly unlock the doors of Dr. Quyen's prison, but our efforts may mean saving him for the work which he has been so nobly doing. We all fear that he knows too much about the evils of the leading family and their satellites to get him released soon, however.

Colonel Sam had told me about the document which he prepared and gave to you two years ago, February. We are hoping that this material has been placed where it may be reviewed during these critical times. He says that he risked his life to get the information and that it all has proven true, and he hopes that the High Officials in the USA will have it at hand when they sit down in Washington to review the data they have been gathering here.

Many of us have been busy preparing the picture of the current Viet Nam which will supplement the military picture, since there are many persons with the Brass whose job it was to gather data on civilian life.

If there is any good way for you to try to call to attention to the document which Sam wrote, it would be of some aid, he thinks.

*My best regards to you and your family. I have been
slated to leave on home trip and return, but some
affairs in which I am active have been delayed
because of "no piasters" and we are hoping to
squeeze the stone and get the work done in the
next few weeks. Then I do not know just what the
decision will be; I think I'll be ready to give the
job to someone else and go to newer and shall we
say "fresher" fields. You may know that the State
Department is letting only the most critically needed
civilians in here now; people on home leave, even
chiefs of party are frozen for some time.*

*Do you see the Ulrichs once in a while? I owe them
a letter and hope to get one off soon.*

Enjoy the football season and the coming snows.

Most cordially,
Agnes
Agnes L. Allardyce
USOM Education Division
Saigon, Vietnam [7]

Reading these letters, I thought about the life I had
been living when all this intrigue was going on. My childhood had unfolded while the country I was living in was
convulsing around me. I had been only vaguely aware of
many of these things at the time. I had all the memories,
and finally the connections were being made, it seemed.

I gazed up at the Colonel. He had a faraway look, as
though with the unveiling of these papers he had moved

back in time and space. He was elsewhere, a place that I couldn't go.

"Did you do anything with these papers? Did you write to him? Did you find *Sâm* after we left?" I asked.

"I tried to give these papers to my immediate superiors. I even went to the Pentagon to try to draw attention at the time to what Colonel *Sâm* had disclosed. Nothing was done," he mused.

I was still going through the documents and had now come across the Depot 704 memos. I stopped to read the final one that had been sent by Lt. General McGarr that finalized any further action with regard to Colonel *Sâm's* reinstatement as Chief of Ordnance. I read it through.

"What do you want me to do with this now, Colonel?" I asked, pulling myself back into the present.

"Americans are confused about the Vietnam War. Revisionists now foster historical amnesia about Vietnam to facilitate the current wars in the Middle East. Americans have no understanding about Vietnam except for the images of war that the media showered them with," he said, chuckling a bit with that textbook summary. "We had no experience with a culture so completely opposite to everything we Americans knew and believed. To this day, we still have not ever bothered to understand the role that history and culture play in relationship to all our conflicts around the globe. We continue to make the same mistakes. Our involvement in the Middle East has the same underlying ignorance that we had of Vietnam!" He looked up, shaking his still-handsome head.

"So, what do you want me to do? Do you want an accurate history on this? What do you see me doing?" I said again, my mind whirling with possibilities.

"You could do an accurate documentary. I can tell you where to go in the Library of Congress. Things are beginning to be declassified and released to the public."

"Okay, but is that what you really want, Colonel?" I was beginning to see I was soon to be under direct orders. There would be no choice in accepting or declining this assignment, so I was trying to get the orders straight right then, or there would be hell to pay later.

"Well, Americans do love a compelling story. Perhaps that would be a better way to go," he said, a twinkle coming into his eyes, a spark that erased any sign of age. "Give them access to seeing this place and these people in a different way than just another war story." He seemed to be gathering his thoughts—slowly, methodically.

"Okay, one compelling story! Why now, Colonel? Why now, after all these years?" I said. The afternoon light was fading. I got up to turn on the kitchen light. Mom was in the bedroom reading, leaving us to talk. I sat down again to focus on what he had to say.

"If you don't understand history, you repeat it." The Colonel paused for a minute, looking up at me. "We went to Saigon with so much baggage. Senator Joe McCarthy's paranoid scare in the '50s about Communism with his domino theory resulted in everybody who knew anything about Asia being removed from government. President Eisenhower propagated the Cold War position as well. Simply knowing about Asia targeted you as a Communist in those days. Their argument was that all Southeast Asia would fall if Vietnam became a Communist country. They didn't realize that this was a country that wanted no foreign rule at whatever cost and would fight to their last dying breath to unify their nation. I honestly believe that, had we not intervened, not violated the Geneva Accord by letting Diệm have his way before the agreed upon elections of 1956, this whole thing could have been avoided."

With that last statement, he got up from his chair. He fully intended to leave me to ponder his statement and the layers of word-filled papers before me. He stopped halfway across the room. Turning, he looked me square in the face. It seemed he wasn't finished yet.

"You know there wasn't an act of aggression in the Gulf of Tonkin. It was all made up to get us into the damn thing. Same as what President Bush did to get us into the Middle East. All this information is coming out of the Library of Congress. People need to pay attention to what the government is up to." He seemed tired. He was old now. His service to his country was finished. He was passing the baton.

"Yes. But what was it that happened to *Sâm* in the end when we left? Didn't you keep track after that? What did you do after you got the letters?" I asked. He paused just before he turned the corner to leave the room.

"Before we left, I met with *Sâm* one day at our house, and he told me he had five ways out. I wanted to get him and his family out when we were leaving and even later, but he said he'd be okay. After I got Agnes and *Sâm's* a year after we came back to the States, I started trying to contact people who knew him when I was there. No one knew where he was or what had happened. Our mutual friend, Colonel Ulrich, had already been transferred back to the States before us and couldn't locate him either. Never did find him or his family," he said, finally exiting the room.

Slowly, he left the kitchen and headed back to his armchair in front of the television. The news blared day and night, announcing the turmoil of wars in foreign lands—American supported conflicts. That night's news was about America's involvement in Afghanistan. Like Vietnam, it seemed unwinnable. No one understood why it wasn't working. I could hear the Colonel talking back to the television and venting his frustration in the other room.

Sliding my chair back from the table, I walked into the living room. He looked up from his armchair as I entered. The lines of age lay like a road map upon the surface of his beautiful face.

"What do you think happened to him, Colonel *Sâm*?" Standing over him and looking down at the top of his graying head, listening keenly, I waited for his answer.

"I think they killed him," he said after a long silence. His voice was filled with an endless agonizing sadness. His was the sullen and heavy heart of a despairing man.

The Colonel died before I could finish writing this story. Somehow, none of us kids, now grown adults, thought death could ever win over him. It came as an utter surprise and shock, even though he'd reached the ripe age of eighty-six. We didn't cry. That wouldn't have been fitting for the children of a military officer or his wife, not for a man like the Colonel. Instead we stood at attention, silent, as the military twenty-one-gun salute was fired and his ashes were laid to rest. In his passing, all the resentment we had ever gathered against him throughout our lives vanished in a single moment, like a wisp of smoke caught by the wind. What was to replace it was the pride we had in being his children. Our respect for him rose to the surface like a geyser that had been capped off and suddenly broke through. We loved him desperately. Every one of us. Only the regret and pain of not having told him enough that I loved him lingers with me now. This pain will stay with me, I'm sure, until I too am gone, my ashes scattered somewhere in the world, perhaps sprinkled over a rice field, thrown into the wind under a vibrant azure sky.

A Moment in History

"Few Americans recall the days of Ngo Dinh Diem. With the turnover of American personnel every eighteen months and the endless series of Vietnamnese military coups, time in Saigon moved forward like an army, obliterating all it passed over. By 1966 even the scenery of the Diem regime had vanished. Of the presidential palace only the outer garden walls remained, enclosing an acre of grass like he wall of a grave yard from which the graves have been removed.

And yet it was strange that Diem should have disappeared so completely. The round little president and his family had ruled Vietnam for eight years – the entirety of the truce between two wars and the whole history of an unoccupied South Vietnam. The Ngos had not been pale cipers for the whole American undertaing in that part of the world: on the contrary, any history of the Diem regime would have to be written in vivid, novelesque colors..."

—*Frances FitzGerald,* Fire in the Lake: The Vietnamese and the Americans in Vietnam, *1972*

The curly headed blond American girl who arrived in
Vietnam in 1960 would never be the same; "the ignorance
of bliss" would be replaced by something else. This
image is how I remember myself in those final days
before departing Saigon in 1962: strong, independent,
a skinny beanpole, saddled with an awareness of the
immensely complex world that surrounded me.

EPILOGUE:

THE END OF AN ERA

The headlines read "Madame Nhu died today," on April 4, 2011, in Rome. So very little said in so few words, not representative of a woman whose power, arrogance, and delusion had determined her country's future. She had been the manipulator of her husband and brother-in-law. Looming at the edges, she had been a definite and persistent part of my life from age ten onward. Colonel *Sâm* had brought her into focus in my world with his stories of political intrigue and through the documents he had given the Colonel. I'd lost track of her as the years sped by, until I read the news headlines about her in a later stage of my life.

Madame Nhu had begun early in her life to carve out a place for herself. *Sâm's* documents, along with what had been written about her by the press in the '60s, confirmed this. "Beautiful Spring" would never be known to Americans by her innocent childhood name. Even her married name, Madame Nhu, would lurk in the shadows, as the world dubbed her "the Dragon Lady." She was an ambitious woman, and Colonel *Sâm's* notes about her showed the early behavior that would be the undoing of her family and, subsequently, Vietnam. She established herself as an advisor to her bother-in-law, President Diệm, and to her husband, as someone they could trust. From there, she moved forward to wreak havoc with the Americans and the Vietnamese alike, demonstrating a singular vengeance toward the Buddhists. Madame Nhu became one of the most detested personalities in South Vietnam, as well as in America.

The world didn't mourn her death. It didn't seem to even acknowledge it, really. She had long since lost any significance in the world. The media simply referred to her as someone once recognized as a member of a cast of players in the drama Americans called the Vietnam War, the conflict the Vietnamese called the American War.

As history shows, she was in the United States on a speaking tour when her husband and brother-in-law were assassinated in 1963. The United States sanctioned the coup by Diệm's military officers, indicating it would not intervene; it was no longer standing on the sidelines as it had in the earlier attempted coup. Madame Nhu's outrageous behavior on her speaking tour in the United States was perhaps the last straw for President Kennedy. She had been traveling around the United States denouncing American involvement in Vietnam and smearing the Washington administration.

The assassination of President Diệm in 1963 wasn't like the bombing of the Independence Palace in 1962. Then, America had mixed feelings about Diệm and Vietnam. Americans still hoped Diệm could pull a rabbit out of a hat. The United States had refused to sanction the Vietnamese military officers' attempted coup then. As Ambassador Durbrow had stated earlier, "We support the regime as long as it stands." By 1963, the American government had reached a point where it no longer believed Diệm could continue to rule, as long as the Nhus were involved in running things; that meant both Madame and Mr. Nhu. The persecution of the Buddhists that the Nhus had unleashed was receiving global attention and could no longer be sanctioned by the United States. Images of Buddhist monks setting themselves on fire shocked the world. Government officials approached Diệm with the request that Diệm remove his brother and sister-in-law from his regime. Diệm refused the request, asserting that he and Nhu would retain control. With that, all bets were off, and a coup took place wherein even those who were supposedly loyal to Diệm turned against him. The Ngô brothers were captured, hiding in Cholon, after they had escaped the attack on the Presidential Palace. They weren't supposed to be assassinated, not as far as the Americans were concerned. But competing factions fearing the brothers would regain control again executed them in the transport they were being driven in from Cholon to Saigon.

The irony of the whole drama, starting with Mrs. *Sâm's* sighting of Madame Nhu entering General Đôn's boudoir in Đà Lạt, was that General Đôn would come full circle in Madame Nhu's life. Trần Văn Đôn was a general in the Army of the Republic of Vietnam and was one of the principal figures in the 1963 coup d'état that deposed Diệm from the presidency of South Vietnam. General Đôn played a key role in this event, which led to the assassination of Diệm and his brother. Madame Nhu and her children would immediately be catapulted to France.

Madame Nhu's children were in Đà Lạt when the assassinations occurred. With the help of an individual from the American government, CIA operative Edward Lansdale, they were quickly transported out of Vietnam to Paris. Lansdale also coordinated Madame Nhu's expedited departure out of the United States. Her disastrous speaking tour left her no choice but to leave quickly. She was united with her children in France. The world then completely forgot about her. She, in turn, closed her doors to all of it.

There were so many explosive triggers in place with Madame Nhu. Her exploits were famous for their complete disregard for anything other than her own self-proclaimed drive for power and single-minded view of the world. There was a moment in this insane drama that many consider the turning point: when the Vietnamese people believed that the "Mandate of Heaven" had changed. In accepting this, the country turned overnight. As the world watched on June 11, 1963, a Vietnamese priest, Thích Quảng Đức, set himself on fire on a crowded Saigon street in protest of the Diệm regime and the persecution the Nhus had rained down on the Buddhists. In true form, Madame Nhu reacted with glee. She publicly mocked this protest, stating, "Let them burn and we shall clap our hands." As far as Americans were concerned, she said, "You Americans are obsessed with Communism." On this, however, she wasn't that far off.

Howard Jones, a historian, says that these comments "all but put the finishing touches on the Diệm regime." They also created open infighting between Madame Nhu and her parents. Her father was then the ambassador for Vietnam, stationed in Washington, D.C., and her mother was South Vietnam's permanent observer to the United Nations. Her father went on the radio to condemn her comments. A Confucian, Tran Van Chuong said that the regime had alienated "the strongest moral forces," implying that it had lost its position with the people. She responded by calling him a coward. Her mother said, "There is an old proverb in my country which means, 'One should not make oneself or one's family naked before the world....' I was sick.... Now, nobody can stop her.... She never listened to our advice." Madame Nhu's brother killed their parents in 1986, and it is assumed that Madame Nhu was the one who directed him to this end. She didn't tolerate any kind of criticism. In retrospect, Colonel *Sâm* was lucky to have simply lost his job and not his life at the time. As to what happened in the end to Colonel *Sâm* and his family, I doubt we will ever know.

By 1963, the situation in Vietnam had begun to rapidly deteriorate. Autumn saw an uprising of students and Buddhists against the regime. Terrorist incidents began to be a regular occurrence, including the bombing of the Alhambra theater in September. The November 1st bloody takeover of the South Vietnamese government from Diệm by General "Big" Minh had him declaring himself in charge of the military junta. On January 30th, 1964, General Khanh staged a bloodless coup d'etat against Minh. By August, students and Buddhists nationwide had forced Khanh to resign. On February 7th, MACV (Miliary Advisory Command Vietnam), the revised advisory corps, put the American Community School under martial protection, patrolling the hallways and riding the buses. On September 9th, 1964, a bomb was set off at the Pershing baseball field. September 13th had the American command concerned when another attempted coup took place. School classes at the ACS were cancelled, with stay-at-home orders given. On September 16th, the Kinh Do movie theater was bombed. The volatile situation in 1964 had military and civilian planners in Washington discussing options for escalating the war with bomber strikes in North Vietnam. Việt Cong staging an intensive mortar attack at Biên Hòa Air Base. On December 24th, Christmas Eve, Việt Cong succeeded in bombing the Brinks building. On February 7th, 1965, Việt Cong staged a major mortar attack on U.S. forces in Pleiku and Qui Nhon. On February 8th, President Johnson ordered expanded air campaigns against North Vietnamese targets and additional ground troops in Da Nang. In 1965, all government-sponsored dependents were evacuated. Those Saigon kids returned to the United States, to a populace that was disengaged from the things that were going on in that small country halfway around the world. The United States had become engulfed in a play that had no script, no clear ending. The final withdrawal of American troops would come in 1975.

In the Far East, there is an expression, "dropping tail." It refers to the tail the gecko lizard will drop to escape, to save its life. I used to touch the tails of small lizards that crawled the stucco walls of our villa and watch in wonder as the tail detached from the body; the gecko would scurry away as fast as its little legs could carry it. We Americans performed the same act when we left Vietnam and the undeclared war we had immersed ourselves in. Instead of a tail, however, we would drop the last of our bombs and Agent Orange as our final act, leaving a scarred and toxic landscape behind us that continues to kill and maim to this day. That is our legacy.

Time carries us forward by its momentum, and Americans have spent decades trying to erase the memory of a time and place called Vietnam. It's a country that my childhood memory recalls through the sounds of throbbing cicadas, clear night skies filled with the scent of jasmine, blue-moon evenings, and the unreality of anything most American kids or adults would ever know. Those of us who grew up there share a past that binds us together as nothing else ever will; we are kindred spirits held together by our experiences and memories. Vietnam will remain a part of each of us until we too become the dust that enriches the soil and brings forth new life. For now, I can only hope for a greater intelligence and understanding of the differences that exist in the world. That an understanding will emerge that recognizes the need to grasp a country's history and culture before attempting to impose our own American culture and beliefs on it. Without this understanding, we are like the elephant whose large foot steps upon and crushes the life below it; in our case, it is a life that might, in fact, be critical to our own well-being.

NOTES

1   From the archives of Colonel George T. Hanna.
2   Ibid.
3   Ibid.
4   Ibid.
5   Ibid.
6   Ibid.
7   Ibid.

ABOUT THE AUTHOR

A resident of New York City and Lambertville, New Jersey, Sandy Hanna grew up in Saigon, South Vietnam and has been telling her story about that experience all of her life. She is an artist and a writer. Graduating from University of Massachusetts, Amherst, with a MEd, with a comprehensive in the Biology of Cognition, her undergraduate degree is from Knox College in Interdisciplinary programs in Science and Literature. She also spent a year studying design at the California Institute of the Arts with post graduate studies at Wharton. She was a designer of children's play spaces, Williamstown Children's Museum, Sesame Place a joint venture between CTW and Busch Entertainment and facilities for handicapped children, as well as a marketing director and consultant for a variety of diverse industries; children's museums, theme parks, modular construction, etc. Her passion, however, is one as a storyteller.